MODERN AMERICA
THROUGH FOREIGN EYES

SELECTED SOURCE MATERIALS

FOR COLLEGE RESEARCH PAPERS

Edited by

ROBERT F. McDONNELL *and* WILLIAM E. MORRIS

OHIO UNIVERSITY

D. C. HEATH AND COMPANY *Boston*

TABLE OF CONTENTS

INTRODUCTION

THE RESEARCH PAPER

THE process of developing new knowledge in most fields of study involves two separate steps: gathering accurate facts, and putting the facts together to see what they mean. The results of this procedure are often communicated to others through a written report which presents the information, tells where and how it was found so that the reader may verify it, and explains what conclusions may be drawn from it. Such a report is called a research paper. The form of the research paper and the steps used in collecting information for it have become standard, for they have been developed over a long period of time. Writing a research paper gives the student experience in gathering evidence in a responsible manner, thinking about it logically, and presenting his ideas to others. The skills involved are useful in nearly every college course, as well as in many professions and businesses. Even more important, perhaps, the research paper gives the student a chance to do the kind of original thinking that develops new knowledge from recognized facts.

The material in this book has been assembled to give you training and practice in developing these skills. In it you will read accounts of the life and travels of foreign visitors in and immigrants to America which, in turn, contain essays evaluating modern American culture and life. The booklet puts the student where the researcher begins, in the presence of raw material which needs to be sorted out, interpreted, and reorganized in a meaningful way. Despite general similarities in experiences, the reactions of the various observers often vary substantially, reflecting diverse backgrounds and attitudes. Sometimes the accounts confirm or supplement each other; sometimes they seem to be, or will in fact be, contradictory. Your first reading should provide a good picture of the subject as a whole, seen from a number of different angles. You should therefore begin working on your research paper by reading this booklet through to gain a general idea of what it contains.

The selections are reprinted just as they stand in the originals. Peculiarities of spelling, punctuation, and grammar are not corrected. The original pagination is supplied in the margin.

The Topic

The success of a research paper depends to a large extent upon the skill with which the topic is selected and phrased. The most common weakness is choice of an excessively broad topic — one that promises much more than can be delivered in a short paper. "Modern America," for example, would be too large a topic. A thorough discussion of it based on this book would require more than ten thousand words — a considerable undertaking for most students and instructors. Length itself is no merit; a paper gains significance and interest in proportion to the depth of the analysis. The first research papers should therefore be written on relatively small topics to permit the maximum amount of analysis and interpretation. "The American College Girl" would be more manageable and could be discussed significantly in two thousand words. For still shorter themes the topic should be narrowed still further: "American Homes," "Sport Conditions Here and Abroad," "The Business of Beauty in America," for example. Discussing a small topic exhaustively provides the kind of training in analysis that you will find useful in all your future papers.

The Outline

After you have surveyed your material and chosen your topic, you should make a trial outline. You should always remember that your first outline is a tentative one. Many students ruin their papers by clinging stubbornly to their original outlines. The final outline must be made inductively; that is, it must reflect what you discover to be important rather than what you considered to be important at the start. You should think about the organization of your paper in all stages of your reading, but you should not make the final outline until you have collected all your material and evaluated it carefully. Follow the outlining techniques recommended by your instructor.

Note Cards

It would be possible to write short papers based on this book without the use of note cards. But to write the longer papers, and even some of the shorter ones, you will find it advantageous to make note cards. You will save time in this way because all the material on your particular subject, which is scattered throughout the book (or throughout the library in your future papers), will then lie before you in small units. You can bring together the cards on different parts of your subject and fit the material logically into your outline or rearrange it to conform to last-minute changes. You will do a better job on your paper because making note cards gives you a better opportunity to analyze your material carefully.

Every note card should be limited to a single topic. This is basic because one purpose of these notes is to enable you to study your material in several different arrangements. In addition, every card should contain three parts: a subject heading, composed by you, placed in the upper left-hand corner; the source, including the page number, in the upper right-hand corner or at the bottom; and the body of the note itself. Placing both the subject heading and the source at the top leaves the bottom of the card open for your own comments which you may wish to add.

The subject heading should be a catch word or phrase which identifies the contents of the card accurately. Such general headings as "American women's attitude toward youth and beauty" or "Youth and beauty" are less useful than more specific ones, such as "American women's worship of youth and beauty" or "The feminine cult of youth and beauty." You will often have several cards with identical subject headings, but this should occur only when the contents of the cards are on the same specific point.

Sources can be identified by abbreviating the author and title if all your sources are before you in one book as they are in this instance or if you have complete bibliographical cards for each source you used in the library. The page number (and the volume number in multi-volume work) must always be included.

The body of the note may be made up of your own summary, a direct quotation from the source, or both. The length of the summary may vary from a brief condensation to a rather complete paraphrase, depending upon the importance you place on the original passage. Whatever the length, the style of the summary must be entirely your own. It is inevitable that you will repeat many of the words of the original, but you must develop your own phrasing and sentence structure. You have not dealt honestly or profitably with your material if you present it in a style that resembles that of your source rather than your own. You must remember at all times that there is no such thing as a "near-quotation." You must present your information either in your own words or in an exact quotation. To fall between these alternatives defeats the value of research writing and leads to failure.

The following is an example of a note card for a paper dealing with the American pursuit of happiness. It is from information found in Mira Gavrilovitch, *You Americans*.

Gavrilovitch, pp. 69-70

The Pursuit of Happiness

Gavrilovitch feels that, "You Americans want to experience romantic movies not only in the theater but also in real life, in order to gain some relief from the intensity of your work and/from the monotonous whir of your machines. You are greedy for excitement, sensations, and record-making."

Note to → yourself

Remember to compare this attitude with the opinions of Cooke and Maritain. Is this really what Americans desire in life?

Although you should use direct quotations sparingly in your first paper, you should learn to use them correctly. When you quote you must be scrupulously accurate. You should observe the following rules, both in the note cards and in the paper.

1. The source must be reproduced exactly, including punctuation marks and misspellings.

2. Short quotations, not exceeding three or four lines, should be enclosed in quotation marks and should be run into the text; longer quotations are preferably

set off by indention (or, in a typewritten paper, by single spacing and indention) without quotation marks.

3. Ellipsis marks (three spaced periods) must be used to indicate omissions within a quotation. If the omission comes at the end of a sentence or extends to more than a sentence, a fourth period is required for end punctuation.

4. Any material inserted by you must be enclosed in square brackets. It may be necessary to supply the antecedent of a pronoun or to insert an identifying name: "I [Maritain] have pointed out a certain number of aspects of American life which seem to me to be typical." If the quoted part contains an error, you may insert the correction immediately following it or you may insert the word *sic* (Latin for "thus") to show that you are transcribing accurately. Archaic and British spellings need not be pointed out.

Direct quotations should be limited to passages of unusual effectiveness or importance.

Writing the Paper

After you have completed all your note cards, you should study them carefully and make your final outline. You should not expect every card to fall neatly into place. Most cards will fit into a logical place in the outline, but a few stubborn ones will resist classification. You must be extremely cautious in dealing with these misfits. They may reveal a weakness in your organization or conclusion. They may point to a contradiction which needs to be explained. Under no circumstances should you discard information to avoid dealing with a conflict. You may never have a better opportunity to increase your knowledge than when you wrestle with the problem of organizing facts which seem contradictory. If you cannot account for an exception to your interpretations of the facts, you should say so and let the exception stand. Throw out only those cards which are clearly irrelevant or repetitious.

After you have organized your material you should review your notes and outline until you feel confident that you can discuss your subject with authority and zest. You must never forget that the research paper is an original, creative piece of writing. It is true that you obtained your facts from your reading, but the interpretation and the presentation are original with you.

You should write the first draft with as few interruptions as possible. Do not bother about footnotes and similar details until later. This procedure is recommended as an antidote to the dull, wooden style that results from merely filling in an outline. After you have completed the first draft you should check it with the outline for digressions and omissions. You should then make corrections, add the footnotes, and rewrite as often as necessary.

The footnotes, which usually appear at the bottom of the page or at the end of the paper, are indispensable in a research paper because you must tell the reader where you got the information that is not original with you. They must be included, not only because the elementary principle of honesty requires you to acknowledge your sources, but also because you must make it possible for your reader to follow up or verify any facts in which he becomes interested.

No matter which system of documentation you use, you should see to it that all your footnotes are clear, accurate, consistent, and brief. The system standardized by the Style Sheet of the Modern Language Association has been adopted by more than seventy journals and is finding favor in many English departments.

The Style Sheet can be obtained for a slight charge from the Treasurer of the MLA, 100 Washington Square, New York 3, N. Y.

Your instructor will tell you whether your footnotes should cite the pagination of this book, or the pagination of the original texts, or both. One good scheme is to begin with some such footnote as this:

[1] All the material used in this paper is reprinted in *Modern America through Foreign Eyes,* edited by Robert F. McDonnell and William E. Morris (Boston: Heath, 1959), hereafter abbreviated as MATFE.

The next footnote could then read:

[2] James Morris, *As I Saw the U.S.A.* (New York: Pantheon Books, 1956), p. 163 (MATFE, p. 108).

Or your first footnote might say:

[1] All the material used in this paper is reprinted in *Modern America through Foreign Eyes,* edited by Robert F. McDonnell and William E. Morris (Boston: Heath, 1959); but my footnotes cite the original pagination, which the reprint supplies.

The next footnote would then say simply:

[2] James Morris, *As I Saw the U.S.A.* (New York: Pantheon Books, 1956), p. 163.

Research papers usually include a bibliography, an alphabetical list of books used in the preparation of the paper. Though a paper based on this book does not, strictly speaking, need a bibliography, you can gain valuable practice by compiling one for your paper, showing the various sources as they would be listed if you had consulted the original texts themselves. For the form, consult the authority you consulted for your footnotes.

Jacques Maritain

Prominent Christian-existentialist philosopher, Jacques Maritain was born in 1882 and educated at the University of Paris. His first experience with America came in 1940 when he took up residence in this country for four years while serving as Visiting Professor at Columbia University and at Princeton University. In 1948, he returned to the United States to become Professor of Philosophy at Princeton, where he has remained. Of his many books in both French and English, some of the better known in the United States are *True Humanism* (1939), *The Rights of Man and Natural Law* (1942), *Christianity and Democracy* (1943), *Man and the State* (1951), and *Creative Intuition in Art and Poetry* (1953).

THE OLD TAG OF AMERICAN MATERIALISM

29 I HAVE spoken of my first impressions on arriving in this country. Since that time I have come to realize more and more the immensity of the human effort which was brought into play to create a new world within the course of two centuries, to give to half a continent a material and moral equipment fit to free men and to build a civilization really and genuinely original in character, capable of astonishing, captivating and seducing the hearts of men.

And I have more and more admired both the creative work which was thus accomplished and the process of self-creation through which it unceasingly continues.

I have already said that the American people are the least materialist among the modern peoples which have attained the in-
30 dustrial stage. . . . / . . . few things, to my mind, are as sickening as the stock remarks with which so many persons in Europe, who are themselves far from despising the earthly goods of this world, reproach this country with its so-called materialism. The power of this fable is so great that sometimes you yourselves are taken in by it. I remember some American ladies in New York who said to me, with a disillusioned (perhaps slightly treacherous) wink: "We are a materialist nation, aren't we?" Well, all this talk about American materialism is no more than a curtain of silly gossip and slander.

In a number of my fellow Europeans the fable in question proceeds from an old prejudice, confusing spirituality with an aristocratic contempt for any improvement in material life (especially the material life of others). In other cases the fable of American materialism (seemingly corroborated, as it is, by some of your exports, like average Hollywood productions) appears as a kind of compensation for the frustrations Europe has endured, and a kind of / solace 31 for the agony which the fact of owing gratitude to another imposes on human nature. And in other cases, it results, contrariwise, from too great an expectation, from the fact that Europeans expect from you an understanding which they fail sometimes to obtain.

I have no intention of denying that in America as in all other places in the world, especially among industrialized nations, large areas in the common consciousness — the most obvious, as a rule, and the most superficial areas — have been infected by the miasmata that emanate from the structures and ritual of our modern civilization; the noise made by a crowd of vulgar assertions, which measure everything either in terms of statistics and facts and figures or in terms of success, fun, and practical power, hold "ideas" to be only something

1

to be "sold" to a possible consumer, silent partner, or sucker, and see human conduct as a by-product either of hormones or of economic factors — this noise is too great not to be heard.

The observer may be misled, it is true, especially when it comes to the answers given by people about their personal aims in life, or about their political choices, by the appearances and facilities of language, /
32 I mean by the fact that as a rule, in our everyday life, we use words in a way which will save our brain cells as much work as possible — and it is much easier and less expensive, in this respect, to have recourse to mean rather than to lofty platitudes. Yet the universal diffusion of a kind of popularized, anonymous positivistic philosophy, to which pragmatist dynamism, in this country, gave higher intellectual standing and additional pep, can only make more real and more insidious the process of materialist contagion of which I am speaking.

I don't deny these things; I do say that to invoke them as a proof of so-called American materialism is to talk nonsense. For, in the first place, they are in no way specifically American; exactly the same symptoms, in relation to similar sociological or psychological areas, leap to the eye everywhere (especially in Europe) where the industrial regime and its congenial ideological fumes are prevalent; only the vocal expression seems perhaps to be a little cruder and more naive here, whereas elsewhere it is either more cautious and sophisticated or more elaborately cynical.

And, in the second place, there are here plenty of other, utterly opposing trends and characteristics, which relate to much deeper
33 and more significant / strata in the common psyche, and which are typically American, and give the lie to the fable of American materialism.

Well, I would like to ask the European critics of this country what are in their eyes the criteria of materialism. Are perhaps generosity and good will the signs of a mate-

rialistic cast of mind? Speaking not of such or such an individual, of course, but of the general cast of mind and the collective trends and customs of the people, what I know is that the basic characteristics of the American people are generosity, good will, the sense of human fellowship.

There are, of course, egoistic individuals in America as everywhere, but America is not egoist; for the common consciousness of America, egoism is shameful.

There are greedy individuals in America as there are everywhere, but there is no avarice in the American cast of mind.

The American people are neither squeamish nor hypocritical about the importance of money in the modern world. Even their frank admission of this importance makes Europeans uncomfortable. For / the average European cares about 34 money as well as the average American, but he tries to conceal the fact, for he has been accustomed to associating money with avarice.

Here, on the contrary, money is cared for openly, because money is considered a means, and must not be kept but rather spent — for improving one's own life, to be sure, and one's freedom of action, but also, and this is fundamental, for improving the lives and freedom of others.

Americans like to give. Of course, there is the exemption from taxes for gifts directed to the common welfare; but this very law about taxes would not have been possible if the astute legislator did not know that as a rule the American people are aware of the fact that it is better to give than to receive. Not only the great foundations, but the ordinary course of activity of American institutions and the innumerable American private groups show us that / the ancient 35 Greek and Roman idea of the *civis praeclarus,* the dedicated citizen who spends his money in the service of the common good, plays an essential part in American consciousness. And let me observe that more often than not the gifts in question are made for the sake of education and knowledge. Frequently people who were unable to have a college education make large gifts to universities.

There is no materialism, I think, in the astonishing, countless initiatives of fraternal help which are the daily bread of the American people, or in the profound feeling of obligation toward others which exists in them, especially toward any people abroad who are in distress.

I shall never forget the work of the rescue committees for European scholars which I witnessed during the war, and all those luncheons which crowds of people eagerly attended in order to have an eloquent auctioneer, at dessert time, extract big checks from their pockets. I shall never forget the admirable devotion with which Alvin Johnson, then President of the New School for Social Research, pursued this work of rescue, nor the fraternal cooperation he extended to our French-speaking *École Libre des Hautes Études* when it was created with the help and on the premises of the New School.

36 There is no materialism in the fact that the American charities, drawing money from every purse, and notably to assist people abroad, run every year into such enormous sums that charity ranks among the largest American industries, the second or third in size, according to statisticians.

Yes, yes, I know, the very fact involves a certain danger that charity itself will become industrialized, or overorganized. Well, people who sit on their money like brooding hens are certain to avoid that danger! And if the collection of money for the needy and the helpless is so well organized here that in giving our contribution automatically each year, we may be tempted to think that we are excused from ever giving our heart (but can we believe that European streets are jammed with people busy giving their hearts?), let us not forget what an immense amount of personal attention to one's neighbor and what personal effort is unceasingly put forth in all the groups which exist in this country, and which spring up every day, to meet some particular human misfortune or some particular social maladjustment.

I would like to mention now other characteristics of American life, namely, the extraordinary resilience and versatility with which the American people face / new 37 problems and adjust themselves to new situations. They don't like to accept things as they are, and to let people shift for themselves by dint of suffering and ingenuity. They prefer to change things and situations. They prefer to find a new arrangement, new equipment, a new gadget, a new line of social activity, for the sake of the human individuals involved. Now, did not Hegel speak of the "infinite elasticity" of the spirit? Such resilience is a sign of a perpetual alertness of the spirit acting as a ferment in the mass.

Let us say, and this seems quite typical to me, that in the immense population of America there is no stagnation. As a result, I don't see America as a mainland, but as a sea, a big ocean. Sometimes a storm arises, a formidable current develops, and it seems it will engulf everything. Wait a moment, another current will appear and bring the first one to naught. A great country, with as many windshifts as the sea.[1]

At the origin of this *fluidity* there is the activity of the mind at work in the people, in the humble ways of daily life.

Many other aspects might be stressed. 38 First, I shall point out the concern of the American people for moral and religious values, their attitude toward moral conscience. I do not say that they always act according to the dictates of conscience — what nation does? I say that they feel miserable, they endure terrible discomfort when they have a guilty conscience. The

[1] May I note in this connection that it would perhaps be a good idea for official propaganda not to seem regularly to ignore the various dissenting currents, the conflicts and oppositions, the more or less adventurous reforming enterprises, which are a sign of American vitality.

very fact alone of nursing a doubt as to whether their conduct was or was not ethically irreproachable causes them pain. The result is sometimes unexpected, as the wave of fondness for the Japanese people which developed after Hiroshima. Let us say that hiring the devil for help will never be agreeable even to your politicians. The common consciousness of this country loathes cynicism, cannot be cynical.

A second aspect is the fundamental part played in this country by free discussion, involving that right to dissent without which there is no community of free men, and which no historical circumstance can impair here for long. There is a perpetual process of self-examination and self-criticism going on everywhere and in every sphere of American life: a phenomenon incomprehensible without a quest for truth of which a materialist cast of mind is incapable.

39   A third aspect is the great battle which is being fought in the educational field to develop the humanities,[2] the liberal arts, philosophy, and to make wisdom the final aim, a battle of which the members of the Committee on Social Thought are especially aware. It is in this so-called materialist country that professors of classics, each in his own great or small college, struggle with unequalled devotion to maintain the intellectual tradition with which they are entrusted; that a strenuous effort is being made by the universities, and by technological institutes as well, to overcome the dangers of overspecialization and the trends toward technocracy which are natural to industrial civilization; and that a reformer of such stature as Robert M. Hutchins has raised his bitter criticisms and insisted on

the necessity for intellectual integration — inspiring or prodding in actual fact the vast academic effort of which I just spoke, though naturally his name is too well known to the public ever to be mentioned on campuses.

A fourth aspect is the thirst, the eager- 40 ness for knowledge — not only with a view to its practical applications, but first of all as a vital necessity for the mind — which I have had the opportunity to observe, year after year, in American youth everywhere in the country. Such a thirst exists in the people as a whole, in uneducated as in educated persons. Here as elsewhere it is not created by education and teachers (sometimes they seem rather anxious to kill it). It is a need of nature, particularly fresh, huge and intense in the American people.

A fifth aspect is the thirst for spiritual life which is deep in the American soul, and the signs of which are more and more manifest, especially among young people. In a number of people it is more or less unconscious, more or less repressed by the conditions of existence and the tyranny of unceasing activity. For all that it is real and alive, and exercises continual pressure on souls.

For many years I was aware of this fact; I am particularly pleased to have laid stress on it at a time when such views seemed more than paradoxical, and my Carthusian friends in Europe told me that the very idea of ever having a Charterhouse in America was completely ridiculous.

In a lecture on Action and Contemplation written / some twenty years ago,[3] I 41 insisted that there were in America great reserves and possibilities for contemplation; the activism which is to the fore appears, I said, in many cases as a remedy against despair, and masks a hidden aspiration to contemplation. I saw in the American inclination to be moved by large idealistic

[2] From among the great scholars who are representing in the United States the tradition of the highest humanistic culture, I would like to mention and pay my personal tribute of admiration to Mark Van Doren, Lane Cooper, Whitney J. Oates, Erwin Panofsky, Huntington Cairns, R. P. Blackmur, Francis Fergusson, who was the first director of Princeton University's Seminars in Literary Criticism, and E. B. O. Borgerhoff, who succeeded him in the direction of the Seminars (Christian Gauss Seminars in Criticism).

[3] This lecture, given in the United States in 1938, was published later as Chapter VII in *Scholasticism and Politics*, New York: Macmillan, 1940. Used with the permission of The Macmillan Company.

feelings an effect of his hidden aspiration. And I concluded: "The cult of action is not specifically American. It is a European idea, an idea of post-Renaissance and post-Reformation Europe. What may mislead us in this matter, so it seems to me, is that the New Continent, with terrible loyalty, has taken some of the Old World's ideas, transplanted into virgin soil, and carried them to their limits. When in America some few come to realize better the value of contemplative activity, its superiority and fecundity, I believe the possibilities I have spoken of will manifest themselves, at least in a small way, but forcefully enough gradually to modify the general scheme of values."

Well, now Tom Merton's books are best-sellers, great classical works on spiritual life are published in abundance and are widely 42 read in the most varied / circles, the Trapp of Gethsemani alone has more novices than all European Trapps combined, and is obliged to multiply new foundations; the monasteries founded by various contemplative Orders are so crowded that they refuse candidates for lack of room; and there is a Charterhouse in this country.

I have pointed out a certain number of aspects of American life which seem to me to be typical. I could continue in the same vein. There is no end to the enumeration of the various features peculiar, quite peculiar indeed, to so-called *American materialism.*

Let me only add that from *Moby Dick* and *The Scarlet Letter* to *Look Homeward, Angel* and *Requiem for a Nun* — from Edgar Allan Poe and Emily Dickinson to Hart Crane, Allen Tate and T. S. Eliot (who has remained an American in spite of himself) — American literature, in its most objectively careful scrutinies, has been preoccupied with the beyond and the nameless which haunt our blood. Man, as it sees him, is a restless being gropingly, sometimes miserably, at grips with his fleshly condition — whom obviously no kind of materialist paradise can ever satisfy. . . .

MARRIAGE AND HAPPINESS

Among the "American illusions" of 137 which I just spoke, the last one — about marriage, romantic love and the pursuit of full individual self-realization — poses, I think, particularly important problems and deserves particular attention.

It is perhaps advisable to try to elucidate the matter a little more by resorting to a few general considerations, and first of all to state more explicitly what I had in mind when I used the expression "romantic love."

To my mind "romantic love" is sexual love when it goes beyond the sphere of simple animality (in which it remains rooted), and bursts into full bloom in the properly human sphere, exalting and ravishing everything in the human being — sentiments, thought, creative activity, which are henceforth imbued with and stimulated by the basic passion of desire.

Such a love carries man beyond himself — in imagination — into a kind of poetical paradise, and makes him believe that he is entirely and eternally / dedicated to the 138 one he loves, and that he lives and breathes only for this one, while in reality this other human person is so passionately cherished first of all for the sake of sexual desire and possession, which remain the primary essential incentive.

This romantic love might be defined as a total intoxication of the human being by sexual desire taking the loftiest forms and disguised as pure and absolutely disinterested, pure and eternal love of the other.

Now, since sexual attraction and satisfaction remain the essential incentive and the essential aim, it must be said that romantic love — *l'amour passion* — being but a transcendent human expression of the strongest animal instinct, is, by nature: first, deprived of permanence and liable to fade away; second, unfaithful and liable to shift from one object to another; and third, intrinsically torn between the love for another, which it has awakened, and its own basically egoist nature.

Consequently, to found marriage on romantic love, and to think that marriage must be the perfect fulfillment of romantic love is, as I submitted, a great illusion.

Mankind has been so well aware of this fact that for centuries marriage, being considered a merely social affair, was regarded 139 as a thing with which per-/sonal inclination and personal love had nothing — or very little — to do. I am thinking of all those marriages which were arranged by parents, for family interests or tribal considerations — even national interests when it was a question of kings and queens. So that sometimes a boy and a girl had never met one another before they were married.

There was some sad, wicked wisdom in this conception, so far as it recognized the fact that romantic love and married love are two quite different things; and that the aim of marriage is not to bring romantic love to perfect fulfillment.

Yet, in proportion as, in the course of history, the human person became more and more aware of his or her own value and own importance, the merely social conception of marriage to which I just alluded appeared more inhuman and more harmful. For, especially in modern times, a result was that in a number of cases men and women looked for mutual personal love, and romantic love (which is an inherent dream of the human being) outside of marriage. Thus people came to realize that if mutual personal love, and even initially an element of romantic love, are not a necessary requirement of the validity of marriage — at least they are a necessary requirement for its intrinsic dignity and welfare.

Finally, the truth of the matter, as I see 140 it, is, first, / that love as desire or passion, and romantic love — or at least an element of it — should, as far as possible, be present in marriage as a first incentive and starting point. Otherwise, it would be too difficult for the human being, if and when an opportunity for romantic love outside of marriage should later appear, to resist the temptation; for what makes man most unhappy is to be deprived not of that which he had, but of that which he did not have, and did not really know.

The second point is that far from having as its essential aim to bring romantic love to perfect fulfillment, marriage has to perform in human hearts quite another work — an infinitely deeper and more mysterious, alchemical operation: I mean to say, it has to *transmute* romantic love, or what existed of it at the beginning, into real and indestructible *human* love, and really disinterested love, which does not exclude sex, of course, but which grows more and more independent of sex, and even can be, in its highest forms, completely free from sexual desire and intercourse, because it is essentially spiritual in nature — a complete and irrevocable gift of the one to the other, for the sake of the other.

Thus it is that marriage can be between man and woman a true community of love, built not on sand, but on rock, because it is built on genuinely human, / not animal, 141 and genuinely spiritual, genuinely *personal* love — through the hard discipline of self-sacrifice and by dint of renouncements and purifications. Then in a free and unceasing ebb and flow of emotion, feeling, and thought, each one really participates, by virtue of love, in that personal life of the other which is, by nature, the other's incommunicable possession. And then each one may become a sort of guardian Angel for the other — prepared, as guardian Angels have to be, to forgive the other a great deal: for the gospel law of mutual forgiveness expresses, I believe, a fundamental requirement which is valid not only in the supernatural order, but in the terrestrial and temporal order as well, and for basically natural societies like domestic society and even political society. Each one, in other words, may then become really dedicated to the good and salvation of the other.

After these general considerations, I come now to the American scene. I shall content myself with a brief outline of my subject — I am afraid a whole book would be necessary to attempt a satisfactory study of it.

Speaking of books, there are, from the point of view of rather superficial but witty 142 and valuable ob-/servation, a lot of interesting remarks in a book by David L. Cohn, *Love in America*, which I remember reading some years ago.

The first thing I would say is that the problem of the relations between the sexes seems to me to be still more important, and still more dramatic, in this country than that of the relations between management and labor, and even that of the relations between races.

Then, I would say that in my opinion American men and women have undertaken with great courage and good will an attempt to found marriage on mutual love (more than on considerations of social standing, clannish interests, expectations of inheritance, and so forth), and to have marriage bring happiness to husband and wife as human persons essentially equal in rights and dignity.

And this is all for the best, indeed, except for the fact that the attempt in question does not seem to be largely successful, and that in too many cases good will ends in unhappiness and conflict: probably, I think, because there was some fundamental mistake in the interpretation of the ideal I just alluded to, and which is quite right in itself but can be understood in a misleading way 143 (if by love one understands / romantic love, and by happiness, individual self-realization).

My final observation is that the problem of which I am speaking, and which risks making the pursuit of happiness a delusion for so many people, will be successfully solved — so far as in human affairs any solution is possible — when the American mind comes to realize two basic verities.

The first verity is that love is not sex, and that that kind of love on which marriage must be founded is not primarily sensual passion, *l'amour passion*, nor romantic love and that philtre by which Tristan and Isolde were divinely intoxicated — but a deeper and more lasting love, into which, as I said a moment ago, romantic love must be transmuted, and in which sex and passion are but a prime incentive. This deeper and more lasting love takes root and develops at the properly human and spiritual level where the one accepts to be entrusted with the revelation of, and the care for, all that the other *is* in his or her deepest human depths, and where the will is fully dedicated to the good and happiness of the one loved.

The second verity is that if one expects from marriage, in the name of the equal dignity of each one, a final assertion and realization of what one thinks of / as one's per- 144 sonality and which is actually no more than self-centered individuality, one prepares for oneself a hell of disappointment and bitterness: because without love, genuinely human love, marriage is a state of servitude, and because love, genuinely human love, is essentially the gift of oneself, that is to say, precisely the opposite of any selfish and self-centered assertion and enjoyment of one's individuality.

As a result, it is through renouncement of such self-realization that real love leads man and woman to a superior form of freedom and happiness, which is purified, and spiritual in nature, and in which the personality of each one is enlarged and uplifted, each one being henceforth primarily centered *in the other*, or having his or her dearest self *in the other*. In contradistinction to love as desire or passion, we have here, I would say, in the etymological sense of the word, love as ecstasy, which makes the human being pass, and exist, outside himself.

I am not suggesting that the two verities I just mentioned are put into practice anywhere in the world more than in this country, or that it is easy to have married life conform to them.

I do suggest that these two verities show us the only way in which it is really possi-

ble to make successful the American at-
145 tempt to found marriage on / mutual love
only, and have it bring happiness to husband and wife as human persons essentially
equal in rights and dignity.

In other words, they express the only
true and really human meaning of the ideal
after which the American concept of marriage is striving.

WORK AND LEISURE

155 Many anti-American cartoons abroad de-
pict Uncle Sam brandishing a dollar as a
symbol of American civilization. There is
more ignorance than malice in this plati-
tude. As a matter of fact, it is not money,
it is *work* which holds sway over American
civilization.

Everybody is working, and working hard.
In this sense all are fundamentally equal,
as working people (and people burdened by
mortgages and deferred payment systems)
who work to make a living, and who, after
their daily hours, busy themselves again
with any kind of task — handicrafts, improving their houses, sometimes building
them, as Dr. Butterfield did, who was so
sorry to leave his frame house, entirely
built by him, when he became President
of Wesleyan University. And they are
more proud of their hobbies than of their
jobs.

American civilization thus lays stress on
the dignity of work and the fecundity of
work transforming matter and nature.
These are basic verities, in spite of all the
fuss that the modern age is making about /
156 them — verities that essentially matter to
man and society, and which ancient civili-
zations more or less ignored.

Yes. And for all that the fact remains
that a certain boredom is caused by the
absolute primacy of work and the disregard
for the human value of leisure. Here is
the dark side of the picture.

Let us think of the American attitude
toward time. There is here, it seems to me,
a certain horror of any span of time which

a man might have at his own disposal in
order to *do nothing*. The great value and
efficacy of standing idle, and lingering over
one's dream, is little appreciated in this
country. One might wonder, for instance,
whether committee meetings and all similar
periodically recurrent administrative nui-
sances have not been invented to prevent
professors, once they have finished lecturing, from having any time for idleness —
that is to say, for thinking at leisure and
pursuing their own research.

Well, friendship requires a great waste
of time, and much idleness; creative thinking requires a great deal of idleness. So it
is that leisure constitutes a serious problem
for American life, especially given the social
and technical progress, the automation, /
for instance, which makes working hours 157
shorter and shorter in industry.

The question will be to have leisure time
occupied in a manner really profitable to
man, and not entirely taken up by the sort
of stupefying passivity that is more often
than not developed by movies or television.
As long as a new cast of mind does not
develop, involving a certain amount of spiritual epicureanism, the quality of leisure in
the modern world will not be on a level
with the quality of work.

If it is true, as Aristotle and Thomas
Aquinas thought, that man cannot do without a certain amount of delectation, so
that when he is deprived of spiritual delec-
tations he passes over to carnal ones, how
be surprised that all over the modern world
the mass of humanity tamed by the general
boredom of mathematized labor, should, if
no superior flame is kindled, naturally become a prey to the obsession of sex (here
the phenomenon, while taking especially
pedantic forms, mentioned in a previous
chapter, has its external or symbolic expression in a curious return to a Greek nostalgia
for the figure of Venus).

No leisure time will be enough for man
to experience the joys of knowledge, of art
and poetry, of devotion to great human
causes, of communicating with others in the

158 dreams and anxieties of the mind, / of silently conversing with himself and silently conversing with God.

Work, which is a fundamental necessity of our existence, is not an end in itself. We work in order to improve human life. But will this very improvement, in ourselves and in others, only consist in working again and working more? Or will it also consist in the attainment of some superior possession, in which we shall rest? There are many kinds of rest. Laziness is sin. Amusement is good, but less good than work. Certain kinds of repose, in which the mind is supremely active, and reaches, however imperfectly, some fruition of immortality through its contact with truth, or with Eternal Love, are better than work.

Higher forms of leisure are no longer leisure but act come to completion. And the highest form is contemplative activity. *Be still, and know that I am God.*[4]

And now, as regards work itself, further considerations may be submitted. The multiplication of technical and artificial facilities for work is intrinsically good, there is no doubt about that. But if these facilities 159 grow at the expense of the natural / energies and resourcefulness of individuals, they might result, *per accidens,* in a sort of over-civilization, removing us too far from our native sources and that keenness of instinct which was a privilege of primitive man. The mental habits produced by the mechanization of work impair to some extent the sensitivity and agility of fingers in certain especially delicate manual tasks, and the average American worker, accustomed as he is to following carefully elaborated plans and standard regulations, happens sometimes to shift for himself in unforeseen situations less well than his European fellow worker. I don't deny the fact. I do not believe that the risk implied will ever develop into a serious threat.

4 Psalms, 45:11 (Vulg.)

Some Americans think that their country, despite the wonderful candor and freshness which are shown by its young people, is rendered older than the Old World by the excess of artificial contrivances and artificial improvements of which it likes to make use. Are they young or old, all these cities where it has become a problem to purchase food products which have not been improved, enriched or energized by a foolish lot of vitamins, proteins, maltose, dextrins, calcium, phosphorus, iron, potassium bicarbonate, milk powder, honey, butter, spices and artificial flavors (fruits are sometimes varnished but not yet injected with anti-histamines or tranquillizers)?

I have never been very much impressed 160 by this line of argumentation. The description just offered was of course slightly exaggerated, for the fun of it. And in general the facilities which art adds to nature only make older, I think, those who have no real youth in themselves. Here, in any case, the instinctive counteraction is not lacking; almost every American dreams of having a farm, and a number of people — not to speak of the farmers themselves — enjoy the real thing. Furthermore one notes, in this highly industrialized country, an amazing fondness for roving about in trailers, breaking new ground, prospecting for the natural riches of the soil, conquering the wilderness, or even leading a solitary life in forests, mountains and lonely spaces.

If it can be said that Americans are not a young people, this is surely not because they like gadgets. The statement is true in quite another sense — in the sense that while they are cheerfully engrossed in building their skyscrapers and their cyclotrons, the age-old experience of the world in misfortune and hard times is secretly flowing back into their hearts, and the unconscious, nocturnal part of their minds is obscurely struggling with all the old dreams, anxieties, and fatigue of mankind, as with haunting ghosts: a revenge that the maliciousness of history is taking on them.

Graham Hutton

From *The Midwest at Noon*. Chicago (University of Chicago Press), 1946. Reprinted with the author's permission.

Mr. Hutton, British economist and author, born in 1904, has traveled extensively in the United States. In the period from 1939 to 1945 he was with the British Foreign Office and Ministry of Information in England and the United States. Besides *The Midwest at Noon*, he has written *Nations and the Economic Crisis* (1932), *Is It Peace?* (1936), *We Too Can Prosper* (1953).

[MIDWEST FARMING COMMUNITY]

78 THE RURAL towns to which farmers repair are an enormous influence in, and a particular feature of, the Midwest. They have generally from one to five thousand inhabitants. They follow a distinctive over-all pattern from Ohio to Minnesota or Missouri with but slight, though important, local differences. They have grown, in the main, from a corner store at the crossing of crude trackways, among a few log cabins, or from a river landing or railroad depot. The pattern of that crossroads is still there at the heart of the town today, often a green square with singular memorials to those who fell in the Civil War and all wars since.

79 Along the sides of the square, if the town is a county seat, are the / county buildings and courthouse, the bank or banks, a battery of lawyers' offices — farmers must still be as litigious as the original settlers, or else land titles are inexplicably confused for so young a country — two or three drug stores, some taverns, barber shops and at least one beauty parlor, doctors', dentists', and veterinaries' offices, the newspaper, and the usual array of hardware, clothing, and other stores. Among the stores are a surprising number of jewelers, for farmers apparently buy much gold when times are good. They were most certainly doing so during the second World War, and jewelry stores have multiplied. Here is perhaps a lingering trace of the farmer-settler's long-pent-up demand for luxuries and distrust of "paper" and banks. During the last fifty years the taverns which used to be, and are often still, called "saloons" have dwindled as the drugstores have increased; a commentary on trends among farmers and their families. The first church — Methodist or Presbyterian or Lutheran or Baptist or (more rarely) Episcopalian — is "on the square." The other churches, like the movie and the grade and high schools, are usually a block or two from it, as the town grew.

The store fronts look modern, if rather cheap and standardized, with neon signs; but, if you cast your eyes upward, you will see good, well-laid Flemish bond or other traditional bricklaying, and windows of the 1860's or earlier. There are no hills, except in Wisconsin or along the Ohio or in Minnesota; so you see no skyline from the center of the town. It is as if the welkin were a big sun umbrella balanced on the central market place. The streets, paved only in the center of town, run straight into a middle distance of overhanging trees beyond which lies open country. Along them brick alternates with clapboard until, still surprisingly near the central crossroads, every building becomes a home and all are clapboard. Before them are little lawns and no hedges or borders, but vines over the porches and flowers by the house. Within a stone's throw of the crossroads are many gas stations, warehouses full of farmers' implements and supplies, and seedsmen's stores. If there is a railroad depot, it is usually a few blocks from the center; it will have one combined waiting-room and ticket office on one side of the tracks. Round it are warehouses; along the tracks are generally loading-pens for cattle and hogs; and there is certainly a sizable truck depot near by. The nearness of the real countryside to the center of all rural Midwest towns is a great and an ever present influence.

Outside the chief public and commercial buildings in summer, and inside them in winter, farmers and local worthies always find time to talk; and good talk it generally 80 is. Everyone uses "first names." They / talk slowly as if they savored it rarely, which is probably the case; and it is simpler Anglo-Saxon, with less city slang in it. During the hours of daylight, as if by common consent, the talk is mainly of personalities and trade and purely local affairs. In the evening, whether in town or at a neighbor's in the country, talk turns to state and national politics and issues of greater pith and moment. The farmer still comes into town with wife and family (except those at school), for his wife has as much to do in the town as he himself, and young children have to be brought with the mother. Where buggies used to line the square and the whinnying of horses was heard on all sides, there are now mute, serried ranks of automobiles of all ages and descriptions, with and without trailers. The farmer's standing can still be roughly gauged by the make and age of his automobile.

There is always one leading hotel in or near the central crossroads, and the lobby chairs are nearly always occupied. Here meet for lunch, on their respective days, if the town is large enough, the Rotarians, Lions, Elks, Kiwanis, Buffaloes, or other service clubs; banquets are given; and local functions take place. It is one of the very few common meeting-places. On the mezzanine or the second floor is usually the local Chamber of Commerce, if the town boasts one. Few rural towns do, but most towns of 5,000 inhabitants and more have one, if only to "boost the town." The Farm Bureau, Grange, or Union has an office or chapter in the town. There are often in the larger towns a Y.M.C.A. and, less generally, a Y.W.C.A. If the rural town is the county seat, there will probably be a public library, but otherwise it is a rarity.

Much of the shape, layout, compactness, communal solidarity, and social familiarity of Lincoln's Springfield still fills these rural towns of the Midwest. In town and county politics almost every voter knows the candidates and they him; or, if they do not, they know someone in town — tradesman, banker, editor — who does. It is much the same in social affairs. Life is intensely personal. Business and politics and social matters are arranged or "fixed" by a few informal talks. A group of worthies runs the community. They trade, talk, and visit with one another. They were nearly all born there or near by. They stay put. They become the arbiters of community life. Each knows, likes, and is liked by a group of surrounding farmers; and in this way the rural town is the social focus of an area often as big as one or two hundred square miles and with an agricultural population of some 10,000–25,000.

If the district is overwhelmingly agricultural — as it will be in central and southern Ohio, Indiana, and Illinois, or most of Wisconsin and Iowa and Minnesota, or the center of northern Missouri — the county / seat may be a rural town of between 5,000 81 and 20,000 inhabitants, and there may well be no other social center of that size within a radius of twenty to thirty miles. This partly reflects the insulation of farm life and small-town life in the Midwest; but it also explains the compact solidarity of these smaller communities and the immense influence they have wielded on the lives of their tradesmen's or professional men's or farmers' children during the last century.

Many a successful midwestern businessman or professional man between his fifties and seventies in the big cities came from these smaller towns or from the farms which serve, and are served by, them. A certain amount of his present outlook, caution, susceptibility to public opinion, toleration, and forbearance will remain from his youth. His successful colleagues and competitors, city-born, do not have these qualities to the same extent. There is much more to be said for life in the public eye of a small community than most people seem willing to confess today. (Perhaps it is just because they fear the public eye.) But in the formation of the Midwest character, the farms and the small country town have done most and best — at least among midwesterners aged fifty and more today. The monotonous life may have driven its sons and daughters forth, but it has left its indelible mark upon them. Much of their success in the cities is due to it.

One of the chief social problems of the farming community and the rural town is the scarcity of diversions; and, as leisure time increases, the problem grows with it. At home there is now the radio, which, however, is almost 100 per cent weighted with "big-city talk" and the characteristics of cities. It has therefore been a disturbing influence on the family life of the farms, while being at the same time a great boon. In summer and fall there is all the sport of the open air; hunting and fishing and boating — there are lakes or rivers within driving distance throughout the region — and motoring to this or that center of amusement or interest. (Water sports are surprisingly popular throughout the Midwest, which may help explain the popularity of the Navy in the inland states.) There are the forests, too. But winter and the so-called spring take up half the farm year. Then rural towns provide the only diversions, and they are limited: taverns, bowling, nickel-in-the-slot machines, one movie house open once or twice a week, and little else. Dances are still arranged by families and societies, as they were a century ago; but there is more attraction for the young, initiated by radio, in the newer kinds of dancing and dance halls, which they have heard of or seen in the cities and of which the religions of the farm belt do not approve. Consequently, social and family life on the farms 82 and / in the rural towns is undergoing great and growing tension. I have been in scores of rural towns in which there was no public library, no community center, no social focus of any kind. (The middle-sized towns and the cities are far ahead in this

respect.) The young have no secular meeting-place save the drugstore or the tavern, though the churches or the Y.M.C.A. and Y.W.C.A., where the latter exist, provide some kind of social or religious focus on some week nights. The service clubs and the city fathers are anxiously trying to find a solution to what, after all, also vexes parents in the largest cities of America and the whole Western world. But meanwhile the thousands of farm communities and rural towns of the Midwest — which has more of them than almost any other region in the world — feel the impact of modernity upon youth much more keenly.

The social life of the parents is simpler and far less pretentious. To that extent we may be on the eve of a great social and familial convulsion in the Midwest, brought on by the automobile and radio. It could easily result in the disappearance of certain original, fundamental, and currently strong midwestern characteristics within a score of years from now. The farmer and his wife today, if they are aged forty-five or over, were not nurtured on radio and gasoline.

I recall many winter evenings with Midwest farmers — in Illinois, Wisconsin, Iowa, Ohio, Minnesota — when, neighbors having been advised (or, perhaps I ought to say, warned), about twenty would foregather in one farmhouse just to talk. The visiting wives would get someone to look after their children and come over to the host's farm to help the hostess with the baking and preparations. They would bring jars of this or that, or a pie, or a cake. The men would bring bottles of this or that, too. The icicles would hang by the barn door, swordlike. The snow would crackle underfoot in the temperature of zero to 30° below. Through the double storm windows far away the little lights of nearest neighbors would twinkle like grounded stars. At six we would see the headlights of cars steadily eating up the straight, white, snow-deep roads and finally snaking along the driveway up to the farm. Muffled, their occupants would come in, greeting each other only by first names: "Ned," "Matt," "Charlie," "Mis'

Clarke." There would be an intense, hushed, and entirely propitious bustling in the kitchen in the rear. The summons would come, and we would sit down, nine or ten aside, host and hostess at either end, the other ladies "in waiting," to a dinner which fairly sang of Midwest hospitality: fresh mushroom soup; two kinds of chicken or pork; lima and string beans, baked potatoes, corn biscuits, preserve of baby straw-

83 berries and butter with the / biscuits; salad of lettuce with fresh cranberry and pomegranate jello thereon; ice cream and maple syrup or three kinds of pie; and coffee. (I know they did not eat like that ordinarily. But I also know they could do it regularly for the enjoyment of their friends and for an evening in their own home.) In the offing, over the banisters, curious and wide-eyed youngsters, regularly shooed off to bed and as regularly returning, would give the false impression of Christmas eve. Afterward the ladies washed dishes — none would dream of leaving that pile for the hostess next morning — and then we would talk, and the ladies would join us.

Of all the talk and discussion I had in the Midwest, I think I relished that in the farmhouses most; and not only because of the preliminaries. It was direct, elemental, simple, often oversimplified, but extremely rational and open-minded. There was an evident readiness to change opinions upon fair, logical conviction. Those fundamental and remarkably searching political discussions in the stores, taverns, farms, and courthouses of Ohio and Indiana and Illinois before the Civil War do not seem so long ago when you go among Midwest farmers today. This may seem very near to romantic idealism; but it goes on. It simply is not heard of by the three-fifths of the population who are city dwellers in the Midwest. And that seems to me a pity for both of the great divisions of the Midwest people. "There is a great gulf fixed. . . . ."

One reason for this division is the greater speed with which the Midwest farming community has assimilated foreign or other-American immigrants to an over-all pattern of rural life. This assimilation is almost complete and utterly unlike the state of affairs in the cities and middle-sized towns. Almost anywhere in the region today, if you take one of the county seats and look at the land titles or records, or comb the area around, you will find American farmers of Anglo-Saxon, Celtic, German, Scandinavian, Bohemian, Ukrainian, and other Slav origins. You will find Methodists, Baptists, Presbyterians, Congregationalists, Unitarians, Episcopalians, Lutherans, Roman Catholics, Greek Orthodox, Jews (only in the town), Quakers, Christian Scientists, Seventh-Day Adventists, Jehovah's Witnesses, and many you may never have heard of before. But if you leave an area with a majority of German or Scandinavian Lutheran farmers and go to one with a majority of Anglo-Saxon Methodists, or to one with a majority of Russian Orthodox (and I have been to some), or to one with a majority of Bohemian Hussites, you will note only slight and superficial differences among those communities, no different pattern of life, and only differences in politics or outlook on national or international affairs.

In one county seat of 14,000 souls in 84 Ohio, for instance, I found Americans of fifteen national origins with twenty-three different churches, excluding different branches of one and the same church. Mason City in Iowa, with 27,000 inhabitants, when I was last there had Episcopalian, Roman Catholic, Presbyterian, Baptist, Congregational, and Greek Orthodox churches and a synagogue; but it had two Methodist churches, five Lutheran — two German, a Norwegian, a Swedish, and another Eastern United Lutheran church — two Negro churches, and one remarkable evangelical, undenominational "radio church" with a big unseen congregation of listeners. The people of the city came from forty different national origins in Europe, including Iceland, and some years ago they were from fifty-five such national origins. Mason City, apart from being the seat of an agricultural county, is partly a manufacturing town and is, in any case, not "truly rural"; it is a middle-sized town. I mention it again in this context because I have described its near-by farmers. But these cases could be paralleled, with variations, throughout the agricultural areas of the region. Yet the social uniformity and single pattern of farm life covers them all.

The morality of the farmers in the Midwest is strict. In both their private and their community life their religions, no matter how great their differences of dogma or theology, have budded forth into an ethic of fair dealing. The sins of the rural families and communities in the region are naturally as human as those of any city dweller, but they are less varied and more elemental: mainly crimes of sex and personal violence, often ascribable to liquor. There is more looseness in sex morality than appears on the surface — or in court! The "shotgun wedding" is still common, even if a shotgun is no longer necessary; and the two parties resume a respected position in society. There is much less theft and almost no housebreaking, robbery with violence, holdups, racketeering, blackmail, and so on. In the farming and rural community, the greater social uniformity is reflected in a greater uniformity of morality. Indeed, there is a more commonly recognized and observed code of behavior there than in the middle-sized manufacturing towns and cities.

I have already noted the unparalleled neighborliness and mutual help of the rural community in the Midwest; but it is worth noting that there are severe and recognized limits to this. Kindness in "trouble" and mutual aid — "trouble" is a capacious portmanteau word in the region — are general and dependable. But the same farmer who will help out on a sick neighbor's farm will not give him an ounce of seed, or yield an inch while bargaining, if he feels that the 85 context is one of / trade or business and not of human need. They are as tender, sympathetic, kind, and hospitable as their womenfolk toward the visiting stranger or the needy; but with the non-needy they drive the hardest and closest bargain possible. And townsmen are an object of initial distrust — with good reason, if you are to go by the history of prairie settlement or the ubiquity of smoking-room stories about the behavior of "drummers."

The severe self-reliance in the farmer's struggle with soil and elements, his geographical insulation from others most of the time, individual responsibility for his acts and decisions, the dependence of his kith and kin and way of life on those acts and decisions, the headship of his little family-community in its isolated acres — all these things make him tend to bring up his children with a sense of the hardness and unpredictability of life. Wherever the children go in the rural community they get the same philosophy, except at school. It is part of the social uniformity. Accordingly, the rural background of the Midwest has been a forcing-bed to so many promising youngsters. The better they were at school, the more, by contrary tugging and opposition and rebellion, did they strive to leave the rural life. Thus the farms and the rural community have engendered much ambition and energy — especially the energy of contrariness and "anti" feelings — and have tended to say what the Scotch say of Scotland or the Irish of Ireland: "A fine country to get away from!" And look what the Scotch and Irish have done in the world — or in England, for that matter — and where they now are in it! The farm boys of the Midwest have been, and still are, its "Scotch and Irish." Again, perhaps it is the contrariness and desire for change which drives so many farm boys away to sea, or into the air, or into the cities. Moreover, there is no room in the Midwest for every son of every farmer to become a farmer, and the room is shrinking.

Few city dwellers realize how pervasive in the Midwest is this influence from farms or rural towns. Some states in the region — Wisconsin, Minnesota, and Iowa — are more dependent on farms and farm products than on anything else. With few large cities, these states form the newest, northwest section of the region. It is predominantly agrarian in its pattern of life and therefore different in atmosphere, political outlook, and attitude from the other five Midwest states. This has significant results. For example, of the roughly two and a half million souls in Iowa, about half form the male and female electorate; and, after less than a century of settlement in the state, a surprisingly large proportion of them actually know, or know of, nearly all political candidates personally and have relatives or 86 connections by marriage through-/out the state. Such social compactness in an overwhelmingly agricultural region is rare. It is not found in Europe or in the East of America, where families have been settled far longer but have forgotten or ignore their relatives. I should like to add here, as a pointer to the impact of war on the farms, that, of Iowa's one and a half million souls of both sexes and all ages over eighteen, more than 300,000 went into the armed forces of the United States in the second World War.

This vast reserve of farming communities throughout the Midwest, always going on with their steady life behind the cities and towns, is of enormous importance to the region as a whole — and to the people of the towns and cities, even if they only think of the farmers when they go motoring or cannot get something for their table. For, vastly different as the life of the cities is, many of the city dwellers' characteristics came, and are still being renewed, from the farming communities. . . .

[NEGRO AND JEW IN THE MIDWEST]

130   Negroes and Jews are two groups apart. The Negro is socially segregated by all whites except those who do the roughest work. The Jews get varying social treatment according to their economic, intellectual, or artistic status.

To the visitor it often seems that the result of the Civil War was not as happy for the Negroes who settled in, or came to, the North as the press and mythology of the North have made out. Society in the South of the United States was, and to a great extent still is, somewhat like a Bach fugue. It takes place within a universally accepted frame-/work of harmony and counterpoint. 131 It moves in an ordered pattern, conventionally and traditionally, easily and logically, toward an inevitable conclusion which is always in the same key as its beginning. The Negro can be on the land or in the city. His position has to be respected, provided he respects the position of the white. There is a rough but practical harmony of duties and obligations. All know the rules to be observed. All, white and Negro, know the penalties. In that southern life, the Negro had, and still has, a humble yet difficult part in the score — just as the coachmen and gardeners of some German margrave in the eighteenth century, fetched in to perform for their master, had to play short but very difficult passages in Bach's *concerti*. All mankind, rich and poor, are happier in a stable and ordered society which performs like a good orchestra. All the players get a measure of happiness out of their little or big contributions to the great harmony of the whole. If you doubt that, pause and think of our society in the leading nations of the world today and try to answer the greatest riddle of all: are we happier for owning more?

But the society of the new Midwest was unordered, unstable, hard, and confused. That of the growing Midwest cities, especially after 1860, was more like a scratch orchestra of gifted amateurs trying to play for the first time a composition by Stravinsky or Shostakovich; but the Negroes, sharing in much of the delight at this new and bewildering composition, were restricted to very few instruments. They did not know how to handle the more complicated and interesting ones, anyway; and they never got a chance. They were given important but limited parts: servants of the public, laborers, and menials of the cities. They could not go on the land. They were and still are largely bewildered by this city life, to such a narrow sector of which they are restricted. And they are equally restricted in the small towns.

The magnitude of the problem as it arose, and the seriousness with which it is now being tackled in almost every Midwest city and town, must not be underestimated. In Chicago alone it is estimated that there were about 360,000 Negroes in 1945, densely settled in a very few localities. They poured into the new midwestern towns and cities after 1865, then as the cities grew, then in 1917 to 1929, and then again after 1940. The movement is still, on balance, from South to North because there is more money to be earned in good times in the northern cities and towns. But it has magnified the social problems of these cities; and, though the Negroes find more money, more possessions, more variety, and more diversions, they do not, it seems, find more happiness. Why should they be any different in that respect from / their white 132 fellow-citizens who have had much the same experience, coming from the farms to the towns or "from quiet homes and small beginnings"? One big difference remains: the white is not "restricted"; the Negro is. His children are born into a fixed status and have to stay in it. Thereby comes yet another form of social tension in the cities.

The case of the Jew was different. Many cultivated Jews and large numbers of eastern and southern European Jews who were less cultivated flocked to the new Midwest. To be "restricted" was not strange to the mass of them. But, unlike the Negro, they were white, they were traders, and they or their children could enter virtually every profession or business. It is very hard for the visitor to find out the cause of the widespread anti-Semitism and social discrimination against Jews in Midwest towns and cities. The feeling seems more vigorous than in the cities of any European country except Germany or Hungary. It is a peculiar kind of anti-Semitism. Individual Jews are well liked. They are and have been outstanding in business, the professions, academic life, and in the making of the Midwest. The most successful of them have been great collectors, donors of art collections and museums, large subscribers to that charity which for so long took the place of social security in Midwest city life, and endowers of schools and colleges and institutions of learning. But the Gentile midwesterner did not, and often does not, like the "lesser breed" of Jews in the towns and cities (Jews do not settle on the land). He calls them by opprobrious names. If it be because they seemed thrusting, blatant, vulgar, and ostentatious — well, so was most midwestern city and town life in its beginnings, and so were most of the Gentiles in it.

The small minority of Jews and Gentiles "at the top" in Midwest cities seem now to understand, respect, and get on well with each other. But below this thin upper stratum, Gentiles still dislike Jews more than the midwesterners of German origin dislike the Greeks, or the Greeks the Italians, and so on. Perhaps it was part of the waves of intolerance, of "anti"-ism, which billowed through America last century and spent themselves in this. It is, of course, quite illogical, because vast numbers of authentic, though unorthodox, Jews transliterated their names into good American, while older and prouder Jewish families preserved honored names but therefore remain unmistakably Jewish. Again, a Bloom or a Blum was recognized as Jewish; but a Virag (Hungarian for "bloom") was not; and so with millions of Magyarized, Russified, Rumanized, Italianate, and Greek names of Jews. The apartment houses, residential districts, clubs, hotels, and vacation resorts which were "restricted" to Gentiles got more Jewish / blood in them than they 133 fondly imagined; but they kept the bulk of the more obviously Jewish, among them many citizens which any country would be proud to own, out of social intercourse with Gentiles. The Jews responded to this kind of challenge by erecting their own clubs, apartments, and so on; and they had the funds. So the gulf was made and perpetuated. Happily it is slowly being bridged, but from the top down, not from the bottom up.

There is an exception to this social gradation. It works only in favor of the Midwest citizen of any grouping below those of Anglo-Saxon, German, Celtic, or Scandinavian origin (except the Negro) who has made a success of life, in trade, finance, industry, arts and letters, academic life, or anything famous or well publicized. It is significant that he does not need to have made merely a *material* success; though that, of course, helps. If he has made that success, he has proved the point of equality of opportunity, the career open to the talents; and for all practical purposes — though not by any means for *all* social purposes or occasions — he has "arrived." His wife and children can practically be viewed as Anglo-Saxon or German or Celtic or Scandinavian. For practically all purposes he and they can move socially among those favored nationalities that form the apex of the social pyramid in Midwest cities. But he must first make the success. He must be a "successful" man. He must be "up and coming," which phrase suggests social gradations, as well as ambition, energy, and ability.

This accent on success is, of course, part of the Midwest's commercial history which is still current. It reflects a real, popular, and general emphasis on material achievements. The successful man is accepted, whatever his national origin — unless he be a Negro or, to a less extent, an "obvious" Jew — because he has paid his dues to Midwest urban society. He has made his contribution to the development of the region. . . .

[RELIGION IN THE MIDWEST]

211   Religion always obtains greater devotion where life is a harder struggle: which is why it is stronger today among the masses in the cities of the Midwest, where the Catholics are most numerous, and among farmers, where the old-line Protestantism is at its strongest.

The first wealthy men in the towns were conspicuous. They lived under public scrutiny. They had deep religious beliefs, and, out of real gratitude, they paid much more than a tithe in charity and good works.

As their children and grandchildren grew to man's estate, social services ate into the sources of private charity. The fortunate individual's duty to his less fortunate neighbor could be performed by paying taxes. Churches, unendowed by state or federal constitutions and needing to grow with the population, became of necessity more and more concerned with ways of raising funds. It was not altogether a matter of materialism. Many of the people *wanted* religion. Indeed, to a great extent the more hectic and materialistic the life of the city or town became, the more people showed that they needed some kind of spiritual life. But material achievements and machines were setting the pace and driving men. Men had to keep up with them. If you had asked Midwest businessmen whether they still believed that man could not serve God and Mammon, they would probably have agreed; but they would also have apologized for having to give up trying to serve God in any other way than by attendance at church and by paying some of their proceeds over to it. They would have said, as so many say, that they had little time. What were the churches for, anyway? Again, that is not peculiar to the Midwest; but it is marked there.

The result today is that at either extreme of religion — among Roman / Catholics, on 212 the one hand, and among fundamentalists, Lutherans, strict Baptists, Seventh-Day Adventists, Jehovah's Witnesses, and similar sects, on the other — there is widespread devoutness and obedience to a moral law. But in the wide space between are a bewildering number of sects, somewhat in spiritual disarray, held together by tradition, cult, good form, and good works, and not quite certain on what doctrinal ground they stand. In the second World War it was among these "midway" sects that most concern was expressed about juvenile delinquency, sexual morality, and so on. The social activities or beliefs of Catholics and extreme evangelicals seem to have more force behind them when the behavior of adults or youth is involved. The sense of vulnerability in the "midway" sects shows itself in acute anxiety over the rate at which Catholicism gains converts. There is more evidence today of religious intolerance than there was in 1914.

The *Christian Century* publishes a special series of eight articles asking whether Roman Catholicism can win America. This reflects Protestant concern at the growth of Catholicism to the biggest single, undivided Christian sect in America, embracing one-sixth of all the people; the richest national Catholic community in the world. In the towns and cities of the Midwest, Americans of Italian, Irish, Polish, and many other origins make it even stronger than it is in the East — despite Boston, Baltimore, Philadelphia, and New York. The religious toleration of the Midwest, on both sides, seems to be wearing a trifle thin. The modernistic evangelists and revivalists stage their rallies for converts with pepped-up music and pep talks, often without a nationally organized church behind them. The Catholics move with the spirit of the times and capture the imagination by celebrations and Holy Name Hours in vast amphitheaters before many thousands of youths and adults alike. The "midway" sects remain in the smaller districts or communities, faithful, instant in good works, but puzzled and disturbed by it all. They are a legacy from the men who made the Midwest. But they are a diminishing minority. Whither are they tending? Even orthodox Jewry finds itself in much the same quandary, with its own "midway" group set between two extremes.

Raoul de Roussy de Sales

From "Love in America" in *The Atlantic Monthly,* 161 (May 1938), 645–651.
Copyright 1938 by The Atlantic Monthly Company, Boston 16, Massachusetts.
Used by permission of Mrs. Raoul de Roussy de Sales.

Comte de Roussy de Sales, French author and journalist, was born in Paris in 1896. His acquaintance with America was long-standing. He was associated with the American Red Cross in France during the First World War. In 1932, he came to America as United States correspondent for several French newspapers. While here he lectured often and translated Hitler's *Mein Kampf* for publication in America. Chancellor of the Fighting French delegation to the United States, he died December 3, 1942.

645 AMERICA appears to be the only country in the world where love is a national problem.

Nowhere else can one find a people devoting so much time and so much study to the question of the relationship between men and women. Nowhere else is there such concern about the fact that this relationship does not always make for perfect happiness. The great majority of the Americans of both sexes seem to be in a state of chronic bewilderment in the face of a problem which they are certainly not the first to confront, but which — unlike other people — they still refuse to accept as one of those gifts of the gods which one might just as well take as it is: a mixed blessing at times, and at other times a curse or merely a nuisance.

The prevailing conception of love, in America, is similar to the idea of democracy. It is fine in theory. It is the grandest system ever evolved by man to differentiate him from his ancestors, the poor brutes who lived in caverns, or from the apes. Love is perfect, in fact, and there is nothing better. But, like democracy, it does not work, and the Americans feel that something should be done about it. President Roosevelt is intent on making democracy work. Everybody is trying to make love work, too.

In either case the result is not very satisfactory. The probable reason is that democracy and love are products of a long and complicated series of compromises between the desires of the heart and the exactions of reason. They have a peculiar way of crumbling into ashes as soon as one tries too hard to organize them too well.

The secret of making a success out of democracy and love in their practical applications is to allow for a fairly wide margin of errors, and not to forget that human beings are absolutely unable to submit to a uniform rule for any length of time. But this does not satisfy a nation that, in spite of its devotion to pragmatism, also believes in perfection.

For a foreigner to speak of the difficulties that the Americans encounter in such an intimate aspect of their mutual relationship may appear as an impertinence. But the truth is that no foreigner would ever think of bringing up such a subject of his own accord. In fact, foreigners who come to these shores are quite unsuspecting of the existence of such a national problem. It is their initial observation that the percentage of good-looking women and handsome men is high on this continent, that they are youthful and healthy in mind and body, and that their outlook on life is rather optimistic.

If the newcomers have seen enough American moving pictures before landing here — and they usually have — they must gave gathered the impression that love in America is normally triumphant, and that, in spite of many unfortunate accidents, a love story cannot but end very well indeed.

646 They will / have noticed that these love stories which are acted in Hollywood may portray quite regrettable situations at times and that blissful unions get wrecked by all sorts of misfortunes. But they never remain wrecked: even when the happy couple is compelled to divorce, this is not the end of everything. In most cases it is only the beginning. Very soon they will remarry, sometimes with one another, and always — without ever an exception — for love.

The observant foreigner knows, of course, that he cannot trust the movies to give him a really reliable picture of the American attitude towards love, marriage, divorce, and remarriage. But they nevertheless indicate that in such matters the popular mind likes to be entertained by the idea (1) that love is the only reason why a man and a woman should get married; (2) that love is always wholesome, genuine, uplifting, and fresh, like a glass of Grade A milk; (3) that when, for some reason or other, it fails to keep you uplifted, wholesome, and fresh, the only thing to do is to begin all over again with another partner.

Thus forewarned, the foreigner who lands on these shores would be very tactless indeed if he started questioning the validity of these premises. Besides, it is much more likely that he himself will feel thoroughly transformed the moment he takes his first stroll in the streets of New York. His European skepticism will evaporate a little more at each step, and if he considers himself not very young any more he will be immensely gratified to find that maturity and even old age are merely European habits of thought, and that he might just as well adopt the American method, which is to be young and act young for the rest of his life — or at least until the expiration of his visa.

If this hotel room is equipped with a radio, his impression that he has at last reached the land of eternal youth and perfect love will be confirmed at any hour of the day and on any point of the dial. No country in the world consumes such a fabulous amount of love songs. Whether the song is gay or nostalgic, the tune catchy or banal, the verses clever or silly, the theme is always love and nothing but love.

Whenever I go back to France and listen to the radio, I am always surprised to find that so many songs can be written on other subjects. I have no statistics on hand, but I think that a good 75 per cent of the songs one hears on the French radio programmes deal with politics. There are love songs, of course, but most of them are far from romantic, and this is quite in keeping with the French point of view that love is very often an exceedingly comical affair.

In America the idea seems to be that love, like so much else, should be sold to the public, because it is a good thing. The very word, when heard indefinitely, becomes an obsession. It penetrates one's subconsciousness like the name of some unguent to cure heartaches or athlete's foot. It fits in with the other advertisements, and one feels tempted to write to the broadcasting station for a free sample of this thing called Love.

Thus the visitor from Europe is rapidly permeated with a delightful atmosphere of romanticism and sweetness. He wonders why Italy and Spain ever acquired their reputation of being the lands of romance. This, he says to himself, is the home of poetry and passion. The Americans are the real heirs of the troubadours, and station WXZQ is their love court.

To discover that all this ballyhoo about love (which is not confined to the radio or the movies) is nothing but an aspect of the national optimistic outlook on life does not take very long. It usually becomes evident when the foreign visitor receives the confidences of one or more of the charming American women he will chance to meet. This normally happens after the first or second cocktail party to which he has been invited.

I wish at this point to enter a plea in 647 defense of the foreign visitor, against whom a great many accusations are often made either in print or in conversation. These accusations fall under two heads. If the foreigner seems to have no definite objective in visiting America, he is strongly suspected of trying to marry an heiress. If for any reason he cannot be suspected of this intention, then his alleged motives are considerably more sinister. Many American men, and quite a few women, believe that the art of wrecking a happy home is not indigenous to this continent, and that in Europe it has been perfected to such a point that to practise it has become a reflex with the visitors from abroad.

It is very true that some foreign visitors come over here to marry for money in exchange for a title or for some sort of glamour. But there are many more foreigners who marry American women for other reasons besides money, and I know quite a few who have become so Americanized that they actually have married for love and for nothing else.

As for the charge that the Europeans are more expert than the Americans in spoiling someone else's marital happiness, it seems to me an unfair accusation. In most cases the initiative of spoiling whatever it is that remains to be spoiled in a shaky marriage is normally taken by one of the married pair, and the wrecker of happiness does not need any special talent to finish the job.

What is quite true, however, is that the American woman entertains the delightful illusion that there *must* be some man on this earth who can understand her. It seems incredible to her that love, within legal bonds or outside of them, should not work out as advertised. From her earliest years she has been told that success is the ultimate aim of life. Her father and mother made an obvious success of their lives by creating her. Her husband is, or wants to be, a successful business man. Every day 130,000,000 people are panting and sweating to make a success of something or other. Success — the constant effort to make things work perfectly and the conviction that they can be made to — is the great national preoccupation.

And what does one do to make a success? Well, the answer is very simple: one learns how, or one consults an expert.

That is what her husband does when he wants to invest his money or improve the efficiency of his business. That is what she did herself when she decided to 'decorate' her house. In the American way of life there are no insoluble problems. You may not know the answer yourself, but nobody doubts that the answer exists — that there is some method or perhaps some trick by which all riddles can be solved and success achieved.

And so the European visitor is put to the task on the presumption that the accumulation of experience which he brings with him may qualify him as an expert in questions of sentiment.

The American woman does not want to be understood for the mere fun of it. What she actually wishes is to be helped to solve certain difficulties which, in her judgment, impede the successful development of her inner self. She seldom accepts the idea that maladjustments and misunderstandings are not only normal but bearable once you have made up your mind that, whatever may be the ultimate aim of our earthly existence, perfect happiness through love or any other form of expression is not part of the programme.

One of the greatest moral revolutions that ever happened in America was the popularization of Freud's works.

Up to the time that occurred, as far as I am able to judge, America lived in a blissful state of puritanical repression. Love, as a sentiment, was glorified and / sanctified by marriage. There was a general impression that some sort of connection existed between the sexual impulses and the vagaries of the heart, but this connection was not emphasized, and the consensus of opinion was that the less said about it the better. The way certain nations, and particularly the French, correlated the physical manifestations of love and its more spiritual aspects was considered particularly objectionable. Love, in other words, — and that was not very long ago, — had not changed since the contrary efforts of the puritanically-minded and the romantic had finally stabilized it midway between the sublime and the parlor game.

The important point is that up to then (and ever since the first Pilgrims set foot on this continent) love had been set aside in the general scheme of American life as the one thing which could not be made to work better than it did. Each one had to cope with his own difficulties in his own way and solve them as privately as he could. It was not a national problem.

Whether or not people were happier under that system is beside the point. It probably does not matter very much whether we live and die with or without a full set of childish complexes and repressions. My own view is that most people are neither complex nor repressed enough as a rule; I wish sometimes for the coming of the Anti-Freud who will complicate and obscure everything again.

But the fact is that the revelations of psychoanalysis were greeted in America as the one missing link in the general programme of universal improvement.

Here was a system, at last, that explained fully why love remained so imperfect. It reduced the whole dilemma of happiness to sexual maladjustments, which in turn were only the result of the mistakes made by one's father, mother, or nurse, at an age when one could certainly not be expected to foresee the consequences. Psychoanalysis integrated human emotions into a set of mechanistic formulas. One learned with great relief that the failure to find happiness was not irreparable. Love, as a sublime communion of souls and bodies, was not a legend, nor the mere fancy of the poets. It was real, and — more important still — practically attainable. Anybody could have it, merely by removing a few obstructions which had been growing within himself since childhood like mushrooms in a dark cellar. Love could be made to work like anything else.

It is true that not many people are interested in psychoanalysis any more. As a fad

or a parlor game, it is dead. Modern débutantes will not know what you are talking about if you mention the Œdipus complex or refer to the symbolic meaning of umbrellas and top hats in dreams. Traditions die young these days. But the profound effect of the Freudian revelation has lasted. From its materialistic interpretation of sexual impulses, coupled with the American longing for moral perfection, a new science has been born: the dialectics of love; and also a new urge for the American people — they want to turn out, eventually, a perfect product. They want to get out of love as much enjoyment, comfort, safety, and general sense of satisfaction, as one gets out of a well-balanced diet or a good plumbing installation.

Curiously enough, this fairly new point of view which implies that human relationships are governed by scientific laws has not destroyed the romantic ideal of love. Quite the contrary. Maladjustments, now that they are supposed to be scientifically determined, have become much more unbearable than in the horse-and-buggy age of love. Husbands and wives and lovers have no patience with their troubles. They want to be cured, and when they think they are incurable they become very intolerant. Reformers always are.

Usually, however, various attempts at re- 649 adjustment are made with devastating candor. Married couples seem to spend many precious hours of the day and night discussing what is wrong with their relationship. The general idea is that — according to the teachings of most modern psychologists and pedagogues — one should face the truth fearlessly. Husbands and wives should be absolutely frank with one another, on the assumption that if love between them is real it will be made stronger and more real still if submitted, at frequent intervals, to the test of complete sincerity on both sides.

This is a fine theory, but it has seldom been practised without disastrous results. There are several reasons why this should be so. First of all, truth is an explosive, and it should be handled with care, especially in marital life. It is not necessary to lie, but there is little profit in juggling with hand grenades just to show how brave one is. Secondly, the theory of absolute sincerity presupposes that, if love cannot withstand continuous blasting, then it is not worth saving anyway. Some people want their love life to be a permanent battle of Verdun. When the system of defense is destroyed beyond repair, then the clause of hopeless maladjustment is invoked by one side, or by both. The next thing to do is to divorce and find someone else to be recklessly frank with for a season.

Another reason why the method of adjustment through truthtelling is not always wise is that it develops fiendish traits of character which might otherwise remain dormant.

I know a woman whose eyes glitter with virtuous self-satisfaction every time she has had a 'real heart-to-heart talk' with her husband, which means that she has spent several hours torturing him, or at best boring him to distraction, with a ruthless exposure of the deplorable status of their mutual relationship to date. She is usually so pleased with herself after these periodical inquests that she tells most of her friends, and also her coiffeur, about it. 'Dick and I had such a wonderful time last evening. We made a real effort to find out the real truth about each other — or, at least, I certainly did. I honestly believe we have found a new basis of adjustment for ourselves. What a marvelous feeling that is — don't you think so?'

Dick, of course, if he happens to be present, looks rather nervous or glum, but that is not the point. The point is that Dick's wife feels all aglow because she has done her bit in the general campaign for the improvement of marital happiness through truth. She has been a good girl scout.

A man of my acquaintance, who believes in experimenting outside of wedlock, is unable to understand why his wife would rather ignore his experiments. 'If I did not love her and if she did not love me,' he argues, 'I could accept her point of view. But why can't she see that the very fact that I want her to know everything I do is a proof that I love her? If I have to deceive her or conceal things from her, what is the use of being married to her?'

Be it said, in passing, that this unfortunate husband believes that these extramarital 'experiments' are absolutely necessary to prevent him from developing a sense of inferiority, which, if allowed to grow, would destroy not only the love he has for his wife, but also his general ability in his dealings with the outside world. . . .

Thus the problem of love in America 650 seems to be the resultant of conflicting and rather unrealistic ways of approaching it. Too many songs, too many stories, too many pictures, and too much romance on the one hand, and too much practical advice on the other. It is as if the experience of being in love could only be one of two things: a superhuman ecstasy, the way of reaching heaven on earth and in pairs; or a psychopathic condition to be treated by specialists.

Between these two extremes there is little room for compromise. That the relationship between men and women offers a wide scale of variations seldom occurs to the experts. It is not necessarily true that there is but one form of love worth bothering about, and that if you cannot get the de luxe model, with a life guarantee of perfect functioning, nothing else is worth-while. It is not true either that you can indefinitely pursue the same quest for perfection, or that if a man and a woman have not found ideal happiness together they will / cer- 651 tainly find it with somebody else. Life unfortunately does not begin at forty, and when you reach that age, in America or anywhere else, to go on complaining about your sentimental or physiological maladjustments becomes slightly farcical.

It is not easy, nor perhaps of any use, to draw any conclusion from all this, especially for a European who has lost the fresh point of view of the visitor because he lives here, and who is not quite sure of what it

means to be a European any more. I sometimes wonder if there is any real difference
between the way men and women get along
— or do not get along — together on this
side of the Atlantic and on the other. There
are probably no more real troubles here than
anywhere else. Human nature being quite
remarkably stable, why should there be?
But there is no doubt that the revolt against
this type of human inadequacy is very
strong indeed here, especially among the
women who imagine that the Europeans
have found better ways of managing their
heart and their senses than the Americans.

If this is at all true, I believe the reason
is to be found in a more philosophical attitude on the part of the Europeans towards
such matters. There are no theories about
marital bliss, no recipes to teach you how
to solve difficulties which, in the Old
World, are accepted as part of the common
inheritance.

Men and women naturally want to be
happy over there, and, if possible, with the
help of one another; but they learn very
young that compromise is not synonymous
with defeat. Even in school (I am speaking more particularly of France now) they
are taught, through the literature of centuries, that love is a phenomenon suscepti-
ble of innumerable variations, but that —
even under the best circumstances — it is so
intertwined with the other experiences of
each individual life that to be overromantic
or too dogmatic about it is of little practical
use. '*La vérité est dans les nuances,*' wrote
Benjamin Constant, who knew a good deal
about such matters.

And, speaking of the truly practical and
realistic nature of love, it is a very strange
thing that American literature contains no
work of any note, not even essays, on love
as a psychological phenomenon. I know

of no good study of the process of falling
in and out of love, no analytical description of jealousy, coquettishness, or the development of tediousness. No classification
of the various brands of love such as La
Rochefoucauld, Pascal, Stendhal, Proust,
and many others have elaborated has been
attempted from the American angle. The
interesting combinations of such passions as
ambition, jealousy, religious fervor, and so
forth, with love are only dimly perceived by
most people and even by the novelists, who,
with very few exceptions, seem to ignore or
scorn these complicated patterns. These fine
studies have been left to the psychiatrists,
the charlatans, or the manufacturers of
naïve recipes.

The reason for this neglect on the part
of real thinkers and essayists may be that
for a long time the standards imposed by
the puritanical point of view made the
whole study more or less taboo with respectable authors. And then the Freudian wave
came along and carried the whole problem
out of reach of the amateur observer and
the artist. In other words, conditions have
been such that there has been no occasion to fill this curious gap in American
literature.

Of course, nothing is lost. The field remains open, and there is no reason to suppose that love in America will not cease to
be a national problem, a hunting ground
for the reformer, and that it will not become, as everywhere else, a personal affair
very much worth the effort it takes to examine it as such. All that is necessary is for
someone to forget for a while love as Hollywood — or the professor — sees it, and sit
down and think about it as an eternally
fascinating subject for purely human
observation.

Mira Gavrilovitch

From "You American Women" in *You Americans*. Edited by B. P. Adams. New York (Funk and Wagnalls), 1939. Used with the author's permission.

Dr. Gavrilovitch, one of the leaders of the Yugoslav feminist movement, was the first woman in her country to receive the degree of doctor of laws and the first woman to become state attorney and judge. Her husband was a member of the Yugoslavian consulate in New York from 1938 to 1946, as vice consul and consul general. Dr. Gavrilovitch now resides in Hollywood, California.

65 OUR HUSBANDS are far less considerate than yours. They like to have us cater to them as if they were Turkish Pashas. They would never think of lending a hand in the house. I was amazed when I first saw American men helping their wives wash dishes, without the least embarrassment.

So, your country impresses me as a paradise for women. Things for which we women in most European states are still struggling, have already become realities here.

Woman's influence here is tremendous in every way. I believe one reason for this is that you American women have realized in time the strength there is in union. No-
66 where in Europe can one find such a variety and multi-/tude of women's organizations as there are here. A second, perhaps more important reason for your influence is that you have accumulated two-thirds of the nation's wealth.

The American housewife has at her command all sorts of work-saving devices, which we either do not yet know about, or which we still look upon as luxuries. One might say that American housekeeping is concentrated in a can. In my country we have to cook on old-fashioned wood stoves; only a well-to-do woman can afford a vacuum-cleaner; and only a few wealthy homes can boast of having an electric refrigerator. In summer our housewives stand for hours by the hot stove preparing winter preserves, fruits, jellies, vegetables, pickles and peppers. Canned goods are seldom used in a private household. In Yugoslavia love is very much dependent on a good kitchen. If cafeterias like those in America were to supplant the kitchens, I am afraid our bachelor problem would become severe. Our women are very much tied down to the house because the men and the children come home at noon for several hours. Insomuch as rents are very low, we have big houses and a lot of furniture, so that keeping house is a full-time task for a woman. . . .

American women worship at the shrine 67 of youth and beauty. Old American women are truly rare — at least, if one is to judge from appearances. Whole new branches of industry have grown up out of their efforts to cultivate youthfulness. Thus, through their search for youth and beauty they have become an important economic factor. It would be superfluous to present boring statistics to prove this point. A stroll through the shopping center of almost any American city, and a cursory glance through the newspapers and magazines, would suffice to show this. The shops for women clearly outnumber the men's stores, and most of the advertisements in the newspapers are devoted to articles of feminine interest. The poor American men!

It is precisely in the world of women's fashions that the principles of successful American business management are seen at their best: it is much less important to have fine, seasonable goods, than to advertise wisely and to set up a truly novel window display. We in Europe always say that good merchandise is its own best advertisement, but here the advertising often outdoes the quality of the goods. Very frequently in New York City I stand in front of the Fifth Avenue windows, and admire more the way the things are displayed than the things themselves. Who in Europe, for instance, would get the idea of displaying in an elegant shop a mannequin whose head is replaced by a stick tilted at a conquettish 68 angle and / crowned with the latest hat? If I were a man, I would make some sarcastic remark about this wooden substitute for a woman's head.

As far as fashion is concerned, you American women are far more fortunate than we in Europe. You wear whatever is becoming to you and are not subject to the European type of fashion dictatorship. Cheap ready-made clothes make it possible for every one of you to go well dressed. You place more value on the style than on the quality. The great range of prices in your articles of fashion is also genuinely American. The price is not determined by the quality of the goods, but rather by the name of the shop where the things are bought. You can dress either at little or great cost, as you choose. The influence of the movies on American fashions is likewise very marked. Hollywood can afford to hire the very best of fashion designers, and the expensive creations for the great film stars are later — thanks to the miracle of mass production — made available to the multitudes.

American merchants are much keener psychologists than the European. The former are well aware of the human weakness for buying bargains, and they know how to capitalize on this. Special sales and auctions are far more commonplace here than in Europe. You American women, in purchasing for your private needs, are very often tantamount to wholesale buyers.

Even in your fashions, your philosophy of life is reflected. In winter your shops display summer things, and in summer there is an advance showing of winter things. This, I believe, is one more indi-cation that you / live fast and think of the 69 future, while we in Europe live more slowly and more definitely in the present.

In your personal life, particularly, I find the one characteristic which I look upon as genuinely American. You are all preoccupied with making money and increasing your possessions. For that reason everyone here works, regardless of the amount of wealth he has. Pressure, speed, and a continual forward drive seem to be the keynote of your life. The workingman has no time to occupy himself with art and science, and leaves these things to young students and women.

Since, however, the human spirit requires romance along with the more serious side of life, it seems that you are more subject to the appeal of the imaginative than we in Europe are. Your films are sentimental, and must always have a happy ending. This makes for the paradox that in capitalistic America, where everything is on a practical basis, your youth enters into marriage with a much more romantic viewpoint than does the European. The movies are a decisive influence in bringing this about. It is not until later that the true life plot is found to work out in a manner quite different from anything that your young people are prepared to meet. If your movies were to end with the difficulties which always arrive with marriage rather than with the evasion of these problems, I believe that divorce would not be quite the remarkable American phenomenon that it is.

You Americans want to experience romantic movies not only in the theater but also in real life, in order to gain some relief from the intensity of your work and / from 70 the monotonous whir of your machines. You are greedy for excitement, sensations, and record-making. Here, much more often than in Europe, great careers are built upon sheer chance, or upon a good idea. Success comes not only to the person who has the good fortune to do something unusual, but also to the one who experiences something extraordinary. It does not matter whether the incident is of a positive or negative nature; the main thing is that it must be something entirely unique and novel. The unfortunate young man who stood on a ledge high up on a tall New York building and threatened to leap to his death, would certainly have had a career if he had not carried out his threat.

Nowhere in the world are there so many devotees to the cult of championships as here. Your desire to make records, however, rests upon the foundations of your democracy and your economic setup. Napoleon's motto, "Free expression for every talent," has been realized by you. Since competition everywhere is so keen, your striving for records rests not only upon the human drive for superiority, but also upon the wish to attain something which may be of economic, social or political value. For similar reasons, your personal life is seemingly more devoted to publicity, and society news columns are also an American specialty.

In view of your general sociability, it is sometimes difficult for a European to comprehend certain aspects of your etiquette. I am reminded in this respect of the experience of a young lady friend of mine, who recently came from Europe. She complained bitterly to me about / your customs, which threatened to destroy her happiness. She came to New York for the express purpose of finding a rich husband here. Inasmuch as she is attractive and refined, she thought that she would not have much difficulty in carrying out her plan. How disappointed she was when after weeks of attending dances and frequenting restaurants and lobbies of big hotels, she was not approached nor spoken to even once by an American man. Only foreigners addressed her, and for that she certainly did not need to come to New York. This little story shows the difference between our outlooks. That which seems to you a personal affront may in the eyes of a European woman be something very desirable. We European women are, alas, more accustomed to being looked upon as females than as human beings with equal rights.

The American woman enters into marriage on terms of full-fledged equality with her mate. Moreover, she retains the control of her own possessions, and the institution of dowries is unknown here. Among us, however, it is customary for the husband to receive a dowry in order to lighten the burden of household expenses. In case the marriage gift is in the form of money, it becomes his property. If the dowry consists of real property, then the husband becomes the legal beneficiary, and has the right to do whatever he pleases with the income. With respect to the free possessions of the wife which are not turned over to the husband as a dowry, there is / in 72 our law a presumption that the husband is the legal administrator; and his wife, in the event that she objects to this, must expressly refuse him this right. But if the wife manages her own possessions, her husband also has the legal right, as it is prescribed, "to hold in check any mismanagement on the part of the woman."

It is unnecessary for me to state how important it is for the position of the married woman that she should have her own possessions and control them herself. It gives her not only more self-confidence, but also more rights. In Europe it is not infrequent that the husband marries his wife's bank account; and if he had his choice, he would withdraw it from the bank and deposit his wife there in its stead.

There is a better side also to the dependent position of our married women. The mutuality of marital life is much more highly developed than it is here, and the wife does not yield so readily to divorce as does her American sister. Since the main theme of life for most of our women centers in husband and children, the supreme effort is made to satisfy and please the man, and a generous part of feminine individuality is sacrificed to this cause. Whenever it is necessary, however, for one of my countrywomen to help out financially, she cheerfully assumes whatever position or work will make it possible for her to promote the welfare of her family. The Yugoslav woman is more self-effacing than the American, and for that reason more easily able to make sacrifices.

The American woman in vocational life stands on an equal footing with men, and 73 she has access to nearly all / occupations. In contrast, our women are legally excluded from certain judicial and governmental positions, and even in the professions that are open to us we can seldom attain a top-ranking position. Generally speaking, we are held down to our "natural" calling of housewife and mother, since, it is argued, we were created for this purpose and are lacking in the higher qualities necessary for responsible positions. The real reason is seldom admitted — that it is not our mental inferiority, but competition, the struggle for existence, which is really the issue. At a meeting where I spoke for the equal rights of the sexes, one of the lords of creation sarcastically countered that we women were left out by nature from the possibility of working side by side mentally with men — for do we not have a much smaller brain than man? I could have replied with the oft-quoted fact that Dante was able to create *The Divine Comedy* despite his abnormally small brain, but I merely asked: "Do you consider oxen wiser than men because they have much larger brains?" In truly male fashion, my antagonist murmured something to the effect that women were obviously not created to engage in serious discussions.

In connection with the independence of American women, I tried to interpret also the fact that many workingwomen here prefer to use the title "Miss," regardless of whether they are married or not. In many countries of Europe we are fighting to have all workingwomen addressed as "Mrs." I understand the psychological motivation for this latter desire. The married woman enjoys more prestige socially, and for this 74 reason the unmarried / woman who works,

wants to compensate for her subconscious inferiority complex. In your case, however, I had logically come to an opposite conclusion, but I find here a certain confusion which I cannot easily understand. I have been told that here, too, in a certain sense, the married woman has more prestige, and that the coming-out parties of your society debutantes are primarily a device for announcing the marriageability of a girl. Even your custom of taking over both your husband's Christian name and surname, seems to me inconsistent with your attitude of independence.

There is only one more point I should like to raise in this general connection, which pleases me about you American women. So far as I have been able to determine, you manage, with few exceptions, to retain your femininity at your work. I feel that this is an excellent thing, for equality, and not identity, with man should be woman's aim. Only when women bring with them into all their life-activities their feminine qualities, only then does their work have intrinsic value for society. Nature itself has decreed that new things can be created only through the joint efforts of both sexes. Thus, the social order can attain a full development only when the influences of both sexes works in harmony and is equally strong.

Furthermore, you American women enjoy political rights for which we still have to struggle. They tell us that we have not yet arrived at political maturity, and that we would always vote for our husband's or father's party; and if we did not do this, family conflicts would / arise. But, if we 75 were to free ourselves from the influence of the men surrounding us, the argument continues, then we would, like immature youngsters, vote for the extreme parties. On one occasion I sought to meet these arguments with instances from history, and pointed out that the few queens who ruled were nearly all great and successful politicians. I was told in reply: "That's nothing remarkable. When women rule they always follow the advice of men, while men

rulers are strongly influenced by women."
What can one say to such an argument?

We European women, who are still fighting for equal rights, owe a debt of gratitude to you American women. You are a living proof that the arguments against equality do not hold much water. Nowhere in the world have so many gigantic things been created as in America. Whenever I stand in front of the Empire State Building and look up to the peak, I ask myself if this is not the symbol of America. The inevitable answer is that this is possible only because there is freedom among you for everyone, men and women, to develop to the full extent of your potentiality.

Your children are educated to become free, independent persons. Very often your schools are unfavorably compared with European standards of scholarship. It is true that when your children finish school they know much less Latin and Greek than our children, and they do not have such familiarity with abstract knowledge; but your children get to know much more about life itself. Graduates of your schools are mature people who / have outgrown child- 76 hood. Your children, precisely because they are subjected to less authority, acquire better habits of self-discipline.

I have mentioned here only a few of my impressions. If I wanted to recount all of them I should have to write a thick volume, for there are myriads of novelties here for the European. America is for us a different continent and another world. It is a land of technical progress, where things which we dream of for the future have already become a reality. Mechanization rides triumphant through this land like some legendary conqueror of old. It is extremely difficult to disentangle the fantastic from the real. . . .

Erna Barschak

From *My American Adventure*. New York (Ives Washburn), 1945. Reprinted by permission of the publisher.

Dr. Barschak, now a psychology professor at Miami University, Oxford, Ohio, took her Ph.D. at Tuebingen University (Germany) in 1925. She has also studied at the University of Geneva, the University of London, and Columbia University in New York. The book from which this selection was extracted is the record of her first encounters with American civilization.

[THE AMERICAN HOME]

36 THE FIRST room which a guest sees in an American home is usually the bedroom, as the guest is requested to go upstairs to deposit his hat and coat. In Europe overcoats and hats are always left in the hall. Bedrooms are considered "private." Time and again in Europe, when I was taken around a newly rented apartment by friends, the hostess, after having shown the living quarters, would say, pointing to a hall, "Behind that door are the kitchen, bathroom and bedrooms. I am sure you will not be interested in them!"

The hostess's customary question asked in a low voice as the guest arrives — "Would you like to go to the bathroom? The second door from the right — you'll find it!" — had spoiled my first dinner party in the U.S.A., and perhaps also a remote chance of a position in a very fine college. I had been invited by very friendly people to meet one of the college trustees, a person who might well be able to help me secure a position. So I had dressed carefully, and thought I looked well groomed. According to the instructions for "intellectual refugees," I had even stopped at a near-by rest room for a final inspection to make certain that everything was still all right. And now this /

37 question: "Would you like to go to the bathroom?" Since early childhood no one had ever sent me to the bathroom like a smelly kid! I felt outraged and uncertain at the same time. Surely something must be wrong with me. Were my hands dirty? My hair out of place? Did something show? I would not have minded my slip showing.

Nearly all women's slips show in this country. This is a national trait.

Not knowing what was wrong, I decided that I had better accept her hint, said an embarrassed "Yes, please," and disappeared in the direction of the bathroom. Not finding anything suspicious, I joined the party downstairs, but quite uneasily. The whole evening was a nightmare. I made, of course, a very stupid impression on the important guest. He did not think much of my English, always repeated everything he had said in simple, short words. With my mind still on the possible causes of my hostess's reminder to go to the bathroom, I missed the point of his jokes and did not laugh in time. All I got out of this evening was the usual:

"Be sure that in case anything comes to my attention at school, I shall certainly let you know!" But I was *not* sure. . . .

When next a kind hostess said, "I am sure you want to powder your nose, the bathroom is to the right!" I was grateful indeed that she specifically mentioned my nose as the offending member, but I did not like the "destination — bathroom!" A teenager would revolt against this offer, I thought, quite upset.

By now I have, of course, found out that such a question, an indication of personal interest, is a kind and considerate offer to restore lost loveliness. But it still gives me a little shock to hear it — there are areas of European sensitiveness, too!

I consider most American bathrooms wonderful sights. Even if the family is comparatively small and the income not high, Americans have frequently more than

38 one bathroom in the / home. Ask any American housewife what her husband could do to improve the house, and in two cases out of three she will suggest, "Let's have another bathroom!" This fact has been attested to by a friend who should know. He is a sociologist by profession, and teaches classes on Marriage and the Family. *His* home has three bathrooms. Real showrooms they are, all three of them: one is all in red; basins, tiles, curtain for the shower, towels, washcloth, even the cakes of soap and the glasses in that bathroom match! The second bathroom is done all in sky blue. The third I have never seen. I guess it is just the bathroom the family uses. And this particular family is not at all in the higher income bracket, just a bit above the $4,000-a-year group.

Sometimes I think the Americans exhaust their creative imagination in designing bathrooms so that not very much remains for the living quarters. After a sightseeing tour through the bathroom with its matching colors, its cosmetics display, its variety of towels, shower curtains, brushes, cakes of soap and cleaning material for the bath tub, the inspection of the living rooms is usually an anticlimax. To be sure, they are lovely, these downstairs rooms; cozy, clean, orderly, yet they do remind me of the nice postcards you can get in the drugstores or in a stationery shop for all occasions: birthday cards, cards for the sick, cards for the well, cards for the absent, cards for all ages and purposes. All are ready made. But a personal word without all the commercial frills from a friend would give me more pleasure than all these cute little greeting cards could ever convey. So would a personal touch in the living rooms of American homes. If you have seen three modern American living rooms of families in the middle-income brackets, you need not see more. You know all of them: "Good Housekeeping Model," 1940; Macy's "265 dollars." This is the usual pattern from San Francisco to Maine: chintz-covered

39 couch, matching / chairs (bright or pastel colors are preferred, with big flower patterns especially popular) matching curtains, a low table with a bowl or a strange pottery animal with a green plant instead of a tail, sometimes a small table with the newest best sellers or magazines.

One advantage, however, of this conformity is that it makes moving easy: you can get the same furniture everywhere. The European housewife knew that she would not move often in her lifetime, at least not from one city or from one state to another. (This was before the war, of course.) But moving from one place to another does not frighten the American housewife. Americans move, young couples especially, from one part of the country to another just to find a better job or a better opportunity or a better climate. And none of their acquaintances consider them as being "restless" or "tramps" or "just like gypsies.". . .

Incidentally, I would like to know (for 40 psychological reasons) where the dividing line between "strictly personal" and "impersonal" starts in the United States. The Americans seem / not to be "sentimental" 41 or possessive at all about most of their belongings. Friends borrow and wear one another's undergarments, stockings, dresses, even formal ones, hats, fur coats, overshoes and gloves. Strangers may rent furnished homes for more or less temporary use. Is there nothing which Americans do not mind sharing with others? It seems to me that the dividing line may start when mechanics are considered. I personally do not mind lending my typewriter to any of my friends. Europeans who have boats or motor cars do not mind lending these mechanical possessions to others. I am not quite sure if American kindness and generosity include the exchange of autos or fishing rods or a tennis racket. Beware of asking for them, O European guest on these shores! You may suddenly find out that there may be a real difference between borrowing an expensive fur coat or a lawn mower, and the temporary use of a completely furnished home or a 1941 Cadillac.

The last room which a guest usually sees

in the U.S.A. is the kitchen. He will ultimately see it when he is asked to help wash dishes after the party is over. This is not meant as a real treat; sometimes it is rather tiresome to lend a helping hand after a good dinner, but one gets used to it. Of course, a pre-war European housewife would rather die than allow any of her guests to see a pile of dirty dishes, much less urge them to join in the post-party drudgery! "The pleasure is mine, so is the work" is the self-sufficient European approach to entertaining guests. The more democratic Americans think differently. They want to share.

"Is this really your kitchen?" I asked Frances when I first came to stay with her.

"What else could it be?" my friend retorted.

"Well, it could be a laboratory, a doctor's supply room, even the dispensary in a nursery school. It looks so professional, / not at all 'private,' and — excuse me, Frances, I do not want to be rude — so empty, if you understand what I mean!"

Well planned, carefully thought out, clean and — empty. Thus do American kitchens look compared with the older European ones. Each little bit of space is used, each cupboard or shelf built according to a certain plan. The emphasis is upon saving time and labor — all except the architect's. European kitchens look as if nobody had spent even a minute in planning them. Why should an architect concern himself with woman's place in the home? And besides: domestic help was so cheap in most pre-war European countries that middle-class families could well afford to hire maids. These maids had, of course, to be kept busy all the time.

For nearly half a century the pattern of middle-class kitchens in Europe did not change much. I do not believe that young Americans can even imaginatively reconstruct a Victorian European kitchen. It certainly seemed a busy place! The walls were covered with china; pitchers, saucers, dishes, pudding forms, plates were fastened with neat blue bows. Once a year all the china was taken down, washed, the ribbons renewed, and then put back again for another year.

When under the influence of modern interior decorators we daughters asked Mother to take all that stuff off the walls, she at first refused. "But do you not feel the kitchen would look too empty?" she said. Even after the daughters' innovation, there still remained enough to make an American kitchen by comparison look empty indeed. All the materials, the tools, were on display in these kitchens: breadbox, jars with flour, salt, pepper, sugar, cleaning stuff, powders on the shelves, soap cakes over the sink, kitchen towels, brooms and sweepers in the corners. You were on the lookout for something all the time. And the hunt for matches! They disappeared the moment you needed them to light the gas for cooking purposes. The / cupboards had glass windows so that the housewife could see with one look that order prevailed. These cupboards were another indication of the lack of foresight and planning. They were always so high that even a very tall woman needed a stool or a small ladder to reach the supplies on the upper shelves. European households were better supplied with glassware, china and silver than the average American home. A good middle-class family had one or two sets for daily use, one set for visits from relatives and close friends, and several for "guests of honor" and for parties. The best sets were stored in the buffet in the dining room. All these sets (sometimes you could find china sets from the famous factories of Dresden, Berlin, Sévres and Copenhagen among them) had to be cleaned periodically — also the glassware and silver, and all the vases and flower bowls, the knickknacks of the average household. . . .

With so much household goods and so little inclination to part from worn and useless stuff, moving is a real task in Europe. The huge wardrobes alone are real headaches. Each member of a family had his own wardrobe; and then there were the wardrobes for the winter garments, for the linen supply. My own was so large that I had to ask a cabinetmaker to take it apart and put it together later on. It would not have been possible to move it through the doorway of an apartment house.

Because there is practically no help available for the American family in the middle and lower income brackets, each member of the family has to share in the household duties. Even the male members of the family do so. I have seen professors washing dishes, doctors fixing breakfasts, and a bank president sweeping the porch of his home. I had to look twice before I trusted my eyes. This democracy in family life seems to me one of the best features of American life. I wish the Europeans would take to it. But I have little hope that they will. The pattern of home life is so fixed over there that one must be transplanted to another continent in order to learn that things can be different. Over here, strangely enough, transplanted Europeans learn. Even refugee males lend a helping hand in the household!

Central heating, hot water, abundant cleaning materials, electric washing machines, electric irons make housework easier for the American housewife than for her European counterpart. But in spite of all the labor-saving devices there still remains a good deal of work for the American housewife. To me she is one of the most efficient, cleanest and most versatile homemakers I have met in any part of the world. Her flexibility, her quickness to change her ways and to adjust to new ideas, amaze me over and over again. She has nothing of the conservative European conception of how to run a household. Her approach to household work has also nothing of that unrealis- 45 tic / attitude which so often has been used in Europe to idealize domestic work. In approaching her chores, the American housewife thinks: "It's not amusing, it's dull, but it has to be done. Let's get on with the job!" And I have often admired, too, her ability

to do jobs which in most European countries housewives leave to experts: fixing electric bulbs, repairing short circuits, hanging curtains, taking off storm windows and putting in screens — and enjoying all the gadgets she can lay hands on. . . .

There are some objects which I miss in 46 an American home: lockers are one of them. I have not yet found the answer to the question, where do Americans keep precious personal possessions, such as intimate letters? Souvenirs? Jewelry? They cannot put everything in a safety deposit box. I also miss doors. This nation seems to prefer living without them. Don't Americans get tired once in a while of even their next of kin, their closest friends? Don't they too ever crave for privacy? But you cannot, generally speaking, have privacy in an American home. You never know where one room ends and another one starts. I also miss bookcases over here. Not books themselves. Americans do have books. Always the newest ones, the best sellers. What happens to these books the following year I have also not been able to discover. Do they throw them away like their broken kitchen knives and worn-out dresses? I hope not. But I miss bookcases filled with old or rare books, half-forgotten ones, books which Grandfather has treasured with annotated and yellow pages, books to browse in, books which people have read not only once but over and over again.

I also miss good pictures on the clean walls of the American living room. I am not the only one who misses them. In a survey by Vernon Pope in *Good Housekeeping* of the opinions and sales records of the leading publishers of prints, department stores, chain stores and mail-order houses, and such organizations as the Chicago Art Museum and the Metropolitan / Art Museum in New York, I read the sad 47 story about the eight pictures which decorate the average American home. The names of the artists are not so interesting as the subject matter: "End of the Hunt," "Christ in the Garden of Gethsemane,"

"The Blue Boy," "Sunday Morning," "Stone City," "Magnolias," "The Calmady Children," "The Samplers.". . .

[THE COLLEGE ADVISOR]

118   The existence of an advisory system on [the Miami University] campus was another interesting novelty to me. In Europe we made only one attempt to guide the student through formal vocational guidance. We helped him to set up his individual program of studies. Nobody had ever thought, at least not to my knowledge, of using guidance experts to help in personality adjustments or to advise in other personal problems.

The American student expects not only guidance but also personal interest from his instructor. I had to learn this very soon. The European professor keeps office hours, but he is not supposed to have more than two or three hours per week available to the students. Even if he is in his office he keeps his door closed and does not expect to be approached about matters other than problems closely related to his field. To approach a professor, a superior human being, about purely personal matters was unthinkable — anybody who has experienced the atmosphere in a German, Swiss, Dutch or Scandinavian university will agree with me. The European professor was not supposed to know the names of all his students. There are many amusing stories about the absentmindedness of some European professors who introduced themselves to their assistants at parties after these assistants had been with them for a good many years. Why should somebody who served science and learning be bothered with ques-
119 tions of "human interest"? The pro-/fessor's realm was the ivory tower — not even lab assistants had access to it.

American professors practice the open-door policy. I have learned to do the same. My office door is always open when I am in, and quite frequently a head looks in and a friendly girl's or boy's voice asks: "Are you very busy or may I come in a minute?" There are various reasons why students want to talk to their instructors: there are quizzes and grades, there may be prospective jobs to be discussed with the instructor, there are term papers and reports, experiments and books to be talked over. But some come in "just to talk to you" and some "have problems."

"I have a problem, Miss Barschak, which I want to discuss with you if you can spare a minute," said Shirley, a slim brunette. At first I thought she looked rather "cheap" with her preference for red colors, deep-red lipstick and matching fingernails, and also red sweaters, socks, with even her necklace and bracelets matching. In her curly hair she usually fixed red roses (artificial ones from the five-and-ten-cent store, of course). She reminded me always of a "Cover Girl" on one of the less refined magazines. Nevertheless, by talking to her, I found out that Shirley was not just a "cutie" but a very eager student of sociology who had already done excellent work on playgrounds and in summer camps with underprivileged children. This preference for loud colors was certainly merely a hangover from early adolescence.

"I really want your advice," she said. "It concerns Mother. She has been lonesome since my brother went overseas and I went back to college. Now, with not much to do, she is running to the doctor's, complaining of this and that. I thought I would ask her to come here for a week end. We live only fifty miles away. Perhaps you could see her and think of something to keep her mind busy?"

Of course, I made a date with Shirley 120 to meet Mother. What should I suggest? Red Cross work? Child welfare? YWCA? . . .

Simone de Beauvoir

From *America Day by Day*. Translated by Patrick Dudley. New York (Grove Press), 1953. Reprinted by permission of the publisher.

Simone de Beauvoir, professor at the University of Paris from 1931 to 1943 and follower of existentialist philosopher Jean-Paul Sartre, is perhaps best known as a novelist (*L'Invitee*, 1943; *Pyrrhus et Cineas*, 1944; *Le Sang des autres*, 1944; *Tous les Hommes sant Mortels*, 1947; *Les Mandarins*, 1954). Widely traveled, she wrote *America Day by Day* after a four months' tour of the United States.

[DRUGSTORES]

21 **B**REAKFAST in the drugstore at the street corner was a feast in itself. Orange juice, toast, white coffee — it is a pleasure that never palls. Seated on my swivel-stool, I shared for a moment in the American way of life; my solitude did not isolate me from my neighbors, who also breakfasted alone; it was rather the actual pleasure I felt in being one of them which kept me apart from them. They just ate. *They* were not partaking of a feast.

But everything was a feast for me. Drugstores were things that fascinated me; any pretext was good enough for me to linger, for they seemed to embrace all the bizarre qualities of America. I had wrongly pictured them as something between a dreary kind of chemist's shop and — because of the soda-fountain — an enchanted fountain of pink and white ice cream. Actually, they are the lineal descendants of the general stores in the colonists' towns and the camps of the Far West, where the pioneers found medicine, food, utensils, and, indeed, everything essential. They are both primitive and modern, a fact which gives them a peculiarly American charm. Everything has a 22 fam-/ily look: there is the same bright cheapness, the same modest gaiety; books with glazed covers, tubes of dentrifice and boxes of candy, all have the same colors — you have the impression that reading these books will leave a taste of sugar, that the candy will have stories to tell. I bought soap, face cream and toothbrushes. Creams here are creamy, soaps soapy; such honesty is a forgotten luxury. But set this honesty aside, and the quality of the goods is dubious. No doubt the shops on Fifth Avenue will satisfy the more exacting tastes — the furriers, the tailors with their international elegance; these are reserved for the cosmopolitan capitalist class. As for the more democratic shops, at first they astound you with their abundance and their glittering choice of goods; but fine though men's shirts may be, the ties are doubtful, while women's bags and shoes are frankly ugly, and a Frenchwoman would have difficulty choosing from all the profusion of dresses and blouses, coats and skirts without violating her taste. And then one soon discovers that beneath the multicolored paper wrappers all the chocolates taste of peanuts, all the best sellers tell the same story. And why choose one particular toothpaste rather than another? This useless profusion only serves to mystify. Here are a thousand possibilities open to choice: but they are all the same. In this way Americans can enjoy their freedom, subject to conditions imposed upon them, without ever noticing that they are not true conditions of freedom.

I was the only one to dally in front of the window displays. Yet those created or inspired by Dali were remarkable; gloves which floated about the trees like birds, shoes stranded among seaweed. In Paris there are only one or two shops which offer similar displays. Had there been an admission fee, there would have been crowds admiring this comedy of fashion; but the show is free, and even women pass by with-

35

23 out a glance; everyone walks rapidly / towards some destination. Other windows, less original, remind one of big stores at Christmas time: here is Broadway throughout the ages, elegant ladies, dressed in the fashion of 1900, getting into a carriage by the light of a lantern. Yes, I am definitely a tourist, amused by everything.

I spent the afternoon and evening with old friends who had sought refuge here in 1940: Spanish Leftists. I know that for many refugees America has been a land of exile: they have not liked it. They say that in New York life is cruel for the poor and for those who have lost their roots. . . .

[GOOD HUMOR]

26   What makes daily life so agreeable in America is the cordial good humor of the Americans. Of course, these qualities have their ugly side. I loathe those imperious invitations "to look at the best side of life," repeated in phrases and pictures as long as the day itself. On posters, for instance, what displays of shining white teeth before Coca-Cola, Lucky Strikes and dishes of Quaker Oats; a smile like lockjaw. The constipated young woman smiles lovingly at the lemonade which eases her stomach. In the subway, in the street, on magazine pages, these smiles pursue me like obsessions. In a drugstore I read on a showcard, "Not to grin is a sin." You sense instructions and discipline. Cheer up! Take it easy! Optimism is necessary for the peace of society and the prosperity of the country. If a banker has generously lent fifty dollars without security to a young foreigner in 27 difficulties, if my hotel man-/ager has taken the risk of cashing my checks, it is because this trust is ordained and implied by an economy based on credit and spending.

Kindness, too, is planned. This afternoon I went to cash a check. As soon as I entered the bank a uniformed employee advanced towards me and offered his services: I almost thought he was expecting me. He took me into a kind of hall where desks were arranged in rows; on each desk was a card with the name of a functionary. I sat down, showed my papers to a Mr. John Smith: he was not an anonymous cog in a machine, nor I an anonymous client, and he showed me courtesy addressed to me personally. He marked my check, and the cashier immediately paid me the money. At home my papers would have been verified on the other side of the counter, without consultation with me, and no doubt harshly; and I should have been treated as a mere number. I am not easily duped, and I know that this respect shown to individuals is quite formal; the polite smile which marks David Brown as an individual is also gratifying to the individual John Williams; nothing is more general than this singular trait which they all take so seriously. You sense a hoax, but it does not prevent the fact that, owing to this personal consideration, the American does not have to be stuck-up to feel his dignity; businesslike perhaps, but the friendliness of salesmen, employees, waiters and porters is, though not disinterested, nonetheless never servile; they are neither sour nor stiff, and their pleasantness is real. We held the German soldiers responsible for the way in which they carried out cruel orders. Indeed, man is never passive; in his obedience he sets limits to his liberty, and in submitting to evil accepts it; as a rule, this acceptance is carried out through invention and initiative which reveal the responsibility of the individual. And, in the same way, Americans do not submit passively to the propaganda of smiles; in an atmosphere in / which 28 optimism is obligatory they gladly become cordial, trusting and generous; a man's pleasant manner becomes less suspect the less interested he personally is in the success of the system; he is more hoaxed than hoaxer.

Whatever my view of American ideologies, I shall always have a warm feeling for the taxi drivers, the newspapermen, shoeshine boys and all those people who suggest by their daily acts that men can be friends. For they create an atmosphere of trust, friendship and gaiety. The man beside you is not *a priori* your enemy; even if he is wrong, he is not immediately guilty; with us, goodwill such as this has become uncommon. I am a foreigner; they found no fault with that, nor did it strike them as eccentric; they did not laugh at my accent, which was shocking; rather, they tried to understand me. If I had no change with which to pay the taxi, the driver did not question my honesty; he helped me to find some: indeed, he would generously let me off a few cents. In any case, I was especially fond of taxi drivers. They talked throughout the entire ride, and it was often difficult to understand them. New Yorkers themselves are at times put out by their accent. Many of them had been in France during the war, and we talked of Paris; each time I thought with emotion: here, then, was one of the men whom we had greeted so joyously, one whose uniform and steel helmet signified our deliverance. It was strange to find them again, each with his name and his private occupation — anonymous soldiers who came to my country from an inaccessible world, a world separated from all our misery by barriers of fire and steel. Their feeling for Paris was a little condescending, like the customs man who greeted me with the words, "You are coming from a beautiful country to a country which is even more beautiful." Their cordiality irritated me after I caught a cold; the fault lay with the New York climate, which changes without warning from hot 29 to / cold; but as they saw it, I was going around with one of those wretched complaints of old Europe. They asked severely, "You have a cold?" They seemed disturbed. A good American is never ill, and it is not polite for a stranger in New York to catch cold. They suggested remedies, and some even produced pillboxes from their pockets and offered them to me.

The other day I mistrusted R. and V. I was in no hurry to judge America, but of one thing I felt certain, in addition to the beauty of New York: there was warmth in the American people. . . .

[HARLEM]

It was more on account of . . . moral un- 37 easiness than of fear that I was glad Richard Wright was accompanying me to the Savoy tonight; I should feel less suspect. He came to fetch me at the hotel, and I noticed he was not looked on kindly by the people in the lobby; if he were to ask for a room here, he might be told that there were no more available. We dined at a Chinese restaurant downtown, for it was likely they would refuse to serve us uptown. Wright lives in Greenwich Village with his wife, who is white and comes from Brooklyn, and she told me that when she walks in the neighborhood with her little girl, she hears the most unflattering remarks. While we were searching for a taxi, people looked darkly at this Negro accompanied by two white women; there were taxi drivers who flatly refused to stop. After that, how could I hope to mingle quietly in the life of Harlem? I felt a kind of stiffness that made me feel guilty.

While Wright was buying tickets at the entrance to the Savoy, two sailors called out to Ellen and me, as sailors the world over call out to women at the entrance to dance halls, yet I felt embarrassed as never before; I should have to be offensive or else equivocal. But Wright, with a word and a smile, arranged everything; a white man would never have found just the right word and the right smile, and / his intervention, 38 though natural and simple, would only have aggravated my embarrassment. I climbed the steps with a light heart: Wright's friendship, his presence at my side, seemed to absolve me tonight.

The Savoy is a huge American dance hall, and in no way exotic. On one side the floor is bounded by a wall against which the band is placed; on the other side are boxes with tables and chairs, and beyond is a kind of hall like a hotel lobby. The floor is carpeted, and there are people sitting in armchairs, looking bored; they are non-drinking customers; they pay only to enter, and in the interval between dances women knit as though at a country dance. We sat in one of the boxes, and Wright put a bottle of whiskey on the table; whiskey is not sold, but patrons can bring it; we ordered soda water, drank and looked on. There was not a single white face. Although this place is as open to visitors as Lenox Avenue, only a few jazz enthusiasts and foreigners feel the urge to venture there from downtown.

Most of the women were young, in simple skirts and short pull-overs, but their high-heeled shoes had sometimes the look of cloven hoofs; the light or dark tan of their skin suits their bare legs better than nylon stockings; many were pretty, but, above all, each was alive. How different from the strained coldness of white Americans. And when these people dance, their animal vitality is not choked by the armor of Puritan virtue, and you understand how sexual jealousy can enter into the hatred that white men in America carry within themselves. However, only a small percentage of lynchings, riots, etc., have a pretext of sexual basis. Although envy goes even further, it is said freely and without spite: "Those people are freer and happier than we." There is some truth in this. What gaiety, what life and freedom in all this music and dancing! It struck me even more in this dance hall, which had about it something of home and everyday life.

39   In Paris, when Negroes dance with white people in the rue Blomet, they are too self-conscious. But here they are among themselves; they have worked all day and have come in search of amusement with their boy-friends; they do not aim at creating an effect. Many of the young women belong to decent families and probably go to church on Sunday morning. They dance simply and in a way natural to them: one must relax completely to be possessed by the music and the rhythm of jazz: and it is also this relaxation which gives vent to dreaming, emotion, naturalness to a degree unknown to the majority of Americans.

Of course, the prejudiced pick an argument here: why should one try to change the conditions for Negroes if they are happy and absolutely free? It is the old argument of capitalists and planters: it is always the workers, the natives who are happiest and most free. Although the oppressed escape the power of the idols which the oppressors have set up for themselves, this privilege is not sufficient to justify oppression.

I listened to the band, I looked at the dancers, drank whiskey; I was beginning to like it. I was feeling fine. The Savoy is one of the biggest dance halls in New York, that is to say one of the biggest in the world; there was something very satisfying in this. And the band is also perhaps the best in the world; at all events, nowhere else does it sound more authentic; the truth is there in the dancing, in the heart, in the whole life of the assembled people. When I listened to a dance band at home, when I saw Negroes dancing, the perspective was never altogether true; it suggested something different, a reality which might attain to greater fruition and of which it was but a doubtful reflection. But tonight I felt its message, I touched on something which was linked to nothing but itself: I had emerged from the cave. From time to time I felt that fullness of spirit in New York which contemplation of a pure idea gives to a freed / personality; that was the great- 40 est miracle of my journey, and it was never more dazzling than today. . . .

[AMERICAN WOMEN]

I ran into college girls again in the train 51 on my way back to New York. I hardly recognized them, for, just like their mothers and their elder sisters, they wore hats with feathers, flowers and little veils, heavy furs and high-heeled shoes. They were far less charming than yesterday. It was obvious that campus dress merely conformed to convention; jeans and a fur coat were two different uniforms. I do not think American women will ever dress for their own comfort or for themselves. First, their

clothes are an affirmation of their standard of life; that is why personal elegance that cannot be estimated in terms of dollars has no value (except in some artistic and intellectual *milieux,* but even here it is based on silks and furs). There is only a quantitative standard; the same coat for those of the same means. A woman's social success is closely linked with the richness of her appearance; it is a terrible handicap for poor people. To work for a certain leading magazine for women, one must go in for refined elegance and a wardrobe even more expen-
52 sive than is / necessary for a siren in a Paris nightclub. Many young women cannot make the necessary approach, and for this reason many positions are closed to those who need them most. When you arrive in New York, the sheen of the women's hair and their tints seem quite miraculous, but the miracle is paid for. Another thing seemed quite absurd to me: even the clothes worn by those American women who defend their independence on every occasion and whose attitude to men so readily becomes aggressive are not clothes designed for comfort; they dress for men. Those heels which paralyze the foot, those fragile plumes, those flowers with wintry hearts and all those furbelows are clearly dazzling effects designed to stress femininity and attract men's looks. European women's clothes are certainly less servile. . . .

[THE BOWERY]

60　The Bowery is an avenue of misery. Streetcars — I think they are the only ones
61 in New York — speed noisily beneath / the "el;" all the houses and shops have the color of gray bread, of unwashed faces. They sell luxury furs and diamonds; these shops are mournful places where various merchants have their counters side-by-side; and there are pawnbrokers, sellers of *bric-a-brac;* festive garments and bundles of old shoes hang around doorway areas; there are tailors, and among them a tailor for fat men, who shows photographs of obese gentlemen carefully dressed by himself and coats and trousers of fabulous measurements. The pawnbrok-

ers' shops hang out their traditional sign, three brass balls; and you can also recognize them by the guitars exhibited in the windows: in the midst of tarnished jewelry, phonographs, watches, cameras and cooking utensils you always find guitars, as noble, despite their surroundings, as any in Picasso's paintings; trumpets and saxophones often keep them company.

Sandwiched between these shops are hotels for men, all along the Bowery; their stained facades and dusty windows touch the heart: they are refuges where for a few cents you can hire a mattress or just a corner of the floor alive with bugs. Poorer still, New York tramps go to the flophouses where they sleep seated on benches, their arms supported by a rope and their heads by their folded arms. They sleep until the rest period they have bought is ended; then a pull on the rope, they fall forward and the shock wakes them.

Those who are even poorer remain in the street. The sick, the old, the down-and-outs, the hard-luck men, all the riff-raff of American life prowl about these pavements. They sleep on the asphalt, regardless of frost or rain; they cower against little stairways that lead down to basements, or else they remain standing, leaning against walls and trying to sleep in an upright position. They have only one object in life: drink; in the dark, cold squalor of the Bowery, neon signs proclaim a paradise in / every 62 bar. But drunkenness must be paid for: they try to sell you, or sell each other, their last shirt, their torn shoes, a chipped knife; over a bundle of rags picked up in a dustbin you will find all the excitement of an auction or the Stock Exchange. But usually they have nothing at all to sell: they beg. My friend, S. L., who works in the district, knows more than one of them: in begging they play the fool; it is the rule here. "The bank is closed, Madam, I cannot cash my check. Could you lend me twenty-five cents?" Sometimes, when she is carrying a book under her arm, she sees two shining eyes: "Lend it to me: I will give it back." They give it back: they have borrowed it to read. S. told me that many women also live in the Bowery, but one sees them rather in cafés than in the streets; one is "the queen of the Bowery," an old woman, once famous for her beauty, who lives in squalor but has a hoard of money.

The most famous bar in the Bowery is Sammy's. It was, until recently, just a bar like all the others, a kind of flophouse, where for a few cents one could drink and sleep through the day and night. In the afternoon its appearance did not change; the sole patrons were tramps, both male and female, who drank cheap beer at the counter or slept on chairs with their heads resting on the tables. But Sammy, the proprietor, suddenly had a brain wave. He got together some ancient actresses, singers and dancers aged sixty to eighty, and at night, decked out in feathers, they offered songs and dances of their youth. The bar was turned into a cabaret, Sammy's Follies, and became a great success. Outside, before the door, men wait in the cold for a nickel to fall from the skies and enable them to enter; those who are in luck tipple happily around the bar; presiding above its array of bottles are the queens of the Bowery painted on the wall. Sitting at the tables are respectable middle-class people, drink-63 ing whiskey and eat-/ing hamburgers. The walls are covered with photographs, press-cuttings, autographs; there are also old colored posters, advertisements for silent films — rape and assassination are forever perpetrated.

As in most New York nightclubs, a woman photographer, draped in black satin, wanders around the tables; with an engaging smile she aims her camera at couples and happy gatherings. We sat beside the platform: a man played the piano, a sad young woman played the violin; she was out of place, conspicuous and unhappy. One by one, the singers paraded. They were purposely selected for their huge size: Mae Wests. Their hair was red or raven black, their make-up extravagantly splashed on: orange splotches on their hanging cheeks, caked powder in the folds of their double chins. Only the eyes, in spite of false lashes, charcoal, mascara and blue circles, remained human: you cannot touch this fragile circle, it evades disguise. All these old hags wore huge hats with green and orange feathers and sparkling jewelry; black silk dresses sheathed their bodies and full bosoms. They sang cowboy songs, sentimental ballads, all the old favorites of 1900; they attempted a few steps and hopped about with bouncing breasts. Many had possessed both talent and beauty and still had fire, life and femininity, however worn. I noticed a woman sitting alone at a table, still young and respectable, drinking whiskey after whiskey while gazing at the stage with a stony stare; other women, whose sight was failing, laughed hysterically.

The main attraction was an octogenarian whose doll-like face, embedded in a shapeless mass of flesh, still suggested beauty. She sang in a coarse, guttural style and kept time with her big hat; she undulated, and, despite her eighty-five years, for a moment recalled the person she had been: when she lifted her petticoats, canary-colored bloomers, tight at the knees, and legs worthy of Mistin-/guette were re- 64 vealed; all the women screamed; hysterical women hitched up their dresses and half-swooned on the shoulders of their embarrassed men. The old woman ran around the room imprinting kisses on the men's heads; she tripped along, and, from time to time, made a gesture as if to raise her skirt behind: a whistle brought her to heel. The public screamed even louder. In the midst of a roll of drums, applause, laughter and wild shouts, the star sat down in a corner of the room, alone; she looked old and very tired. Tomorrow she would begin again.

Of course, this story is not very attractive: they make fun of miserable old women. But what do serious-minded people who protest against it offer them? After all, Sammy gives them the means of earning a living. The Bowery exists; Sammy is not to blame. And the Bowery is the reverse of Wall Street. You must look further if you want to find reasons for being indignant. . . .

[PSYCHOANALYSIS AND OPTIMISM]

67 Psychoanalysis is a huge enterprise undertaken for social rehabilitation; its sole object is to permit each citizen to resume a useful place in society. There is at present a whole category of individuals whom they seek to rehabilitate: the G.I.'s who came back from Europe or the Pacific troubled by their experiences overseas. D.P., whose method is to submit psychological cases to tests, told me that there are a considerable number of war veterans among them. One can understand why, after breathing the air of American optimism throughout their youth and after having lived in a country which denies the existence of evil, these young people were quite overwhelmed when roughly confronted with the world at war; their experience no longer fits in with the system in which they must somehow or other find their place again. Those who have the courage to believe in this experience represent a new force, but many continue to feel themselves lost. To adapt oneself here is, in fact, to resign oneself; to be happy, one must obstinately blind oneself. Many things would be changed for Americans if they would only admit that there is ill-luck in this world and that misfortune is not *a priori* a crime. . . .

[DEATH AND BURIAL]

85 People do not talk willingly of death in America. True, I often caught sight of neon signs illuminating the night with the words: Funeral Home. But the name is supposed to be comforting; from the outside, they look like bars or cabarets. I had read the words on posters. *Funeral Home: Reception Rooms, Children's Playrooms, Cloakroom, Low Prices.* It is there that, prior to burial, the dead man gives his last party: his face is exposed, made up in glaring colors, and he wears a gardenia or an orchid in his buttonhole. His friends all come to greet him for the last time. As for me, these engaging "Homes," wedged between bars and drugstores, give me the creeps: I always ex-/pect to see some zombie 86 or vampire emerge from them; the truth of death is vainly denied, but in the cemeteries it is revealed, and it is this which gives their funeral parks an unexpected charm. All of a sudden, in this country where health and happiness are guaranteed by the most modern processes, you discover death, and life recovers a dimension it had lost in trying to conform to the lines suggested by advertisements for Quaker Oats.

On Broadway, despite the weighty skyscrapers, in Queens, despite the dreary uniformity of the working class sections, and at Arlington, despite the marble serenity of the Capitol, the cemeteries remind you that each life is individual and everyman is finite in himself; they remind you that life is carnal, and that even conditioned air is breathed through the lungs. Returning to dust, man shows that he is not a machine; he is flesh, and real blood runs in his veins. In America, it is the graves that affirm man's humanity most authoritatively. I do not know if Americans are sensitive to this, or if they feel more tenderly than they admit about that sleep which will give them rest from their breathless business of life: the fact is, their cemeteries have more character than their cities. Among these headstones, half sunk into the ground, one finally escapes from the trivialities of daily life. . . .

We drove for a long time before reaching 125 the place we were to visit: the "optimistic" cemetery which is called Forest Lawn Memorial Park. It covers a great hill where wide roads twist about, as at Arlington. It is a green park shaded with fine trees. Here and there on the lawns a gravestone has been raised bearing a single name. It is as though the dead have been buried under the turf with rustic simplicity, as in Corsican cemeteries: there are neither monumental tombs nor mortuary chapels, and one imagines simple wooden coffins sunk in the ground. In fact, the turf covers great works of masonry with a light crust, and the graves are made of concrete. The coffin is let down by means of winches and pulleys. The gravediggers are not gardeners but mechanics, and as for the grass which disguises the cement, it is supplied in broad strips which are rolled out like linoleum: it must be mass-produced somewhere. N. told me that even the coffins are watertight; the air cannot penetrate, nor can worms live in them. The bodies are mummified more or less perfectly according to cost. The intestines are always removed, and the face is made up and painted. They remain exposed to friends and parents for one or two days in the Funeral Chapel.

From the top of the hill there is an immense view over Los Angeles, the sea and the mountains beyond. There is a chapel here, but most astonishing is *The Book of David*, a copy of a book at least the height of a man, open at the middle page, and on this page one reads in letters of huge size an inscription of which this is the substance: "How beautiful it is to dominate the city of the living and the city of the dead from this majestic height. You are on one of the high peaks of the world. But what you do not see is this: below the sides of this hill are the biggest water reservoirs
126 of Los Angeles: they contain / many million gallons of water, and it is thanks to them that our lawns are always green. Such is the greatness of man!". . .

[A WRESTLING MATCH]

207   Since there were no cockfights, a professor took me, after my lecture, to a wrestling match; if not especially representative of Texas, it was, at least, typically American. We arrived, toward the end of the match, at an immense sports arena filled with a frenzied crowd. Women were raucously shouting, "Kill him! Kill him!" In the ring, the wrestlers were circling one another, their eyes filled with hate, studiously aping the movements of King Kong. It was obvious from the start that the
208 match / was "fixed": one of the wrestlers threw the referee out of the ring; the other pinned his opponent to the canvas, and the

loser suddenly feigned rage, furiously ground his teeth and threw himself upon the winner, who fled in sudden terror: they chased each other up and down the aisles and fought, while the crowd screamed hysterically. Surely they knew it was all sham, yet they refused to believe it; besides, they were getting their money's worth: there had been hard blows struck, and blood had flowed. . . .

[NIGHTCLUBBING IN NEW ORLEANS]

In the morning we returned to the places 217 we had seen the day before. At noon we ate creole food in an old / French restau- 218 rant. Then we took the boat that goes up and down the Mississippi for a few miles. There were four decks, one above the other, and each had a bar, a cafeteria or a dance floor. At night there was a band and people danced, but in the daytime they just sat about in chairs and drank. Actually there was little to see. The excursion was pleasant enough because of the sunshine, the sky, the sound and smell of the water. But the river flowed between factories and warehouses and was in no way remarkable. The captain took up his stand before a microphone and relentlessly explained the scene. It was always the same story, as at Niagara Falls and the Grand Canyon: nature must be served up to the tourist in a "homogenized" way by a human intermediary.

We dined in a patio, different from the one we saw yesterday but just as delightful. We were struck by the color of the sky: it was pearl gray, luminous as the dawn, as if lighted by some mysterious searchlight. Once we were back in the street we understood: a soft mist enveloped the city. Tall buildings on the other side of Canal Street had retreated; they were far away and ghostly. The mist smothered the neon signs, but it made a screen above the roofs where all the lights were reflected. The sky was almost white, the air quite moist. It was gentle but stifling and seemed to presage a storm.

We met our friends again at *The Old Absinthe House*. We were proud of their company, proud to feel ourselves in league, not with the people who listened dumbly, but with the musicians. There were more people tonight: some attentive students, bored couples and gay parties. At one of the tables an old gentleman began to sing. He had a fresh, pink complexion and fine white hair, gold-rimmed spectacles and an air of quiet assurance that comes from a well-stuffed pocketbook. He was of a common and particularly detestable type. The 219 band obligingly accompanied / him. He began another song, and I got mad. The little Italian smiled; he explained that anyone in the audience had the right to sing providing he paid for it: the money went to the musicians. And I saw indeed that the obtrusive singer had put his dollars on the piano; he loved music in a strange way.

R. and C. wanted to go to a nightclub reserved for colored people to which they had entrée. But it was Holy Week, and New Orleans is a pious city. Tonight the place was closed. They took us to another bar in the *Vieux Carré* where there was a good Negro band with saxophone and trumpet; the trumpeter was young and played with youthful zest. He had a natural gift, so complete in itself that his whole being seemed to be concentrated on each note. It is here in these unostentatious nightclubs and among these unknown players that jazz attains a real dignity, far more so than in Carnegie Hall or the Savoy: there is no showmanship, no exhibitionism, and no commercial flavor. It is, on the contrary, a mode of life and a *raison d'être*; it gives to art, poetry and printed music the pathetic privilege of making immediate contact, like the moments whose very substance it transfigures. If these men's lives are often so tormented it is because, instead of holding off death at arm's length like other artists, they are conscious at every moment of the marriage of life and death. It was against this background — the background of death — that the inspired music of the young trumpeter rose up. You could not listen to him merely with your brain, for he conjured up an experience in which you felt you had to let yourself go utterly. He conjured it up, but in what a desert! The people here have not even the respectful enthusiasm of concert-goers; they are amused by jazz and despise it on racial grounds, their prejudices being as firmly rooted in their morality as in their money. It was with a similar arrogance that the / great lords of the past amused themselves 220 — with buffoons and jesters. R. questioned the trumpeter, they exchanged a few words, and the dark face lit up; he smiled at us as he played. Like the musicians at *The Old Absinthe House*, he felt he must play for someone, and it was a chance he seldom got. . . .

[THE NEGRO IN THE SOUTH]

Seen through the tempests, the sun, the 223 dank nights, the pearly colors, New Orleans seemed worthy of its legend. But I knew it was also one of the most wretched cities in America, one where life is bitter; its stagnant luxury already seemed ambiguous, and we would have liked to penetrate further into its heart and live the reality of its daily life. On departing, I decided to return. . . .

Right through the day the tragedy of it 224 all pursued us like an obsession. Even the traveler, confined to a bus and waiting rooms, cannot escape it. From the moment we entered Texas, and everywhere we went, there was hatred in the air, arrogant hatred on the part of the white race and silent hatred on that of the black. At the stations, middle class women, respectable but badly dressed, looked enviously at pretty Negro girls in brilliant dresses and flashing costume jewelry, and the white men resented the nonchalant good looks of Negro youths in light suits. American kindliness no longer found its place; in the line outside the bus the colored people were jostled: "You're not going to let that colored woman go in front of you!" a woman said to a man. She sounded furious.

The Negroes were crowded humbly in the rear seats, in the heat and the jolting, which are extra hard at the back of the bus.

They tried to obliterate themselves. In the afternoon a woman with child fainted; her head bumped against the window whenever the bus jolted. We listened to the sneering, scandalized voice of a college girl who cried, "That woman is crazy!" The driver stopped the bus and came back to see just what was happening; it was only a Negro woman who had fainted, everyone told him, these people always cause embarrassment . . . They shook her up a bit, brought her to, and the bus started off again; we did not dare to offer her our place in the front, for everyone would have 225 opposed it, and she would have / been the first victim of their indignation. The bus continued on its way, the woman continued to suffer, and when we stopped in a town she fainted again; the passengers went off to drink Coca-Cola without bothering about her; there was only an elderly woman who came with us and tried to help. The pregnant woman thanked us, but she seemed anxious, and she went off quickly without accepting our offer of further help: she felt guilty in the eyes of the white people, and she was frightened. . . .

[TWO AMERICAN COLLEGES]

249   I spent three days at Smith and Wellesley colleges. I slept in white guest rooms which reminded me of clinics and monasteries, and I talked a good deal with the professors and students. The atmosphere at Smith is gay and intimate. Wellesley is more sumptuous, with its slate-blue lake, medieval keeps and trees. As at Vassar, here, too, students are serious (even though the French scholars think them superficial, and the American girls are disconcerted, when they come to Paris, by the difficult examinations in law, letters or political science). They admit only young girls well thought of in their high schools. For those who don't want to work, but whose social standing demands that they go through college, there are milder establishments. Near Wellesley I saw one of the most aristocratic colleges where they accept students who have been refused elsewhere and who gen-

tly pursue their studies in near-luxury: they live in charming clubhouses / scattered 250 throughout the country and never worry about anything other than their appearance and their "dates." They look down on the Wellesley girls, who, in turn, despise them.

There is a far more democratic spirit in the big colleges: for instance, the sororities, about which the college girls at Smith spoke so harshly, have been suppressed. They are, they say, idiotic institutions, and the only pleasure in membership lies in the knowledge that certain other girls have been excluded — a cheap kind of superiority. The traditional practical jokes new girls are submitted to are both brutal and stupid; nothing positive is accomplished in these clubs, they have no object other than their existence, no reason for existing other than snobbery. They expressed these opinions in pure and rapid French; on some points, at least, their knowledge is sound.

The more I talked with these girls, the more difficult it was for me to form an opinion — more difficult, indeed, in that the colleges represent a kind of selection; all the girls come from rich or more or less comfortably-off families, they belong to different milieus and regions, and, despite their conventionality, each one is an individual. At Wellesley I saw upper-class students who seemed to me as deep and serious as others appeared frivolous. "Even those who seem frivolous are not always so," they said. "You must understand that, with us, frivolity has a certain snob value; one would be afraid of being taken for a blue-stocking if one took ideas and studies too seriously; but many of the students are interested in important questions; they hide it only because it is looked down upon. No, we are not primarily interested in finding a husband, and we shall not be content with a job that will only keep us busy for a year or two. We want to take up work which is useful. We want to see the world and enrich ourselves intellectually." Many of them said with conviction, "We want to make ourselves / useful." They are pre- 251 occupied with social and economic questions and specialize in these fields in the hopes of basing a career upon them.

I was touched by the freshness and warmth of their friendliness. Of course, I am writing of an elite class, but in French secondary schools and universities there are not many young girls who would voice such views with so much sincerity. This desire to be of use does not spring from any need for compensation: on the contrary, those who spoke to me were among the prettiest and most charming. They added that it would be altogether wrong to judge their generation by the big, impressive colleges; in the humbler specialist schools or the State universities, where it costs far less to study, most of the students without private means work harder than here; they know they must count on themselves, and this gives them a strong sense of independence. Here independence is the rule, indeed, almost an institution. The students freely criticize their teachers' methods, and the teachers take note of their remarks; but they often criticize for the pleasure of criticizing; they willingly air their views, often originally and trenchantly, to prove a personality as yet not acquired. One also finds these defects among our own young people, all the more so because of their greater conformism and idleness: their stress on originality is also a form of convention. Do college girls like the superficial paradise in which they live, or not? That is a question on which they are divided. Many are delighted by it; they find life with their parents boring and stifling; they are frightened of leaving college. Others regret being cut off from the world and would prefer to live more like our students at home. . . .

[INTELLECTUALS IN COLLEGE]

270   There are two sorts of universities in the United States. Those financed by the state are modestly endowed; the buildings are sometimes poor, the professors sometimes badly paid. Tuition fees are low, thus the schools are full of young people without money who either must or really want to learn. The students often have some other occupation which enables them to live. Unfortunately, however, as salaries are low, the most distinguished professors flock to the great private institutions. Financed by wealthy patrons, by gifts and legacies, they have magnificent buildings and campuses. Their staffs are amply remunerated, and their prestige is greater than that of public institutions. Their tuition fees are very high, which adds to their attraction. It is, naturally, at Yale, Princeton, Harvard and Columbia that many of the most eminent scholars and men of letters teach. This results in a paradoxical situation: poor students who wish to study get mediocre teaching on account of their social status; the soundest and most brilliant instruction is offered to those who are richer and who sometimes care least about intellectual quality.

A remark made by a Harvard student struck me; when I expressed astonishment at the contempt shown by many of his friends for intellectual values, he said: "In Europe / students are intellectuals, but not 271 here." He was paying a compliment to European students; in France, the departments of Law and Medicine at the Sorbonne are full of young people who are in no sense intellectuals. But the fact is that this remark is strikingly true of the great American universities. They are thronged with the sons of the rich, who feel they must have a distinguished education, and, for the average among them, it is just a gay and elegant way of passing the time of youth. They form clubs and busy themselves with club life, committees, and with the inner organization of the university, all of which gives them an illusion of independence and activity. They take a certain interest in sport and indulge in heavy drinking bouts. Intellectual distinction and culture are ignored in the clubs and fraternities, and brilliant academic achievement is generally avoided. The college girls at Wellesley had spoken of this snobbery rampant among them; it almost takes on the aspect of caricature at Yale or Harvard. Young men want to be taken for "gentlemen," not intellectuals, and the two categories seem incompatible to them.

There are five grades awarded in examinations, A, B, C, D and E. The one coveted by the gentleman-student is C, called, for this reason, "gentleman's C"; D or E would mean failure; these grades would mean you were incapable of reaching the standard you yourself set; but A or B would mean base pedantry. Professor T., to whom I talked for a long time, told me that students often came to him and asked what to read, what lectures to attend and how much time to give to their major subjects in order to pass with a "gentleman's C." And A. E., a scholarship student at Yale, told me that, to make a little money, scholars wrote theses for the wealthy students; they also tutored them during the last two months, giving them everything they needed to know for the examination, in 272 digest form. Fees varied ac-/cording to whether those who paid were after an A, B or C. He added that it was difficult to aim precisely so as not to achieve too good a record.

Of course, despite all this, there is an *élite* which takes work seriously. I met mostly students in the French department, and they spoke good French. But nowhere did I stay long enough to get a clear notion of the value of the instruction offered by the professors or the level of the students. What I was told, and what I could sense for myself, was that teaching is highly specialized. They turn out linguists, chemists, mathematicians, sociologists, but they do not form minds. Specialization in literature is suspicious to them. Literary people are considered aesthetes; they themselves derive a certain glory from this distinction, and they isolate themselves; nothing disturbs them more than the idea of "literateur engagé"; they loathe it. For them, the realm of art, poetry and the word is cut off from the rest of the world. Here again I ran into the tendency which had struck me, not among writers, but among intellectuals in America. Its roots go deeper than the

taste of specialization. I shall return to the subject later on.

Philosophy is not at all here, as in France and Germany, the most inclusive of the intellectual disciplines; it is divided into completely heterogeneous branches: psychology, sociology and logic treated as though they were exact sciences, as isolated within their spheres as physics or chemistry. As for metaphysics, it hardly exists at all. Dewey's philosophy, the most widely recognized, is neither metaphysical nor ontological and even refuses to pose this kind of problem. At Yale they are seriously interested in phenomenology and the various forms of existentialism, but this case is almost unique. Professor T. who is a European Jew, a philosopher and a physicist, told me he had met with complete failure in trying to initiate some stu-/dents into phenomenological 273 methods and in trying to explain the method of Cartesian thought; they find speculation useless, idle, and nothing interests them less than the history of ideas; they care only about positive results. Even in the sciences they care little for demonstrations and are content with conclusive formulae. T. told me that one day, when he had a difficult physics theory to explain, first he stated the law, and then he proceeded to prove it. He was politely interrupted: "Don't worry! We believe you."

"When war breaks out between America and Russia, which side will France be on?" I heard this question frequently. It was typical of that fatalism I found so frightening. Public opinion carries great weight in America, and Alain's idea is even truer here than anywhere else: this resignation to war is the first factor which makes it possible. Many people added, "Naturally, war is a dreadful thing, but, if we don't go to war now, who can guarantee that Russia will not make war as soon as she is stronger than we are?" Propaganda for a preventive war makes headway among students as easily as among drugstore waitresses.

This evening, in Boston, P. and D. were angry about the anti-labor laws, but they do not even think of seeking a way to make their protests heard: "Don't you see," P. said, "D. must go into his father's business, and I, too, must make a career in business. You know that at the moment there is a 'Red scare'; we have only to proclaim our left-wing views for people to say we are Communists, and that would be enough to compromise our future." I was touched by the naive sincerity of this confession; in France, a well-born youth would have shown more malice. But this was all the more shocking in that P. and D. were honest and well-meaning. They are caught up in a social mechanism from which only real heroism can free them. Their professors will not preach courage; / they have little 274 influence and complain of being ignored. A university professor is an even less important person in this country than in my own. But perhaps this is because they do not try in any way to serve as spiritual guides. This is a vicious circle. They have no share in the administration of the establishment in which they teach, and they know they would soon reap their reward for an imprudent word; all they can do is to serve the regime with exemplary docility.

The inertia I observed at Oberlin, as well as in California and the East, is not just the result of laziness and timidity. It is this, indeed, that is disturbing at first. Individually, these young people often seem most highly gifted. They are paralyzed not by any interior malady but by the situation itself. They all have the impression that America is too vast a machine with too complicated a structure. One American said to me, "This country is like a whale, with its tiny brain — the East — and an endless body." The tiny brain does not feel capable of controlling the mass of flesh. One of a number of factors, a tradition of intellectual defeatism, has established itself in this country, so new, yet already so old. Myrdal has described and analyzed it with great penetration in his fine book, *American Dilemma*. He says that the political tendency of *laissez-faire* is strong in present-day

social science. It has very typically developed into a general theory, and sociologists merely reflect the great mistrust which all educated classes in America feel for politics and legislation. The democratic American mind's fatalism in regard to the *res publica* is a current disease which is on its way to becoming chronic. The American, says Myrdal, generally regards indulgently and tolerantly the politics and administration of his country, as though they were things for which he is not responsible; he does not look upon himself as a legislator, nor does he try to coöperate in / the organization of 275 an agreeable social life. He is even inclined to disassociate himself from politics as from something despicable.

This is part of what Lord Bryce called "the fatalism of the multitude" in America. This fatalism and this lack of participation create a vicious circle: they are both cause and effect. It was certainly this vicious circle that I, too, felt during these conversations and that seemed to me so sad. Nobody can do anything, for everyone thinks he can do nothing. . . .

[THE ATTRACTION OF AMERICA]

The great attraction held for me by 328 America, where the memory of the pioneers is strong, consists of the fact that it appears as a realm still in transcendence; its history is contracted, of course, in time yet stretches splendidly across vast spaces; it is the history of the creation of the whole world. For this reason skyscrapers always move me; they proclaim man as a being who does not stagnate but who is, instead, filled with enthusiasm and a desire for expansion and fresh conquest. In the shameless profusion of goods that one finds in the drugstore there is poetry as fantastic as in a baroque church: man has taken raw matter in the toils of his desire and has asserted over it the power of imagination. New York and Chicago reflect the existence of this demiurge, with its imperial dreams, and that is why they are the most human, the most uplifting / cities that I know. There is no 329 room here for any of the dreary caution of the *petit bourgeois* in his carpet slippers, whose only object is to stay at home and wait for death, as the sonnet puts it. To devote one's life to that is living death. Americans in this sense are truly alive; inertia does not appeal to them. A man is judged by his acts: to exist you must do something. The great iron bridges, buildings, Grand Central Station, Park Avenue, the air terminals, the highways and mines, all proclaim this faith.

It would be difficult to tear myself away from these splendid visions of hope; and yet I knew their wiles. In America, life also ebbs away in the effort to survive. "I've been out since 10 A.M.," a taxi driver told me at 10 P.M. "You bet I want to get home!" I remembered how people rushed to the ferryboat that took them across to New Jersey. All my friends had told me how hard the working days were in this city of distances, especially for women who have a job and a home to run at the same time; they are exhausted when night comes: I have often seen them too tired to accept an invitation to go out. I have come to understand that if people drink so much it is not because they have a mania; they need a spur at the end of the afternoon.

That is not all. One has a premonition that anything might happen. But what is actually happening? What do they do with their time and the money they earn? No doubt, I did not get to know the ruling class, those who invent, study and speculate; but they make up only a small minority. Americans, for the most part, are like those with whom I rubbed shoulders; they let their lives go around in circles. They have neither a liking for, nor the sense of, collective life; nor have they any concern for their own personal destinies. This is the source of the sadness that I often felt when with them. This world full of generous / promise crushes them; and its splendor soon appears barren, for no one controls it.

330

Each civilization offers in the "banality of everyday life" a means of escape, but what strikes one here is the point to which this escapism is organized. Neither his education nor the atmosphere in which he develops are designed to shed light on the inner self of the individual. He is aware of himself not only as a human body but also as an organism protected and prolonged by a whole arsenal of devices; he goes from floor to floor by elevator, travels by subway, speaks into the telephone, typewrites, and sweeps the floor with a vacuum cleaner. Between his stomach and the food he eats there is a world of canned food factories, refrigerators, electric cookers. Between his sexual desires and their fulfilment there is the paraphernalia of moral precepts and hygienic practices. He is hemmed in by society from childhood. He searches outside himself, among other people, for his models for conduct; hence what is called American conformism: Actually, individuals are just as different and just as isolated one from another in the new world as in the old, but here they find easier means of escape from their individuality and the feeling of "forlornness"; or perhaps they do not find them, but then, at least, they seek them more stubbornly. Like everyone else, they know dissatisfaction, boredom and doubt, but they try to rationalize their own confusion by posing "problems": instead of drawing strength from solitude, or overcoming it by plumbing its depths, they cling to the given facts; they see the source of values and of truth in things, not in themselves.

Their own existences are things of chance to which they attach no importance. That is why they are interested in net results, and not in the spirit that engenders them. In much the same way, they think they can isolate the part from the whole, as witnessed in the call for specializa-/tion 331 that one finds in the sciences, technology and education. To use Hegelian terms, one can say that the very negation of the subject leads to the triumph of understanding over the spirit, that is to say, the triumph of abstraction. And that is why in this country, which seems to turn so decidedly toward the concrete world, the word abstraction so often came to my lips; the object set up as an idol loses its human values and becomes abstract, for concrete reality is that which actually envelops object and subject simultaneously. That is the paradox of all positivisms, all pseudo-realisms which forsake humanity to proclaim the importance of things; they are lacking in the object itself, and never attain to anything more than concepts.

I often felt, while listening to American jazz or talking to Americans, that the very time in which they lived was abstract. They respect the past, but only insofar as it is a thing embalmed; the idea of a living past, integrated with the present, is foreign to them. They only want to recognize a present cut by the course of time, and the future they visualize is that which can be deduced mechanically, not one whose ripening, or whose sudden explosion, implies unforeseeable risks. They believe in the future of a bridge, for instance, or of an economic plan, but not in the future of an art or of a revolution. Their time is "the physicist's time," an exterior concept which doubles that of space.

Because they refuse to accept the durability of things, they also refuse to recognize their quality; it is not only for economic reasons that "craftsmanship" does not exist in the States. Even in leisured occupations qualitative success is never sought for: food is cooked, just as fruit is ripened, as fast as possible; in every walk of life one must always hurry, lest the result be already outdated by the time it is achieved. Cut off from the past and from the future, the present has no weight. Nothing is 332 more foreign / to Americans than the idea of regarding the passing moment as a repetition of time, a mirror of eternity, and of anchoring oneself to it to grasp truths or values that are in themselves timeless. To them, the content of the passing moment is as fragile as the moment itself. Because they will not admit that truths and values *become,* they do not know how to conserve them in the movement that leaves them behind: they just deny them.

History is a great cemetery: men, deeds, ideas die almost as soon as they are born. Each individual existence has a flavor of death; from one minute to the next, the present is merely an honorary past. It must constantly be filled anew to dissemble the curse it carries within itself; that is why Americans like speed, alcohol, horror films and sensational news. The demand for new things and ever newer things, is feverish, since they find no rest in anything. But here, as elsewhere, life repeats itself, day after day, so they amuse themselves with gadgets, and, for lack of projects, they cultivate hobbies; in spite of these crazes they pretend to accept daily life. Sport, the movies and comic strips are distractions. But they end by going back to that from which they tried to escape: the arid basis of American life is boredom. Boredom and solitude.

It has been said a thousand times, and it is true: these people about me are lonely. Because they flee in terror their essential solitude, because they run away from themselves, they have no real self-possession. How are they to extend themselves? How can they receive from others? They are open and friendly, capable of tenderness, passion, sentiment and cordiality; but they rarely know how to create deep love or enduring friendship. They are far from stony-hearted, yet their relations with one another are superficial and cold. They are far from lacking in vitality, enthusiasm or generosity, but they do not know how to devote themselves to the business of their lives, and, to / be a Julien Sorel or a Ras- 333 tignac, one has to take one's self in hand, not run away from one's self. There are very few ambitious people here. They worship heroes, but in a capricious way; few want anything more than to be raised a few rungs on the social ladder; a young man anxious to distinguish himself will wish, at best, to distinguish himself as a citizen rather than as a man; he will not dream of emerging far beyond the set conditions of life, the dream of which is the tree where Julien perches and the hill from which Rastignac proudly looks down over Paris; ambitions of greatness are the source of many disappointments and failures in ways that Americans do not know; they have virtues born of indifference to themselves. They are not embittered, persecuted or ill-willed, envious or egotistical. But they have no inner fire. As a result of losing themselves in pursuit of the object, they find themselves without any object. They experience in another form the "forlornness" that their civilization tries to screen from them. It is the very contrast between their secret fragility and their proud edifices that makes them so pathetic.

I think it is because of the abstract climate in which they live that the importance of money becomes so disproportionate. These people are neither mean nor avaricious — on the contrary, these are faults of which they justly accuse the French; they do not want money in order to amass it; they spend it readily, for other people as well as for themselves; giving comes naturally to them. Nor are they pleasure seekers, for they do not desire money in order to satisfy extravagant appetites. If money is the sole object for so many it is because all other values have been reduced to this one denominator and because it has become the measure of every human accomplishment, whereas it is really only the abstract sign of true riches. It is because they cannot establish or affirm 334 real values that / Americans are satisfied with this empty symbol. Actually, they are not satisfied; with the exception of the leading capitalists, they are as self-conscious of their wealth as they are of their leisure.

This is one of the reasons, undoubtedly, why American women have become idols: the dollar is a doleful divinity. Man does not mind justifying his work and his hard-won earnings by dedicating them to a flesh and blood being. Yet their cult of women, like the cult of money, is only a substitute. The existence of the American male would have no meaning if he were unable to give a concrete meaning to that abstract entity, his liberty. This is a vicious circle, for in order to fill this empty liberty,

he would have to change the social and political conditions in which he lives and which govern his inertia. Thousands of Americans are daily working to break this circle, and, naturally, there are thousands to whom these remarks do not apply. But insofar as one can generalize, it is the vast majority who are victims of the machine. The escape from solitude and boredom holds them fast to solitude and boredom; through wanting to lose themselves in the world they have lost command of themselves.

One thing which struck me most forcibly was how much they hate to question themselves and existing conditions. They want to believe that Good and Evil can be defined in precise categories, that Good already is, or will be easily, achieved. I felt this from the beginning of my stay, but I have recently had striking confirmations of this. For one thing, I almost incited a riot among the students at Columbia, Yale and Harvard, when I talked to them about the question of conscience in Rousset's book, *The Days Of Our Death:* what criteria should someone employ in making his choice if he found himself in a position to save the lives of two or three people in a camp of deportees? They stubbornly replied, "No one has the right / to dispose of 335 human life," or, "What would give him the right to choose?" When I objected that not choosing meant saving no one, and that, in any case, the positive act of saving two lives was worth more than a murderous abstention, they remained silent. I think that they, for their part, would have preferred to let them all die, rather than assume too heavy a responsibility. Or rather, they could not even imagine a situation in which they could have been forced to contribute to an evil. People here refuse to do this, even though it is the only way to fight evil. Even people of goodwill refuse to visualize the actual conflict between justice and liberty, and thus the necessity for inventing a compromise between these concepts; they prefer to deny justice and the lack of freedom. The fact that the complexity of the situation creates problems beyond any virtuous solution is something they will not admit. Evil is a residue which they will eliminate by progressive stages, by applying more rigorously certain institutions which are wholesome in themselves — that is what many idealists think; and if this optimism appears too easy, they will try to create a type of anti-God: the U.S.S.R. That is Evil, and it only needs to be annihilated for the reign of Good to be re-established. This explains why so many of the students, who have such respect for their fellow beings, complacently talked of dropping the atom bomb on the Soviet Union.

If then, in conclusion, I advance so many criticisms, why, in spite of everything, was I so sad to leave? First of all, because one could formulate other criticisms — just as depressing — of our European civilization, and of our French civilization to which I would return. We are unhappy in other ways and false in other ways. That is all.

The judgments I made during this journey were not accompanied by any feeling of superiority. I see their faults; I do not forget our own. Embedded in all that I like and / all that I loathe in America is something which fascinates me: the tremendous opportunities America offers, the gigantic risks it actually runs today — things in which we all share. All human problems are posed here on a tremendous scale; they will be solved here, but whether we will find these problems, in retrospect, greatly clarified or buried in the darkness of indifference depends largely on the solutions themselves. Yes, I think that is what moved me so strongly as I took my departure. America is one of the world's pivotal points: the future of man is at stake here. To like America, or not to like her: these words are meaningless. Here is a battlefield, and one can only be stirred by the struggle she carries on within herself, a struggle whose stakes are beyond measure.

336

Hugh Willoughby

From *Amid the Alien Corn* by Hugh Willoughby, copyright 1958, used by special permission of the publishers, The Bobbs-Merrill Company, Inc.

Mr. Willoughby, a young English agriculturist, came to a large Midwestern university in 1955 for advanced study of American farming methods, and *Amid the Alien Corn* is a product of this visit. Willoughby holds a master's degree in history from Oxford University.

[GADGETRY AND GOOD HUMOR]

25 LA DOUCEUR DE LA VIE PHYSIQUE, or gadgets and how to use them. If you want pure comfort and a society organized for comfort, this is the place to come and wallow. Typical examples of American comfort: the gum on envelopes — it's flavoured (take your choice, strawberry, chocolate, or vanilla; however, I failed to find Pimm's 1 thru 5). I work under a reading lamp. The switch gives three types of light, so you can choose how bright you want it. A small point, but very typical.

26 The university has a big carpark, about 600 feet by 250 feet. (This is the main one, not the only one, of course.) At one side of it is a little wooden rack holding six bicycles. Over a third of the students own cars. In front of the engineering school is a carpark. One day at the beginning of class the professor asked, "Where is Smith?" A student responded, "He will be along in a minute. He couldn't find a place to park his car."

I actually heard this.

Also, a friend was telling me of a friend who works in the Pentagon. There are so many cars parked in the park that it takes him forty minutes to walk from his car to his office.

On some roads there is a notice: "Warning. Radar traffic control." Somewhere some cop with his feet on the mantelpiece is watching you.

Travelling by Pullman is the most comfortable way of moving I have ever struck. Short of substituting champagne for iced water . . . , I really don't see what else they could have done.

One very noteworthy thing — morale is good. Everybody around here seems to be enjoying himself. Working in a cafeteria, selling stamps, singing in church, waiting for a lecture to begin, nobody looks worried or strained. They all seem in good spirits — no moaning, no *carfard*, ennui or spleen.

The people are nowhere near so noisy 27 or so crude as I had been given to understand. Their idiom of courtesy is not ours. They are certainly less formal officially. But the general impression is quite like home.

Friendliness is pervading and natural. Everybody seems to like everybody else and we all get along fine. There is nothing about Being Nice to Poor Foreigners. You are there, so they are friendly to you. And the people whose job is to be helpful really are helpful and apparently enjoy it thoroughly.

Typical American phrase when you say "Thank you" for something — "You are welcome.". . .

[THE CAR]

The country is run on the assumption 30 that everybody has a car — there are railroads, long-distance buses, town buses, but no country buses. Or more accurately, everybody has a car over here because the rural pattern makes it necessary.

To me one of the most conspicuous points in the countryside is that there are no villages or small towns, but only farmsteads and fairly big farms, say 100 to 200 acres. The first settlement I struck going north was Battleground, which calls itself "Battleground Incorporated City." It is eight / 31 miles from the university. Its population, I found in a gazetteer, is 888.

So if this place were Oxford, there would be buses to Birmingham, London and Bristol and good town buses. But there would not be any country buses to Woodstock or Witney because such places don't exist.

Bridget and I sometimes go out for country walks over the week end. Nobody else does. We haven't seen anybody of any type anywhere going for a walk.

It is most amusing watching the few cars that pass us on the gravel roads (we keep off the main roads). Their drivers tend to slow up and we can see them watching us in the driving mirrors (rearview mirrors over here) as they pass us. We can almost hear them saying, "No, they don't look quite like hoboes; we haven't passed a wreck anywhere; they seem quite sane. . . . Hell, there must be *some* rational explanation. . . ." (Incidentally, a wreck in America is a smash, a ditched car.)

It would be quite an interesting subject for a thesis: "The Place of the Car in American Culture." Not just as a means of transport, I mean.

On this side of the Atlantic the car is (1) an index of your social position, and (2) a subject of or for conversation. The folks here discuss the finer points of cars 32 just as the Italians discuss the / finer points of wine. The same disinterested and delicate approach. Colouring in particular provides a source of endless discussion. . . .

[THE QUALITY OF AMERICAN
COLLEGE EDUCATION]

64 English people are accustomed to sneering at American universities. Exceptions to this general rule are a few of the very famous ones. How justified are these sneers?

I have heard quite a lot of discussion 65 on this / subject, from Americans and Europeans, some students, some staff. I get the following picture:

The American B.A. (at a middling university) would hardly rank in Europe as an academic distinction. An American M.Sc. is about the equal to a European B.Sc. However, by the time you get to the Ph.D. stage the two are about equal.

The reason, it appears, is *not* in the university. European folk over here tell me that the equipment here is first class. Certainly the instruction is good. Systematic, orderly, well planned and very patient. (I cannot compare what I am doing here to what I did at Oxford, where I studied a different subject in a much different way.)

The fault, it seems generally agreed, is in the high schools which are sometimes shockingly poor. I have heard all kinds of stories about the weakness in the high schools. But it seems fairly clear that the university has to spend much of its time teaching people things which they should have learned at lower levels. Hence, it takes some time for the student to catch up.

There are other things too. Firstly, the far higher proportion of people over here who attend college — Indiana with her four million people has three big universities, with perhaps thirty to thirty-five thousand students or more in all. Secondly, American students work a lot on their vacations. This, of course, lowers academic standards. But / the real point, everybody says, is the 66 poor quality of so many high schools.

In certain courses I am very struck by the almost drill-manual type of instruction. This is particularly the case in farm management. The students are given a sort of checklist, a technique to apply to any problem. You want to know what to do under specified conditions? Right, ask these questions in this order. Then check the answers with the list on Page 14.

This method has several advantages. It means that students are taught to use method, principle, system. It means that you all start square — that is, you are given a bag of tools and if you are conscientious you can do just as good a job as the bright boys. It reduces the "variable" of human quality. It also means that you can make considerable use of student instructors (chaps taking the M.Sc. or Ph.D. who also give classes). This is good for the chaps and cheap for the university. And, because of the type of course, it is not too hard on the students.

More generally, it is all part of the engineering outlook on life which is so typical of America.

A Ph.D. is a very valuable union card over here. It gets more and more valuable as a key to good jobs as the number of B.Sc.'s increases. But it is a long job, on an average, three years. And that is after four years on the B.Sc. and at least a year, / 67 often two years on an M.Sc. It grieves me to see fine people in their late twenties still grinding away at theses, often not on very important or interesting subjects, often not because they are particularly interested in the work, but simply to get that union card. They would be much happier and better employed out in the world, at a job. And the Ph.D. stage should be one of the most exciting times of one's life. But over here it has too often become a chore, an investment of time and energy for future benefits.

And how these boys work! It jars me. Never have I seen people work so hard. And they have already done, say, five years on a campus. Prima facie, I would have thought such a prolonged, intensive grind would have been too much for general health and efficiency; I would also have expected it to discourage reflection, insight and imagination and to encourage straight pedestrian fact-grubbing, especially as they take such little recreation, at least in the winter. A few play indoor basketball, but most play no games.

I don't know enough about it to make a proper comparison. But health and spirits don't appear to suffer very much, though there are noticeable signs of individual strain. Their research theses certainly follow defined procedure pretty closely. They are rather machine-made, and usually painfully constipated in style. But this, I think, 68 is the / result of convention and tradition rather than intellectual fatigue.

This work, of course, explains the high standard of American doctoral degrees as opposed to the low standard of bachelor's degrees. It is in this last stage that they catch up. It certainly pays them, in the higher salaries they can command with doctorates. But glory, they earn it!

Classes are, broadly, compulsory. If you miss over a certain amount you get penalised. It is assumed that the university knows what the student should be doing better than he does.

You take a course, say, one semester on farm management, course Number 450. This consists of classes (lectures) and labs, which are practical work, plus assignments, homework. Periodically you are given tests. Generally, these are purely factual, sometimes the true-or-false kind, sometimes short answers. Very little of our essay-type question. Plus labs, which are major problems on which you turn in, in effect, a report.

You are graded (marked) on these tests, all of which are partial; they are on the stuff you have learned since your last test, *not* on the subject as a whole. So you deal with the subject bit by bit; you don't have to see it as a whole and pass an exam in it as a whole. You study a lot of little packages in detail — in great detail. Immense emphasis on facts. There is a very heavy pressure on time. Little time to reflect, think, order the subject in / your mind. Series of 69 spurts instead of a straight run.

Remember, however, this is a technological university. The courses and outlook are adapted accordingly. The university is operating under severe pressure of numbers — 12,000 in 1955, 30,000 expected by 1975. The departments can't get enough professors, have to make use of graduate students as instructors, are developing television talks by professors, etc., etc. Are even planning a series of standardised courses for degrees, so that the student will have little choice in what courses he takes. Some of the professors are fighting this — and I should hope so, too.

There is nothing in the nature of tutorials. But you are expected to "participate," ask questions, join in class discussions. Classes often transmogrify into a sort of free-for-all discussion group, with the professor as moderator. These discussions are often extremely good and the professors handle them very well. I have learned a lot from them. This is one of the reasons why classes are compulsory. The student is expected to bring something to class, to make his contribution to discussion so that other students can benefit.

Within limits and on particular points, you can go and see your professors individually. They generally have office hours when they are "at home" and students can come to see them. But, of course, you generally go with some particular problem or difficulty. It is not like a regular tutorial. . . .

[AT A DANCE]

Bridget and I went to a dance. This was 81 fun. It was also curious. Everybody was even smarter and better groomed than usual. The appearance side of the job was fine. But they don't quickstep — they jive. They jive well and it looks good. More peculiar, they go in couples and they stay in couples. No Paul Joneses nor nothing. We met several / (American) friends there 82 and we foregathered in between dances, but nobody would have dreamed of asking anybody else's partner for a dance. This makes, to our eyes, for monotony. The reason? Basically, I think, this marriage-market outlook on life. You want to get people to commit themselves. You may dance for fun, but you never lose sight of the main chance.

Kenneth Harris

The selections from Kenneth Harris, *Innocents from Abroad* are reprinted by permission of and arrangement with Houghton Mifflin Company, the authorized publishers.

Mr. Harris was an undergraduate of Oxford University in 1947 when he and two other members of the University's debating society, the Oxford Union, toured the United States and competed against American college debaters. During their five-month tour, the three Oxonians visited some sixty American colleges and universities and traveled through forty-three states. Harris's book — which gives a detailed account of the tour — was originally published in England in 1949 under the title *Traveling Tongues*.

AMERICANS AT COLLEGE

50 OUT OF THE Pullman car window, the prairie stretches away back to the horizon — land, land, land, brown and yellow, rising and falling gently, limitless like the sea. Not even a wire fence borders the track; the line is at ground-level, and the metals look like cotton strips, neither strong nor deep enough to stay in place. Through many a fair-sized midwest town the train has passed plumb, with only traffic lights to warn the motorcars and the walkers that they must not cross the un-gated road. Through Ohio villages and Missouri townships, the westbound express thunders across Main Street at all hours of the day and night, whistle moaning like a banshee; bell clanging, and the huge head-lamp sending a broad beam two hundred yards ahead.

Walking down the corridor, past the ice-water fountain and the bright reproductions of Cézanne and Matisse, we come to the diner. Only the headwaiter is a white man; 51 he wears a / dark suit, with a grey-striped waistcoat. From the breast pocket sticks out a clump of pencils. He gives one to each passenger so that he can write out his own order.

"I'd like another whisky."

"Sorry, sir. No drinks."

"But dash it; I had one only five minutes ago."

"Yes, sir. But since then we've crossed a state border. This state's dry."

As we finish lunch, the whistle begins to blow short jerky blasts. The bell is clanging. Scattered homesteads are appearing, one or two big sheds, a road — like a thin strip of sticking-plaster on the brown face of the prairie. Now there is a warehouse, a lofty building with the name of a big cereal firm on it. The train is slowing down to a halt. This is our next stop: Rocky City.

When we get out, we find that there is no station. We have alighted right in the middle of the street. The booking office is between a barber's shop and a garage. Cars drive up and down on either side of the track.

"Pardon me. Are you the three gentle-men from Oxford?"

"We are."

"That's fine. I'm Jack Erlinger from the Speech Department, and this is Bob East from the Union reception committee who'll look after you while you're with us. What about your bags?"

"I'm afraid there's an awful lot of them. Nine."

"That's O.K. — we've got a car. Ah, here's Professor Jameson."

There are more introductions. Professor Jameson is Pro-/fessor of Speech. He is not 52 so sanguine about carrying all the luggage — it is his car. Somehow we all squeeze in.

The way to the university takes us straight through the town. It is like a thousand others in the midwest. The main road is thirty yards broad, with a wide pavement on either side. On each side is a long low line of shops, each with big sheets of glass

56

in their fronts, and bright Neon signs. "Eat," orders a green one; "Church of St. John," announces a deep purple; "Dance," gasps a red one; "Elite Burial Parlor," says a fourth. Through gaps between the bus station, the bank, the liquor store and the drugstore, the brown prairie seems to seep in, through the small, wooden, detached residential houses behind the shops, right on to the main street. The atmosphere is one of unapologetic utilitarianism; the town looks hard, cold and spiritless; impermanent and hasty. Age has not softened it. All its history was made in a ten days' battle with the Indians, followed by fifty years of frontier vigil. Remembering, you have a sudden vision of a covered wagon on that street, and the whole place leaps into life and warmth.

"There's the campus," says Jack.

Five hundred yards ahead, the road forms a circle, about two hundred yards across. Inside it the grass looks smooth and fresh; it is planted with trees and shrubs. Around it stand the university buildings, the new-looking concrete and stuccoed walls in odd contrast with those of the town. There is the library, the art gallery, the museum, the lecture rooms, the block of dormitories and the slim masts of the radio station. Over on the far side stands the football stadium. It is tall and U-shaped so that the light can 53 come in at the end. The / dressing rooms are full; we hear that the bachelor ex-servicemen — the veterans — are living there; the married ones live in the cluster of "trailers" and cream-coloured hutments through which we are just passing. Over on the right is the university's airport; a few monoplanes stand glinting in the sun.

"We're putting you up at the Union," says the Professor of Speech. "It's more comfortable than any place in town." He pulls up at the centre entrance to a long high building looking like a municipal government hall. The doors are ornate, and handsome steps lead up to them. Inside, the hall is lofty; it is panelled in a light, yellowish, polished wood. A log fire burns upon a fine open hearth; the reflected light flickers on the dark leather of the saddleback chairs. Behind the desk, where we register our names, the two young men are students, clerking part time to pay their fees.

The following morning I stroll round the campus. It is eleven o'clock. Some hundreds of students are crossing from one lecture room to another. They are all brightly dressed, and blithe. The boys wear trousers and lively shirts, and the girls tartan skirts and white jerseys. Some wear "blue jeans" — long blue dungarees rolled up to just below the knee — and short white socks. The boys are not all as good-looking as film stars, but they are lithe, and smart on their feet. The girls use their cosmetics with craft. Many of them have been using them since they were fourteen. They seem to bring out the individuality, not the sameness, of their features. Their hair looks free, luxuriant, vital; each hair style seems to belong to its owner, and to no one else. They seem to have a better sense of colour than English girls who, on the other / hand, have a 54 better sense of cut. If English girls' legs are not as good, if they do not walk as well on them, they are certainly better at posing — against the rocks at Brighton or, windswept, with a golden setter. They hang much better on straps.

Young men and women walk arm-in-arm in groups or couples, over to the "coffee shop" for elevenses, or to the library, to whisper while they work. Some lie on the grass under the trees. Co-education, clearly, means far more than sitting together in class. One or two are yawning. They were out last night dancing till one A.M., and lectures this morning began as usual at eighty-thirty. To miss would have been to lose some "credit."

"Did you say you wanted to see the School of Journalism?"

"If it's not inconvenient."

"Couldn't be easier. Hey! Luke! C'mon here. This is Luke Manheim, editor of the campus daily."

"This sure is a break. I've been looking for you debaters all over. I wanted to interview you. What you think of America?"

"Wonderful."

"Say, somebody's told you. What d'you think of American women?"

"They've got jungle dignity. You know, they move along so gracefully, and with such natural poise like a great cat."

"What? Say, that's good. 'Got Jungle Dignity.' That's a quote. That's good. Now is it true you've got royalty with you?"

55   "*What?*"

"Haven't you got a baron in the team?"

"Oh, I see. Well, yes. Edward Boyle is a baronet, that's a kind of knight——"

"Did he get that on the field of battle?"

"No. One of his ancestors was made a 'Sir' for his services to the nation, and, as it's a baronetcy, it's handed down."

"I get it. Now how should he be called? We don't know much about titles over here, but we hate to get things wrong, especially with people visiting."

"Well, officially he's Sir Edward Boyle, but mostly on the campuses he gets called Edward or Ed."

"I get it. Now what about the Honourable Benn?"

"He's the son of a viscount——"

"You call that 'vyecount'?"

"Yes. Incidentally, in Britain it's either Mr. Benn or the Hon. A. W. Benn."

"I get it. What do Sir Edward and Mr. Benn think of your king and queen?"

"Well, er—I think, like all the British people I know, they think a great deal of them."

"Sure. I meant personally."

"You'd better ask them. I don't think they know them very well personally."

"But they're aristocrats, and the British crown rests upon the aristocracy, don't it?"

"That doesn't mean they're all in and out of Buckingham Palace all day. You only go there if you're asked."

"Uh-huh! Guess there'd be a kinda crush 56 if it was all free. / Well, here's the School of Journalism. You just go in and ask for Professor Madison. I'll be seeing you."

Professor Madison was a keen young man of about thirty-five. Rocky, apparently, had been losing journalism students to other state universities. Funds and prestige had sunk together. Madison was out to re-establish Rocky's old reputation. Outlining his plans, he took me through the morgue, where clippings of the leading national newspapers were kept, past the library of books and articles on various aspects of newspapers and writing. He opened the door into one of what he called the "laboratories": about a dozen young men and women were standing at high desks, each fitting in advertisements on a dummy newspaper page. As they did so, they jotted down costs and accounts in a notebook. The first one to finish his page took it with the accounts up to the instructor. "Just like the real thing," said Madison. Next door, there was a sub-editing class. Here, the teacher was talking about how to deal with incoming news. In a kind of cupboard behind him were two Associated Press tape machines. The news was dribbling gently into a big tub. "Now supposing the editor sends down . . ." said the instructor.

But before I heard what would happen I was in the picture library. From there we passed through the photographic plant room. "Trouble about this stuff is that it costs good money and gets broken," said Madison. He picked up a brand-new reflex camera, a shining box of tricks in black, dark blue and silver. There were six more on the shelf, and a few gross of flash bulbs. "Good as the London *Times* gets," he / said, "and any kid here can use it. Now 57 come and see the real workshop."

We walked up the corridor, and pushed past two baize-covered doors. We were in a complete printing works. Along one side ran a shining press, of about the size that an up-to-date county newspaper would be using. There were Linotype machines, compositors' stones, even a furnace for melting down the lead. The students worked the plant, supervised by the expert printer, aided by a man to work the lead.

"Everybody looks pretty busy," I said.

"Certainly they are. They bring a paper

out every day. Four thousand circulation."

"Who pays for it?"

"We try and make it pay for itself. It sells for a couple of cents, and we get plenty of ads."

"Are these people working here doing it spare time or academically?"

"Academically, you might say. They get credit for it, anyway. Now you want to go over to the radio station." He looked round the room at the busy figures. "I've got to take a class on 'Interviewing,'" he said. "I'll get one of the boys to take you over. Bill, will you take this gentleman over to the radio shop?"

"Why sure, Professor."

We walked round the campus circle toward the radio masts. "So you're going to be a journalist, Bill?"

"Oh, no," he said. "I'm going on studying English literature. In order to major ——"

58   "What's 'major'?"

"Well, I suppose it's your bachelor's degree. To get it I've got to get credit in two other subsidiary subjects. So I'm putting in thirteen hours on journalism and thirteen on music."

"Hours?"

"Yeah. That's how you get credit, putting in so many hours."

"But don't you get an examination?"

"Examination! I'm telling *you* we get examinations."

"But not one big one, what we call finals, at the end of two or three years?"

"No. We do ours in sections, a bit at a time, spread out over whatever the period is — two or three years maybe."

"As far as 'majoring' is concerned then, you can forget what you've learned as soon as you've passed the section."

"Sure. But you don't want to forget it. It's all so interesting and *useful.*"

At the radio station vestibule we met Herb Cantello. Half his time he spent as programme controller, the other half as a postgraduate student working on his Master's thesis. First we saw the gramophone library where two student "disc jockeys"

were preparing for a thirty-minute recital, and another was busy cataloguing. Then we looked in at a small studio where a girl was reading a newscast. When she had finished, a young man came forward and delivered a lyrical advertisement for a local firm.

"Damn it," I said. "I'd have thought the university radio station could have kept its programme uncommercial."

"But why?" he said. "The fees we get 59 from them make it possible for us to put on the music and the talks. Besides, it's what happens on the air outside. Our students don't get any illusions about what keeps culture on the air."

Through an elaborately equipped sound-effects room we came into a small auditorium. About a hundred desks were arranged in sharply ascending tiers. In the front was a rostrum. Behind this was a large plate-glass window. On the inside it had thick curtains which could be pulled by a cord. When the window was uncovered the auditorium looked into the main studio. There was a two-way radio system connecting them. "Demonstration room," said Herb; "programme goes out from main studio. Class sits and looks on. Professor pulls the hell out of it."

"Do you take much interest in the British Broadcasting Corporation here?"

"Yes, a certain amount."

"What do people think about it?"

"Our students think a great deal of a service which doesn't have to get mixed up with commercials. And they know what a high level of entertainment it hits compared to ours. But those who were over there and heard it, well, they figured it was a bit dull."

"What do you think of the Third Programme?"

"Never heard of it."

"We have a special programme in the evenings only and on a special wave-length of music, plays and talks. It's understood that only a minority will want to listen, and that they will want culture rather than pure entertainment."

60   "Gee! That sounds pretty good. That's really revolutionary!"

He walked with me to the door. Two men were coming in. One was the Professor of Economics, and the other was one of the state's leading Congressmen. They were going to have a broadcast battle on the subject of price controls. "That reminds me," said Herb, "I'd have been seeing you and your two friends tonight anyway. At the discussion."

"Discussion?"

"Yes. In the main studio there. With the Rocky debaters at seven o'clock. Going out on the state network."

"But that's the first I've heard of this! What on earth are we going to talk about? Where's the script?"

"We don't want to hear you boys read. We want to hear you talk."

"Good Lord!"

"That'll be O.K. You'll enjoy it. You know, that Congressman of ours is going to have his tail twisted this afternoon by Professor Davies, but he'll put up with it. He doesn't get a script either."

Outside, I stood in the sun for a moment feeling a little dazed. Suddenly there was a light musical hail. "Hullo there! Oxford!" A young lady was walking along the opposite side of the road. She wore a flowing red cloak. Her hair was like smooth pale gold, and her eyes as blue as the English cornflower.

"I wanted to tell you boys how much I enjoyed that debate last night," she said. She had the American girl's knack of looking at you as though you really mattered. "You boys aren't at a loss for a word, are you?"

61   "We boys are going to be at a loss for one tonight," I said. "We've got to take part in an impromptu discussion without a script."

"What d'you think of American radio?"

"Well, I've heard some of these fifteen-minute love and suffering serials, these — er ——"

"Soap operas?"

"Yes. And I must say I think they're pretty frightful."

"They're meant for just some listeners. Plenty of other stations on the dial."

"Pah! I can't think who can listen to such awful tripe."

"Chiefly women. Women who look after the house. It's not much fun, with your husband at work all day, and the kids at school, and the dishes to wash and the clothes to mend. They get lonely and tired ——"

"Tired, with electric mangles? Lonely, with a thousand people living in the same block?"

"Say, why don't you come out of New York? That's the trouble with you British. You come out here, all of you, lecturers, painters and singers and writers, and you either stay on the east coast, or hop right over to California. Or you stay in Britain, complain that Hollywood films are far-fetched, and swallow them whole. Everybody's rich out here, and everybody listens to soap operas. We get it both ways."

"Sorry."

"Oh, well; I guess we swallow it too." She looked at her watch. "Where are you going now?"

"Nowhere special," I said. "Where are you going?"

"I'm going to a drama class. Want to come?"

"Yes please."

"C'mon."   62

The theatre stood outside the rim of the campus circle. We walked about a quarter of a mile down a side road to get to it. It was built of pale-coloured brick. One side bulged out into a big wing. It held the properties. Above the stage end, the roof rose sharply to make a great cage for the drops and the back cloths. We passed by the gilded portals and ironwork flambeaux of the main entrance, and entered by a side door.

"Want to see around first?"

"Please."

The stage was as big as the one or two

I saw in New York. Practically the whole of it was on the circular piece which revolved at the touch of an electric button. Including the wing, there was more room behind than in front of the proscenium arch. About six hundred people could sit comfortably in the plush armchairs which were set on a steeply rising ramp. The stage- and house-lighting was more elaborate than anything I had ever seen outside a West End theatre. Every light was controlled from a small, compact, desk-top switchboard in the soundproof room behind the back row of the stalls. It was the kind of theatre that is a producer's dream. And it was for students.

"It's magnificent. What play are you putting on next?"

"*Dracula.*"

"H'm."

"Don't say it. I know. They wanted to do something low-brow for a change. C'mon. Let's have a quick peek behind."

63   Under the auditorium were a number of rehearsing studios. Stirring lines from *Henry V* resounded from behind a half-open door, and as we walked on down the corridor my ear caught the hollow groan of a Greek chorus. From another door came an even more familiar sound. "Well!" I said. "I've only been to a few universities so far, but this is the fourth one to be putting on *The Importance of Being Earnest.*"

"It's got everything we haven't got."

The drama class was held in the Green Room. We set back in basketwork chairs and smoked cigarettes. There were about twenty boys and girls there, sitting on the floor, perched on the furniture or leaning back in the chairs. At length the instructor appeared. He was about thirty. Everybody called him "Huck." He wore a pretty shirt which, he told us, had once been a Japanese girl's kimono. He told us how the kimono had become a shirt. He was a charming raconteur, and a very pleasant personality.

"Well," he said. "Let's get to work."

We were going to discuss the production difficulties of *The Importance.* "Now, first of all, let's talk about its qualities," he said. "What would we aim to bring out?" We had a long discussion. Eventually we decided we would aim first to bring out the Englishness of it. Then its humour, its elegance, and its sophistication.

"Huck," said a boy, thoughtfully, suddenly looking up from his notebook. "Stylization. Would that be a good word to use about it, Huck?"

We moved on to the casting of the play. "First, let's cast it in terms of personalities in this class," said Huck. We did / this. 64 "Now people we know on the campus. . . . Now, film stars."

An hour went by very agreeably. Around me the girls and boys had garnered a rich harvest of notes. Huck brightened his instruction with anecdotes and illustrations drawn from his experiences in Hollywood and Broadway. "Now, something to work on for next time," he wound up. "Choose a scene from *The Importance.* Make your production notes on it — choose your furniture, the setting, and sketch out the movements. O.K.?"

"O.K., Huck."

The girl in the red cloak guided me back to the Union. "Now you're ready to start producing on Broadway," I said.

"If I wanted to be a prodoocer," she answered, "I'd learn on the stage."

"What *do* you want to do?"

"Be a nurse."

"Well why on earth do you want to know what furniture to use for a play?"

"Can't nurses know something about the theatre?"

"Of course. But they can pick that kind of thing up as they go along."

"Go along where?"

"Well, where they work or where they live."

"Where they live! See here, I'm a farmer's daughter. I live right out in the prairie, three hundred miles from here. When I'm at home, I don't see twenty people my own age from one year's end to another. And you say I can pick up something about the

theatre. I don't come in here to fill my /
65 head with book stuff mainly. I come in to
meet people, and to live a bit. Huck, now.
He's been to Hollywood, and he's been on
Broadway. He wasn't great shakes there,
but he was *there*. Talking and listening to
him's as near as I'll ever get. In England,
I guess, you can't be farther than a couple
of hundred miles from London wherever
you live. Over here you can be a couple
of hundred miles from the nearest town.
It's the people who don't understand that
who find education over here so comic."

"I don't think anybody finds it comic."

"You people from England do."

"Well, all right," I said, "we do. And it's
up to you to tell us why we shouldn't."

"Well, you take my aunt. She lived out
in the prairie with my uncle, almost on her
own for fifteen years, having children and
helping him on the farm in the bad times.
D'you know the first thing she wanted to
do when the littlest kid was raised and my
uncle had enough money for her to quit
working herself to death?"

"No."

"She wanted to go into town, twice a
week, drive sixty-five miles in and sixty-five
miles out, to take lessons— in musical
appreciation."

"What did your uncle say?"

"He said she was crazy."

"Well, quite frankly, I think she was."

"Maybe. But it isn't important whether
she was crazy or not. What's important is
whether she really wanted to do it, or
whether she did it just to show off. I can
66 tell you: she / was dead serious about it.
When you people criticize the things we
do to get educated, you forget that we're
dead serious too, as serious as any of those
monks or friars, or whatever they were, that
got your universities started."

We got to the door of the Union. "Here
you are then, Oxford," said the girl.

"Here we are then," I said. "There's one
thing you can be sure of. When I get home
to Britain, if there's one thing I'll bear
witness to, it's that Americans take education pretty seriously."

"That's right. And that doesn't mean we
gotta put on gowns and say the grace in
Latin. O.K.?"

"O.K."

That night I sat in the rooms of Professor Arthur Y. Westinghouse. The "Professor" and the "Arthur Y." meant nothing
to me. We had been up together at Oxford
before the war, and as far as I was concerned he was still "Barney." "Have a look
at this, Barney," I said. In front of him I
put the following account:

"In Britain, one person in a thousand is
at college or university: in America, one in
seventy. This is not only because the Americans can afford to spend more money on
education than we can — they can afford to
spend more money on their back gardens,
but don't — but because their view of education is different from ours. Their society
being still so young, nature being so dangerous as well as bountiful, there are always
a thousand urgent tasks, mental and physical, to be done. The hands and minds to
tackle them will be trained at the uni-/ver- 67
sity. This is why, at so many of them, you
can take a course in anything from Egyptol-
ogy to hotel management; why one treatise
is written on the 'Publishing Trade in
Fifteenth-Century London,' and another on
'Eighteen Ways of Washing Dishes.'

"Even today, when they may be serving
far more Arts than Science students, some
of the largest universities and colleges look
back to the days when they were created
to teach engineering and agriculture. Then,
building machines and coaxing crops from
the virgin soil were more pressing needs
than seminars for philosophy. The vocational approach is still strong: subjects are
often treated as techniques to be mastered
rather than as intellectual or esthetic experiences to be understood and lived
through: history, philosophy and literature
seem sometimes to be taught in the scientific, formal, tabloid layout of a book on
'How to Grow Tomatoes.'

"All other aspects of the American's attitude to education are overshadowed by one:

his unbounded faith in it. In Britain, many self-made men, businessmen and adventurers, will often ask, 'What is the point of a university?' and say that they believe in boys being pitched out to learn in the hard school of the world as soon as possible. You never hear that kind of remark in the United States. Millions of business men and women, who might otherwise have been 'self-made,' take part-time courses, go to night school, until late in life. There is a great respect for the university, from the tycoon down to the taxi-cab driver. Perhaps it is because they are so confident that their universities are 'useful,' and because so much of the 'hard school of the world' has 68 been caught, tamed / and forced into textbooks, and taught in the class and lecture room."

"Yes," he said, "that's all quite true."

"But the thing that gets in so many gizzards," I said, "is that you're so keen, over here, on educating everybody, that the standard of education enjoyed by any one person is bound to be pretty low."

"Pretty low compared to what?"

"Well, say, to what he'd get at a place where each pupil had far more time and attention devoted to him personally, but where there are far fewer pupils. The few being selected by competition; scholarships, and so on."

"Well," said Barney, "you've always had an aristocratic tradition running through your educational system. First, the well-born people went to Oxford and Cambridge, then, as democratic ideas became more efficient, that handful of aristocratic vacancies became available through open competition; and so on, through the newer universities. But over here, we had to deal with the masses almost from the start. And our educationalists came into a society which had already made up its mind that whatever was going ought to be shared out equally all round. You might say that we care more for the equality of the product than we care for its class."

"Do you really believe in the American

type of education, Barney?"

"I don't know. But I'm sure of one thing, which is that the answer to our problem can't be imported from Britain. Or from Germany, or from France. That's the mistake we've / made in the past. We forgot 69 that when people started building Oxford in the thirteenth century they didn't have any blueprint, any 'The Ideal of a University' to work from."

"What're you getting at?"

"This. I think education in America may want a tremendous amount of thought, and a lot of criticism. But it shouldn't be criticized in terms of standards and methods which have been successful in other kinds of community. Not unless the community is like ours. It's when we copy you we look foolish. Evelyn Waugh or Eric Linklater can come over here and make a midwest university look like a burlesque show. Though as a matter of fact, James Thurber could do the same for Oxford. Anyway, a community gets the kind of university it deserves and needs in the long run. And I suppose we'll hammer out our deserts and needs in time too."

"If you don't mind my saying so," I said, "I think your people deserve and need better than they've got at present."

"You're right," he said. "Well, we'll hope for the best; for leadership, and the right people to come and teach."

I looked out of the window to where the little ring of culture ended, and the vast plain began again; on all sides, like a sea. "By the way," I said. "When you came down from Oxford, you said you were going into business."

"That's right. I went into business, at that."

"Didn't you like it?"

"Sure I liked it. Very much. It was just that I thought I'd like teaching more."

"Why didn't you stay on the east coast?"

"Well," said Barney, looking in his turn out of the window, / "I guess there were 70 two reasons. First, I thought a spell out here in the sticks would give me a chance to find out how much I learned at Oxford was the real M'Coy. Second . . . well . . . if it hadn't been for this particular university popping up on the prairie I don't suppose I'd have got to Oxford at all. I'd have been punching cows a hundred miles down the line."

He looked at his watch. "Time you went," he said. "Your train leaves at eight tomorrow."

I got up to go. "There's one thing about it, Barney," I said. "You Americans do *believe* in education."

"Yes," he said. "We do. We always have believed in it. And now that we can see the new tasks and responsibilities we've got to take up in the world, well, I guess we believe in it, and hope from it, a great deal more."

He got up and crossed to the door where his Oxford B.A. hood hung on a hook. He took down the broad-brimmed Stetson which made him look more like a farmer than a don and put it on.

"I guess we'd better leave it at that for now," he said. "Let's go."

AMERICANS HIT THE ROAD

71 An American can leave New York, fly twice the distance from London to Moscow, and find himself still in his own country.

Even those people who do not leave New York can get an idea of distance in the United States. The railway train speaks of it, as it stands humming and hissing in the station. It lacks the characteristic shape of the British engine, the long round belly of a boiler, the stunted funnel, the tall broadspoked wheels. The American locomotive is a great long metal box, the engineers walking round the diesel units inside like electricians in a powerhouse. On the platforms, signboards show where each train is bound for: this one to Chicago — 1000 miles, this one to Miami — 1400 miles, and that one, over there, ready to start its passengers on the 3000-mile stretch across to the west coast.

Travel by train is more of a campaign than an assault. Security, comfort and sure 72 arrival, rather than speed, are the / main features of the arrangements. Wealthier passengers take "drawing rooms," containing two or three bunks, a sofa and a lavatory. They take their radio set and typewriter with them. There are compartments which are comfortable coaches by day and shadowy, green-curtained sleeping shelves by night. There is the ordinary coach where, if you can grab a double seat for yourself, adjust the seat and the foot rests and hire a pillow, you can sleep in comfort. At stations, a little band of functionaries will come on board, like islanders coming out to a passing ship. The "Butch" sells milk, coffee, fruit, sandwiches and chocolate from a big basket. Another man sells newspapers and books, and a third comes round to deliver or collect telegrams. The businessman sitting opposite you is sending another cable: he may have done three or four business deals by the time he gets off this train. Last night, you recall, people boarding the train wore overcoats. This morning, new passengers are wearing panamas and open-necked shirts. Along this fifteen-hundred-mile descent from north to south, the train drops through different climates like an elevator through the different floors.

A glance at an airport shows this even more vividly. La Guardia, one of New York's two big flying fields, is a national and an international hub. Two-engined aircraft are taking off every few minutes to fly, at about a pound a hundred miles, to nearly every fair-sized town in the East. Bigger two-engined planes are flying to Chicago in three or four hours. Now and again a four-engined giant sweeps in from San Francisco, the Pacific Islands, or from Europe. Travellers to and from three continents get in and out of planes as casually as if they were / crossing a country, not a 73 world. They stand chatting in the airport vestibule, men carrying fur coats rubbing shoulders with men wearing linen jackets.

People write in the same slang, and mail the letter for five cents, to relatives and friends a thousand miles across country. Children go to their grandmother's funeral by airplane. Students thumb a lift across a continent for the Christmas holidays. Trips into Canada, vacations in the West Indies, hang like scalps at the money belt of those who have a couple of hundred dollars a year to spare. There are still millions of Americans who have never been out of town; but the present wave of prosperity has borne millions more into mountains and forests miles away from their homes.

All this combines to form the present attitude of the American to the matter of getting from one place to another at any time. There is only one word for it, and the word is casual. They take distance in their stride. It does not worry them.

One morning we left Peoria by air for Chicago. We were due to arrive there at noon, in order to catch another plane to get us to Madison, in Wisconsin, in time to debate at eight P.M. We were late, and the connecting plane went off without us. We explained our predicament to the young ladies at the desk. They listened with a sympathetic but calm air. When they turned to their timetables for a substitute route, their manner was unhurried. They were used to routing the unconnected over a continent. They discovered quite quickly that if we flew to City A, we could catch a train to City B. Thence a bus would take us to Madison, where, with luck, we would be ready to debate at eight-thirty.

74   At that point one of us remembered that we had made a promise on the boat to ring up Professor Cleaver of Chicago University if we ever passed near. (Just to say "Hullo!") While Edward Boyle and I marshalled the suitcases, Wedgwood Benn went to the telephone box. In a few minutes he was back, looking rather bewildered. "Cleaver says there's no point in messing about with buses and trains," he said. "He says he'll come up with his car and drive us to Madison."

"He can't possibly do that," I said. "It's more than five hours' driving. And he'll have to come back alone."

"And what about his classes?" said Edward.

"He's not lecturing till noon tomorrow, and he says he can get back by then," said Anthony. "In any case, there's no point in us arguing. He's on his way here."

Cleaver arrived in about twenty minutes. He was wearing an old suit and a floppy hat. He looked as though he might have just come from mowing the lawn. His luggage consisted of a large paper bag in which his wife had hastily packed fruit and sandwiches. "O.K., boys," he said. "Jump in."

We drove steadily up the 200-mile stretch to Madison. "You boys rest your voices for tonight," said Cleaver. "I'll talk till you tell me to hush up." We talked chiefly about Socialism in America, and the question of how to reconcile what was going on in Britain with the old Liberal ideas of individual freedom. "All very well you British saying we Yanks don't know how tough things are, and how much freedom has to be sacrificed because of an emergency. But you don't verbalize enough about what you're doing. You don't explain."

We arrived at Madison at seven. After a quick wash we / marched into the Union 75 restaurant where our hosts were waiting for us. "This is Professor Cleaver," we said. "He's brought us all the way from Chicago, otherwise we'd never have got here."

"Why, thanks, Cleaver," said the Professor of Speech. He sounded very grateful, but not at all surprised. As for Cleaver, he had already seated himself and plunged into a conversation about Marshall Aid.

At quarter to eight we all got up to go to the debating hall. We heard Cleaver say that since he would be getting up before dawn next morning, he had better go early to bed. "Well, good-bye, Professor," we said. "And thank you again."

The Professor stood for a moment in thought. "On second thought," he said, "I might just as well stay and hear you boys shoot."

All through the debate we could see his spectacles gleaming cheerfully in the gallery. It was like having an old friend up there. Afterwards he was pressed into joining a small party given by the Professor of

Speech. "Well, O.K.," he said. "As long as I get to bed pretty soon." But at midnight he was on the station platform seeing us off to our next university. "You boys get into your bunks right away," he said. "Talking all the time, you need plenty of sleep."

On a lovely day in the Canadian autumn, we were being given lunch at the University of Toronto. "You must see Niagara Falls," said our hosts. "The American side looks bigger, but more water goes over ours."

"We'd love to," we said. "But we've got to be in New York tomorrow morning, and the trains are very tricky."

76 There was some whispering across the tables for the rest of the meal, and a little semaphore up and down the room. "We've got two cars fixed up," said one of the faculty members as soon as the meal was over. "If we leave by four, we'll get there soon after six."

We arrived at the falls by six, having driven just under a hundred miles. When we got there one of the cars broke down. While it was being mended we had a very merry dinner party. At nine o'clock the car appeared. We prepared to leave — the Oxford men to catch the train to Buffalo; the Canadians, we imagined, to drive back home.

"Good-bye," we said.

"Good-bye nothing," they said. "We're driving you boys over to Buffalo."

We drove the seventy-odd miles to Buffalo. The Canadians waited till our train came in at eleven-thirty, and then began the five-hour drive to Toronto. Three of them were due in the office at eight-thirty the following morning. When we heard this we clucked sympathetically; they stared at us as if they did not understand. I was never with eight people who seemed to get on better together, and in the train I said so to Anthony. "I thought the same thing myself," he said. "But one of them told me that he and his wife had never met any of the others before, and I know that

those two girls have only been in the place a week."

Mitchelmore College was the one place we visited twice. We left it for the first time on a Friday morning. It was a sad parting. "You must come back," they said. "We'd love to." 77

"Well, why don't you?"

"We've got to debate at Surrey tonight."

"You can come back tomorrow."

"Well," we said. "If Surrey aren't expecting us to stay the week-end, we'll come back and spend it with you. That is, if we can get a train."

"O.K. If the trains aren't too good, we'll come halfway and fetch you. Call us up tonight and tell us what's happening. O.K.?"

"O.K."

We got to Surrey. We gathered that the week-end was our own. Just before the debate began, we rang up Mitchelmore to say that we would be coming over next day, and would wire when we knew what train we could catch.

The debate finished at ten. There was a variety show going on in a hall on the other side of the campus, and the debating squad escorted us over to see it. The show lasted till eleven. As the final applause died down, I looked around for my two colleagues. Just then I felt a tap on the shoulder. "Well, here's one of you, anyway," said a voice. I turned and saw an American debater standing in front of me. "Ready?" he said.

"For what?"

"Why, to go."

"Oh, don't you bother," I said. "We can find our own way down to the hotel."

"Might as well go in the car," he said. "I suppose you've all packed?"

"*Packed?*" I said. "Hell, we've only just 78 *un*-packed. We needn't pack till morning."

"Hell, too," he said. "You're gonna be back in Mitchelmore by morning."

It then dawned on me that he was a debater from Mitchelmore, not Surrey. It seemed that he happened to have been in the Speech Office when our telephone message came through. As he "wasn't doing anything much that evening," he thought he might as well come over and collect us right away. "We'll be there for sure by three," he said.

"But wasn't it lonely, Johnny, driving one hundred and twenty miles at this time of night?"

"No," he said. "I brought the wife."

There she was, out in the big, battered car — fluffy-haired, bright-eyed, as fresh and lively as though she were bound for a cocktail party. Husband and wife and a debater squeezed into the front, two debaters and nine suitcases crammed into the back, and off we roared at eleven-thirty along the straight prairie road. At one in the morning we stopped at a roadside drugstore and ate hot dogs washed down with coffee. For the next thirty miles our driver sang sweet, haunting cowboy songs about cattle on the skyline and faithful ponies. The wife stayed awake, throwing away one and then lighting another cigarette for the man at the wheel. The Oxford debaters fell asleep.

That week-end at Michelmore was unforgettable. The second parting was even more sad than the first, except that having returned once we began to feel that no parting need be final. On the Sunday, to 79 make sure that we had time to / stay for lunch, instead of putting us on the noon train the young Professor of Speech insisted on driving us to our next destination. It was 150 miles away.

In the hotel at which he left us, we said good-bye. It was late, and we were a little worried about him. "I just don't know what you boys are fussing about," he said. And his face showed that he didn't. "I'm fine," he repeated. "I'll just call my wife and tell her how things are going."

He went to the telephone in the hall, and picked up the receiver. "Is that you, honey?" we heard him say in a few moments. "Yes. Very nice trip, too. Look here; seeing I'm over this far, I might as well go round by Beltonville and look up your ma. It's only a few miles out. I'll be in about four. O.K.?"

"O.K." we heard faintly from the other end. And O.K. it seemed to be.

The American's casual attitude to travel gives the European visitor the feeling that he has been brought up under a tub. Professor Smith has just gone to Honolulu to give a memorial lecture. The boy next door has gone a thousand miles to try to market his firm's new gadget. Johnny across the street is motoring four hundred miles to be best man at his cousin's wedding. Here lives and multiplies a people with a real world-sense. It does not come out of a religion preaching the brotherhood of man, nor from an economic theory of his interdependence. It grows naturally out of the big broad land in which the Americans live. They inhabit a world, not a country. This is why they learned so soon the technique of a global war. It should make them leaders in a global peace. /

AMERICANS AT HOME

No door is more open to the stranger 80 than the American's. This is true of him whether he is a well-rooted midwestern descendant of an Anglo-Saxon family or a first-generation Hungarian on the edge of Manhattan. It may be the handed-down memory of the frontier days which makes it so, or reaction from those first few days on the bleak unfriendly beaches of a new world. Certainly the size of the country keeps the heart of entertainment warm. Whatever the cause, the door is always open.

The first American home I stayed at was half an hour across the Hudson River from New York. I went over by bus. "Here it is, bud. Melville," said the driver-conductor. He gave me some change from the tiny cash register on his belt, and, without leaving his seat, pulled the lever which automatically opened the door. "Where'd you want to get to?"

"Lincoln Avenue."

81   "Up there; go past the funeral parlour and the bank. Turn left when you see No. 17 school——"

"Number what?"

"No. 17 school. Schools in New York have numbers, not names. Hope you find it O.K."

The bus, long and narrow, hissed off round the corner. I began to walk up the hill. All the houses seemed built of wood, white or light-coloured timber in overlapping planks set parallel to the ground. Most of them were a step or two up from the ground, with a veranda in front. Their steep roofs, the high gables and the white wood, made them look Scandinavian rather than British. Each stood back from the asphalt pavement and away from each other, at regular intervals along straight streets. From the air it must have looked like an army camp.

"Excuse me. But am I going right for Lincoln Avenue?"

"Sure. Cross over by the Pantarium and——"

"What's the Pantarium?"

"Where you get your trousers pressed. While you wait."

Each house had its own plot of ground. There was full scope for privacy, but this community of individualists seemed to prefer not to take it. Though there were variations in their design they had one thing in common: there were no hedges or fences between them, and no wall to part them from the pavement. Children and dogs ran without let from one front to another. Along the kerbs of the side streets were green strips of turf and an occasional tree in blossom. But there were few lawns and few flower gardens. Not even a window box seemed to challenge the encroaching 82 city. The good peo-/ple of Melville had delegated their gardening to the local government. In the Welsh valleys, rising from the coal dust, and in the Lancashire towns, shining through the mists that keep the cotton damp, the bowl of hyacinths, the allotment and the straggling runner bean proclaim that the industrial worker still feels the call of the soil. The Americans are great landsmen; but once they leave the farm they seem ready to leave it for good.

The first American door opened to me. "C'mon in," they said, as a hundred other families were to say in the same welcoming voice. As I was to do on dozens of occasions all over the country, I took off my coat and hung it on a coat hanger, not a hook. "Sit down," they said. They didn't have to say "Make yourself at home." They hung up your shyness for you with your hat.

An American meal is a medley of the food of two worlds. Frankfurter sausages from Europe, but packed in American nylon. Hamburger steaks, but coming from the butcher in round, hard discs which rattle like quoits as they drop in the pan. Beer tasting like lager, but poured from a can looking as though it held bicycle oil. Old World water, tinkling and sparkling in ice-filled long-barrelled tumblers. White bread soft-crusted, and delivered already sliced. A side plate of lettuces, with mayonnaise, cream cheese and a peach in the centre, to eat between courses. Ice cream with the sweet. In some houses, we ate no butter: it was five shillings a pound. The margarine was colourless till, without taking off the cellophane wrapper, the hostess kneaded from one corner of it a blob of brown dye. In a moment or two the whole was a rich yolky yellow.

In Meadowville, Jim Wilson, a big, bald, 83 perspiring bank manager, asked me round to supper. "C'mon in," he said. He was in his shirt sleeves, his trousers held up by tags at the hip. "Kind of warm. Take off your jacket." I took off my coat. "What d'you wear suspenders for?" he asked. He looked at my braces as though I was displaying some piece of intimate medical apparatus. "What d'you think of this house of mine? I've just had it built."

I looked around. One end of the very large room on the ground floor was made into a recess by two short protruding pieces on opposite walls. From the recess, in which stood a dining table and chairs, an arch led into a tiny writing room, and a swing-door into a large airy kitchen-breakfast room. The front door led straight from the big room out onto the fly-netted veranda. There was no hall. The stairs rose from just inside the door to the first floor — second floor in America — where there were two large bedrooms, two small ones and a bathroom. "It's very well designed," I said.

"What kind of a house would someone like me have in England?"

"Well, in England," I said, "however small the place is, we try and make it into separate rooms with a door to each."

"Why?"

"Well, I suppose we like having a number of separate rooms, and each one being shut off. Privacy, you know."

"You can have the privacy. Give me convenience. If I want to be private, I reckon I can go to bed."

Not till I had passed through another twenty-five states did I see a house which might have been built in Britain. It was a country house in South Carolina, square 84 and solid-looking, / with thick stone walls and small lofty rooms. Everywhere there were doors which we opened and shut as though shaking hands with old friends. Elsewhere even the houses of the rich were divided on the ground floor into a number of rooms, all opening through wide arches into the centre hall. From the front door you could see and hear what was going on in every room.

When central heating is a common feature, doors do not become as necessary as they do when every room has to guard its fire's heat jealously. Quite modest American houses have an oil furnace in the cellar, sending the hot air through concealed chimneys or swirling up through gratings in the floor. The absence of a fire gives many an American room an unfamiliar look to the British visitor. Though there may be a fireplace, the room does not look towards it. The easy chairs do not face it, the pipe rack and the favourite bookcase are not handy by its side. The furniture seems often to face all ways or no way. To an Englishman who had not realized how the fireplace had dominated his unconscious mind, the aspect of American rooms was comfortable but never cosy. Americans love their homes; but they seem not to have our feeling for the hearth.

"So you think we Americans love our homes, do you?" said one American.

"Yes, I think so."

"I'm not sure. Seems to me we're always trying to get out of them. Clubs, theatres, ice rink, movies, sports, parties. And not just entertainments, you understand. Evening school, voluntary services, helping with the church work, run-/ning charity 85 drives. All we seem to use the home for's to eat, sleep and keep our clothes in. It's not that we're just doing it for fun, you understand. It's just because we kind of like getting together. We're friendly. Ah, well, I guess human beings weren't meant to be alone anyway."

"I don't call being home with the family 'being alone.'"

"No. Sure. I guess some of you British think even that's a crowd. I knew a guy in London who used to go out of the house to get some solitude, he said."

When the American does go out for the evening, he seems able to stay out later and enjoy himself more thoroughly than most British people would. Whether it is because of a richer, meatier diet, more physical energy, a drier atmosphere, or just the American way of life, he seems to manage on far less sleep. Going to bed and getting up at routine times does not seem to matter to him. Like the animal, he lies down when he is tired, and gets up when there is something to be done. It seems to do him no harm, though under the eyes and round the mouths of American boys and girls of twenty are often lines and shadows which super-fatted cosmetics and after-shaving lotion don't conceal.

To cope with the Americans' late-night needs and desires, entertainments, restaurants and hotels work pretty late. Our first breakdown in schedule landed us in a fair-sized midwest town, unheralded and unbooked, at a few minutes before midnight.

As we lugged our suitcases off the train, our hearts were low at the prospect of sleeping on benches without any chance of supper. When we got into the station vestibule, our spirits rose. People were getting 86 off and on to trains as / though it were twelve noon. Restaurants were steaming and hissing with frying eggs and bacon, and humming with the conversation of travellers. We ascended to the hotel. The vestibule blazed with lights, and the reception desk bustled with activity. In the lounge people sat around and drank cocktails, the sounds of exciting dance music and energetic feet floated down the long corridor to the hall. The main doors opened and in came another dozen or so people, talking and laughing. Their bright faces and high tones suggested that the evening was just beginning for them. The light, the laughter, the music, infected us with a sense that it was almost beginning for us.

A boy stood near me while his girl deposited her coat. "Is there a dance here?" I said.

"Yeah."

"It sounds very gay."

"Think so? Ordinary supper dance."

"D'you mean it's like this every night?"

"Sure."

"Well," I said. "I don't know how you Americans can do it."

"Do what?"

"Stay up so late every night."

"We don't. Me, f'rinstance. I'll be up till two or three tonight, but tomorrow I'll go to bed early. I'll be in bed by twelve, at the latest."

One of the things British people miss in the United States is the village inn. In the big towns there are expensive, smoothly got up cocktail bars, and the small towns have 87 their / liquor shops or bars. But on the whole, apart from the lounge in some hotels there is nothing in between. The American does not walk round to the local two or three times a week with his wife or with his son, to have his pint, his chat with the neighbors, and then his walk home. He

does not take out the dog last thing every night, and break his journey with a quick one at The Crown. He either goes out on a flashy binge with a party at a cocktail lounge or has a really good soak with "the boys." Drinking in America outside private houses is, on the whole, a raw business, and the regular drinker in the city bars, when he has had a few, is more likely to say something rude than to sing a song. Over there fewer women seemed to drink than here. But those that did seemed to leave off rather later than British women.

One of the things that the Britisher has to get used to is the patches of Prohibition with which the country is still dappled. When the whole state is officially dry, like Kansas, one knows where one is. But when one county, or town, is dry and the next is not it becomes confusing. One hot day I got into a taxi in a town in Florida. "English?" said the driver.

"That's right."

"Bet you miss that beer of yours down here."

"I certainly do. Still, I'll get a bottle of lager at the hotel."

"Oh no you won't."

"Not even that canned stuff?"

"Not even that canned stuff. This place's dry as dust."

"But I didn't know Florida was a dry state!"

"It ain't. We got local option. We voted, and the vote said 'Dry.' You'll have to have a chocolate soda."

"Might it ever change to wet?"   88

"Naw. What's the point? The teetot'lers like it as it is; the liquor sluggers drive five miles down the road to the next county and load up with a case or two. Everybody's happy."

Some towns, though "dry," sold bottled beer as freely as Coca-Cola. In others you could buy "hard" liquor in one of the state-controlled "liquor" shops if you had the necessary official "liquor book." In South Carolina I could not buy anything but beer across the hotel bar; but if I brought in a bottle of whisky or gin, as some of the residents did, the barman would make it up into cocktails for me, or sell me soda to drink with it.

"A man who could tell you just what you could and couldn't do for a drink in every state," said Tom Brown, an Englishman who'd been fifteen years in America, "would have to be a walking encyclopaedia."

"You've seen both countries," I said. "Don't you think that British people use drink more than the Americans do to get 'eased up,' get a party warmed up, and that kind of a thing?"

"Yes," he said. "They don't need much priming over here. They start off warm. Last night, now. Half a dozen of our neighbours came in. We had a thoroughly gay time on a cup of cocoa with a marshmallow in it."

"You know, Tom," I said. "In my first few days over here some of the people were so easy to get on with, so cheery and forward, I thought they must have been drinking."

"Cocoa with a marshmallow," said Tom. "I noticed this friendliness, this unself-consciousness among the neighbours / when I came over." He looked out of the window at the comfortable, double-decked, detached houses across the street. "Now take this place, for instance. In Britain, you'd call it a middle-class — perhaps a lower-middle-class — residential area. You know, bank clerks, secondary schoolmasters, lawyers, doctors and so on. Now back where I lived in England, in a similar kind of background, people were very cut off. They called on each other, and that kind of thing, but they weren't really matey. They put up a little screen of discretion around all their goings out and their comings in. The only thing they were prepared to have their neighbours know was their success. Now over here the neighbours come busting in on your failures as well. They come and give you a meal when they hear the wife is sick; they come and help

89

you mend the car. If they hear you're not doing well and they're thinking of going to live in some other part, they come in and tell you what they think."

"Do you like it that way?"

"Well, if you stay here, you've got to have it that way. It'd drive many an Englishman I know crazy. But his children'd do better on it than they would back there."

All the American's casualness and kindness comes out in the way he treats his children. All his optimism, his belief in human nature, his hope for the future of the man next door, go into the freedom and trust he gives them. For him, they seem to be not *his*, but so many other individual members of the family. He does not believe that they should be seen and not heard. As soon as they are big enough they sit at table. They horn in on the conversation almost as soon as they can / talk. In one house, a little boy next to me was interrupting every two minutes. "Junior," said his mother at last, "for Pete's sake give your father a chance." The children I met looked at me solemnly but not shyly. They were polite, but once they had heard it, they called me by my Christian name. It was "Ciss" and "Tom," not "Auntie Ciss" or "Uncle Tom," and I heard lots of children call their parents by their Christian or by some family name. American children are more mature than ours are, though in an engaging, not a precocious kind of way. They talk better and more freely earlier on. They do not suck their thumbs and they cry less. If they want to show off they don't stand twisting their dresses in their fingers while their parents coax them to recite some little poem. They go and ride like mad on a tricycle in the garden.

"It's the ruin of our education," said the High School headmaster, as we stood in the school yard at "recess."

"What is?"

"The things we do for our children."

"Sounds funny."

"We make things too pleasant for them. We reckon that children have got to have

90

a good time. They've got to grow up with a good memory of being young. Not too many textbooks, not too many hard lessons. Any spare cash, spend it on a new stadium, or a new pool, or a new dance floor. Any darn thing, as long as school doesn't get *nasty*."

"Not a bad thing up to a point, surely."

"Sure. But it's got beyond the point. The universities are infected. Apart from the big private places — they're O.K. — college is just a glorified school. Not a place where 91 real in-/tellectual scholars work on a super-adult level, while the youngsters extend their intellects by craning upward. It's the other way round. Our so-called scholars sit and think out smart ways of getting down to the student's level. We ought to toughen up on our kids. Hell, when you come to think of it, they're all this country's got." He looked over at where a bunch of boys and girls were chattering. "Jessie," he said. "Come over here."

Jessie ran up. "Here's a gentleman from England," he said. "Say hullo to him." Jessie said "Hullo." When she went away again, he said: "How old do you think she is?"

I looked after her slim figure, her made-up face, the well-rouged lips and pretty hair. "Sixteen? Sixteen and a half?"

"She's thirteen. She's having a hell of a good time. She oughta be smacked a bit, but it's not allowed. By the way, all these grade schools are going to get psychiatrists permanently on the staff."

"That's very thorough."

"Sure. Childhood in America is a thorough time. A lot of time and money and energy go into it. No wonder we don't want to grow up."

Whether it is due to the co-educational system or to the freedom of the American home, young Americans seem to be much more open about their relations with the opposite sex than they are over here. They begin talking about "dates" and "dating" at an earlier age. Boys visit girls in their own houses, call for them and take them for walks, at an age when in Britain they would still be rendezvousing behind the chapel or in the back row of the cinema. Whereas in Britain many / a girl will see 92 a boy a couple of dozen times before she plucks up enough courage to take him home to tea, in America she might try him out on the family the day after she meets him first. The word "Date" itself has a kind of accepted jargonized ring, and even highly educated and sophisticated people use it as good verbal currency. The wife of a university professor will tell you that you have missed seeing her daughter as she is "out on a date." A leader of provincial society might volunteer to you, almost over the teacups, that she doesn't know what will happen, but "Dorothy has been dating steady with John Smith" for nearly six months. Sometimes after a debate there would be a dance nearby. "Would you Oxford gentlemen like to go?" The Oxford gentlemen would. "Shall we fix you up with 'dates'?" You might be standing in a group at a party talking to a young lady. "Oh, by the way," she might say suddenly, pulling on the sleeve of a contiguous male, "I want you to meet my 'date,' " or "You don't say? Well! I must tell that to my 'date.' " Having, or being on, a "date" sounded rather a formal and full-time affair. The young lady would have to be fetched, escorted, protected, and taken home. If a young man "dates" a young lady for a big dance, he must send round a corsage for her. This must match her dress and suit her taste, but he is expected to achieve this without asking her what she wants. "What about a 'date'?" says the boy at a party to a girl who has taken his eye. There is no shy beating about the bush. Both know the minimum that they are in for. Having had one date together, neither of them will assume that another need or should follow.

There is a natural connection between dating and the Ameri-/can motorcar. It is 93 comfortable, it is fitted with radio and electric heater, ash trays, cigarette lighter. It has doors. It is about the only place in America where there is any privacy. The house is a busy thoroughfare; hedges and shady arbours belong to the Old World. It would be unjust to say that the auto has become a substitute for babies. The car is the bridge by which Americans pass from the inhibitions of always living in public to a private life. The Ford V-8 is the American Lovers' Lane, and the crooners deputize for bird song.

A visitor from Britain would notice one thing about any American home he entered — the comparative simplicity of the family's life. There would be quarrels and snaps, the usual tensions of the blood-relationship and of people living together in a small place, but all much lighter than they seem in Britain. The relationship between American father and son are much more truly brotherly than they are over here. There is none of that unmanning shyness which is papered over here under the "old boy" and "old son" of that pseudo comradeship to which some Britons are still committed. For his mother, the American boy's feelings are more complicated. The days when an Indian raid could destroy a community's hope of posterity are not so long ago, and the realization of the vulnerability of society through the mother is still vital enough to put an edge on his chivalry towards her. The women, especially the mothers, are more dominating than they are in Britain. Hearing the strength in some of their talking, sensing their independence of the man they have married, you remember that their grandmothers were born with the smell of gunpowder in their nostrils. It is round the 94 mother that the / family's feelings centre. It explains why American men, beneath the toughness, can be so tender.

The freeness, the candour, the naturalness of the American home rises out of the way the children are treated — as fully-fledged members of the family. In British families, a visitor is conscious of the "ranks" which still linger: the head of the family, the head of the family's wife, the eldest son, the eldest daughter. Over there, there are two old people and a lot of younger ones. American parents seem to demand much less and expect less than British parents do. They accept the consequences of toleration cheerfully.

One Saturday night, in Melville, I could hear the boy next door arguing with his father. "Why cain't I take it, Dad?" he said once or twice.

"Because it's new, and I don't want it scratched," said his dad.

"What's going on?" I asked Tom.

"Jim wants to take his father's car down to a dance on the shore," he said, "and his dad won't let him."

Jim was sixteen. The hour was then eleven o'clock, and the shore was half an hour's drive.

"Well, I don't blame him," I said. "Sixteen years old, driving a car out to a dance at this time."

"Oh, that ain't what his paw's grousing about," said Tom. "He don't mind the kid goin' in his *own* car. It's lending him his that he don't want."

"Well," I said, "you may think I sound a prig ——"

"What's that?"

I explained.

"We don't have 'em here. But g'wan."   95

"I may sound a heel," I said, "but I think that kind of freedom's going too far."

"Well, I guess you're right maybe. But we let the kids get on with it. See, we don't figure it's logical to wrap 'em up in cotton at seventeen, and send 'em out to bomb Berlin a few months later. But maybe you're right." . . .

Alistair Cooke

Mr. Cooke, perhaps most popularly known as the host of the *Omnibus* television program, has been an American correspondent for a number of prominent English periodicals. Since 1948, he has been with the Manchester *Guardian*. The book from which the extracts in this volume were taken, *One Man's America* (1952), is comprised of several adaptations of radio talks for the British Broadcasting Corporation. Of his several other books, *A Generation on Trial: U.S.A. vs. Alger Hiss* (1950) is the best known.

GETTING AWAY FROM IT ALL

10 THE REAL end of the American year is not the thirty-first of December but the old festival of Labor Day. It is the day when the summer is put away, the swimming-trunks squeezed for the last time, the ash-trays in country cottages filled with mouse-seed and rat-paste, the storm-doors hammered into place, the lock turned for the last time on your private world of sun and sand and picnics and the pride of growing children. Labor Day brings you back to the world of schools and offices, to sniffling colds and insurance policies, to taxes and radio commentators, to dark nights and the dark horizon of politics.

We sat around for the last time in our beach house at the end of Long Island. We had brought in the furniture from off the porch and the rusty barbecue grill we haven't used in four years but always put out in the sun at the beginning of summer as a symbol of our pioneer instincts. We had phoned the electric company to turn off the current. Called up the phone company to disconnect same. Left a note for the garbage-man, same for the milkman. What else has to be done? Defrost and clean the

11 refrigera-/tor. Draw the curtains across the windows on the east and west sides. Sprinkle moth-flakes on the rugs. Try to hide a smelly fishing-rod in a dark closet, and fail — your wife coming at you saying, "Could this be bait?" It is. It is a poor, dried-up piece of squid that was chewed on by a whole school of porgies and sucked dry.

We sit around finishing a last bite. The baby is snoring placidly in a house reeking of camphor and good old mouse-paste. We bury and burn the last load of garbage. We pack the car while we wait for the baby to wake. Some of the grasses on the dunes have started to turn the fall colors. So children who normally treat them as considerately as bulldozers now develop a collector's passion for bayberry and pine branches and feather-grass. Somebody sees a phonograph record worn so gray you'd think it had been played with a poker. It is *Good Night, Irene,* and it too is suddenly an object of tenderness. We finally leave, with the rear end of the borrowed station wagon looking like an army camouflage squad, bushes and plants and a bedstead growing out of each side of *Good Night, Irene.* We are on our way.

We stop and say good-by to Mrs. Horton, who sells eggs and collects antiques. . . . We wish a good winter to the Ryskos, who sell groceries; to Grathwohl, the builder and sometime carpenter; to the Doroski brothers, who run a gas and service station; to Josie Wanowski, the little bent old toothless Polish woman who has taken in washing these many years and for many of them kept a crippled husband, and who raised four astonishingly handsome chil-/dren, 12 two straight beautiful girls with shining teeth, who might be movie starlets but are in fact a nurse and a schoolteacher; two boys, one in college, one ex-army air forces.

It is much the same as any other leave-taking in the fall. But there is an ominous note or two. The bank manager is off to Riverhead: there is a meeting of the new civil defense evacuation committee — a committee, that is, to plan the evacuation of doomed New Yorkers to the potato-fields of Long Island. A young man who came out of the navy four years ago, who chose to be a potato-farmer the year of the big drought and went into debt for two thousand dollars, is not around any more. His troubles were all scattered by a letter one morning from the President of the United States, beginning: "Greetings!" — a cordial invitation to come back into the service, or else. Eddie, the boy who drives the grocer's delivery truck, says, "Well, I'd better say good-by," in a strange shy way. He too has had his call.

These little things give you a shock, and you wonder about them on the way up to the city. Everything looks like the familiar fall, the maples turning, a milky stream of smoke from burning leaves curling up into a blue, bottomless sky. But as the swift twilight comes on we are at the end of the parkway, past La Guardia Field, over the Triboro Bridge, and there are the vertical city and the plunging spires: New York again, splendid as ever in the autumn light. Not quite the same, though. We curve round and down off the bridge and pass a billboard advertising a new de luxe apartment-building somewhere. The big sign has stars against the features it is specially proud of: thermostat heat control in each 13 flat; all-electric / kitchen, with deep freeze, laundry and dish-washing machines, and garbage-disposal unit; air-conditioned units available in summer; two bathrooms for every four rooms. The last item, the last star, says: "Adequate sub-basement atomic bomb-shelter." One of the children reads it aloud, and it makes a pompous sound, so that the baby claps her hands and chortles like a wise old man. And we all laugh.

Back in the city, people with copper tans who ought to be congratulating themselves

on being able in the first place to get away from the New York summer, began in recent years to find themselves fingering the real-estate sections of the Sunday papers and peering through advertisements for "desirable country houses." Why should lucky and comfortable people be so fretful and restless for more idleness? It was not idleness such people sought but a more dreadful thing: safety. Lately the phrase "getting away from it all" has taken on a sadder and more furtive meaning in the minds of parents who live in industrial cities. It needs no winks or meaningful glances to arouse a fear that everybody feels and a few talk openly about. It is the padding fear of the atom bomb.

I heard of a man who lives in Washington who had quit his job, fallen back on his savings, bought a little place deep in the hills of Arkansas, and gone off there to farm with his wife and five children. Far off in the Black Hills of South Dakota, some pessimist as thoughtful as Noah has bought a mountain cave and invited prudent couples — one male, one female — to abandon their regular lives and batten down underground at an annual cost of two thousand five hundred dollars per person, all found. This may / appear to be the 14 furthest pole of lunacy. But during the San Francisco organizing conference of the United Nations, the citizens of the Black Hills, bidding for a lasting fame as the chosen headquarters of the United Nations, challenged the delegations with maps (Dakotas projection) to find a spot anywhere in the United States more swiftly accessible by air to Moscow, Cairo, Tokyo, or London. Maybe this pessimist was acting from the same melancholy discovery.

Then in the late 1940's businessmen caught the epidemic. Businessmen, I should say, who have factories in the East, in the ring of cities round the southern rim of the Great Lakes, or out on the Coast. An aircraft company in Bridgeport, Connecticut, announced it had decided to move bag and baggage to Dallas, Texas. Now, this is quite an undertaking. The company worked on a million and a half square feet. Its factory cost ten million dollars. It employed about ten thousand people. The company invited its skilled workers to go with it. As an American migration, this one would not be without its epic and humorous side. Bridgeport is a typical New England industrial city, except for the untypical fact that it has a Socialist government. Its workers are mostly of Italian and Czech, Hungarian and Polish stock. They are used to cold winters and New England ways. It would be quite a sight to see them in West Texas, mimicking the Texas accent, being baffled by the Mexican foods, wondering when the hot dry winds of spring and the steaming misery of summer would ever end in — as the song says — "that Texas town that never seen ice or snow." For a few excitable weeks, the unskilled men had a happy time joshing their superior brothers who had / signed up to go. They bandied around the nicknames Sagebrush, and Tex, and "Hi, there, Dallas!" Jokers appeared in ten-gallon hats and called a work-gang "you-all." But however gay the workers felt, the company's announcement caused a nasty jolt to other defense industries along the East Coast. Any company that would make a move as dramatic and costly as that must, they figured, have "heard something." The Defense Department was rattled by telephone inquiries verging between anxiety and hysteria. The callers were told in as noncommittal a way as possible that there was no "immediate" plan to go underground, to move industrial cities, to decentralize the basic industries that surround the Great Lakes. It was made officially plain that the Bridgeport company had made up its own mind and the National Security Resources Board had given its nod. The company's work had to do with testing jet-planes, and the directors had decided that the congested seaboard was a poor place to accommodate, without an expensive new airport, the special and alarming habits of jets. The Texas central plain is — if Texans will pardon the expression — flatter than Kansas. It seemed just right. But many

industries, big and little, leaped to the conclusion which they dread and which — by the peculiar chemistry of deep fear — they half-hope to have fulfilled.

The telling point about the Bridgeport story is, I think, the current emotional disposition to believe the worst. The atomic age offers us the raw material of a civilization larger, more efficient, and more humane than any that has gone before. But this promise and this challenge are lost sight of in the energy that goes and must go into making / weapons of war. This energy has the real excuse that never before in history have free men faced the threat of a tyranny so large, so merciless, and so painstaking as that with which the Soviet Union confronts us. Dangling between these two unique worlds — a world of unequaled slavery and a world of incomparable riches — we build the storm-cellars and hope for the best.

Most men find the problems of political power insoluble and tend to despair before a world that has shrunk in scale and enlarged in complexity, so that the knowledge of how it behaves seems more and more to be open only to the specialist. There never was a time, except perhaps in the fearful pestilences of the Middle Ages, when men hungered more for a decent private life, and when they are tempted to match in their joys the intensity of the sorrows all around them. I believe that this impulse, far from being an escape, is the only right way of asserting that human dignity which gives sense to the phrase "an appetite for life." What reasonable hope can an ordinary man have for himself and his family? Must we oscillate like crocodiles between panic and apathy? What more adult way is there of coming to terms with the alternatives of the atomic age?

I should like to have the wisdom and the knowledge to suggest something at once practical and noble. But all I can think of is an incident from the American past that comes nearer to home every day and seems to me as sensible as anything written since Hiroshima.

The time was the 19th of May 1780. The place was Hartford, Connecticut. The day has gone down in New England history as a terrible foretaste of Judgment 17 Day. / For at noon the skies turned from blue to gray and by midafternoon had blackened over so densely that, in that religious age, men fell on their knees and begged a final blessing before the end came. The Connecticut House of Representatives was in session. And as some men fell down and others clamored for an immediate adjournment, the Speaker of the House, one Colonel Davenport, came to his feet. He silenced them and said these words: "The Day of Judgment is either approaching or it is not. If it is not, there is no cause for adjournment. If it is, I choose to be found doing my duty. I wish, therefore, that candles may be brought."

Ladies and gentlemen, let candles be brought. . . .

ROUGHING IT

34 A hundred years ago the first ship sailed out of New York bound for San Francisco and the American River, where, according to the reports that had drifted East, you lowered a pan into a sluggish stream, shook it several times, and sifted out a fortune in gold. By ship round the Horn was only one way, the most tedious and the safest. You could go by way of Panama and Nicaragua and run the risk of malaria or yellow fever. You could sail down to Mexico and face a shorter journey across its width through almost trackless desert and the chance of epidemics and slaughter by bandits.

Most people in the East who for one reason or another felt the urge to Go West decided to go the overland way. Today it is impossible to experience the human ordeal of that great migration, one of the last epics of purely human function before the Industrial Revolution transformed our lives. These people, in New England, and New York and Maryland and Ohio, sat down and planned to walk nearly two thousand miles from St. Joseph, Missouri, or Independence, where the locomotive and the steamboat ended / and the Middle Ages 35 began. Independence was a more thriving place a century ago than it is today, because it was the outfitting center for the Forty-Niners. From there you were on your own. You went by mule and drove your wagons and cattle along with you for the remaining eighteen hundred miles. You used a route map drawn by somebody who had once made it and survived. You depended very much, too much, on the hearsay of these people to know where the water-holes were and where you could take a short cut through the mountains.

There was no archetype of the Forty-Niner. They were of every human kind. But early on they learned that they had better travel in packs, and most of them elected what they called a captain and two lieutenants. A quartermaster was chosen to look after the provisions. They may sound very martial in a noticeably non-military nation. But they knew, the later companies at any rate, that there were certain unavoidable hazards: flash floods, the rotting of their food, Indians, disease, and the constant challenge to their discipline and courage of reducing the weight of their pack — their implements, even their food supply — when the route was too much for their animals, who set the pace. They figured correctly that no group of human beings, however individually noble, would be likely to stay noble in the desperation of thirst, or spontaneously organize themselves in the event of attack. By the time they started the long journey from Missouri, most of them had formed themselves into companies and agreed on written or unwritten laws. Many of them spent weeks in the East before they left, drawing up written constitutions. Some of these / were abided 36 by all the way to California. Others were torn up in anger, stuffed down the captain's throat, or buried with a dead cow.

Most of them through the late spring of '49 took far too many provisions. It was said that the summer companies had the routes laid out for them by trails of abandoned stoves, pillows, beds, pots and kettles, crowbars, drills, plows, harness, trunks, bellows, and dishpans. These, they found, were luxuries to a pioneer. And the word got across the continent that what you needed was one wagon to carry the supplies for every five persons, a mule apiece, rifles and shotguns, a rubber knapsack, an oilcloth cap, two pairs of boots, eight shirts, an overcoat, one pair of drawers, three blankets, a hundred and fifty pounds of flour, twenty-five pounds of bacon, fifteen pounds of coffee, twenty-five of sugar, some baking powder, salt and pepper.

That's as far as I want to go in describing the famous journeys across the plains. But I suspect that any American who started out today, fitted out just this way, and got to California, even if he stuck to the countless cement highways that slam across hundreds of thousands of miles north and south and east and west — such a man would become some sort of national hero or crank. He would be paced by the newsreel boys, met at intervals by the advertising salesmen of whoever's flour and bacon he was carrying, he would be greeted by the Mayor of San Francisco, he would in the end be flown to Washington and shown in all the papers shaking the President's hand in the White House.

Nothing persists more in the fancy of Europeans, and in the superstitious pride 37 of Americans themselves, than / the conviction that Americans are tough and rough and ready, scornful of the European niceties and primmer ways of travel. The last thirty years have turned this belief into unmitigated legend.

One of the most precious books to American book collectors is a copy of Baedeker's *United States* for, I believe, 1906. In the conscientious Baedeker way, it warns the comparatively domesticated European of the coarse pleasures and inconveniences he will have to settle for if he decides to take a holiday in the United States. It is always Baedeker's consolation, however, to the intending tourist that no matter how constant the public spitting, how hard the beds, how ankle-deep the roads and primitive the hotels away from the big cities, the traveler who has any pioneering spirit in him will never regret his courageous visit to the United States because nowhere else will he see the singing color of the New England fall, the blossom of the South in the spring, the grandeur of the Yosemite, the Yellowstone, etc., etc. This guidebook is greatly sought after precisely because today it reads like such a gorgeous joke. If you changed the place-names and made them European, an American could read it with a straight face, since it would record most of his grouches about traveling in Europe today. The application of American technical genius to the mechanics of living has not merely turned the tables on Baedeker, it has turned the American, however reckless or self-reliant his individual character, into the world's most urbanized, most petted traveler.

Mr. Richard Neuberger, who lives in the Far West, in Portland, Oregon, has taken up this theme in a magazine piece. He was in Alaska during the war having, as he puts / it, "the sort of experience we had 38 read about eagerly as boys, in the tales of James Fenimore Cooper, Jack London, and Zane Grey." And, he adds, "we hated it . . . we talked nostalgically of percale sheets and fluffy towels, or breakfast in bed and tiled bathrooms." They complained — in Alaska, this is — about "drafty privies and the lack of dry-cleaning facilities." Mr. Neuberger concludes that "with a few bold exceptions, we Americans have come to regard the steam-heated hotel and the internal combustion engine as indispensable to any foray in the open." Nowadays, more millions than ever before (the latest annual count was 15,057,443) visit the American National Parks. But according to the Department of the Interior fewer and fewer people each year attempt the two-day hikes, or even drive up the highest peaks, or, having looked at the Grand Canyon, will undertake the day-long mule journey down to the overnight camp at the bottom. It is very hard to say how Americans would compare with other peoples in this new-found lassitude. Driving around most of the National Parks is pretty strenuous in itself. If you could put Yosemite and Yellowstone together, you would have something about the area of Wales, whose geography is a combination of Switzerland, Persia, and the Day of Judgment. But even so, these parks were lovingly created two generations ago by men who chopped through thousands of feet of lumber, who rode into them on a horse, who discovered the sublime with an ax, a botanist's kit, a piece of bacon, a tent and a stout heart. Now through all of them, even over the hair-raising pass into Tuolumne Meadows on top of the Yosemite, American engineers have built incomparable cement highways, 39 blasted through prehistoric rock, en-/circling mountains where no other race would dream of cutting out a dirt road.

This suggests a cheerful contradiction. That even if the traveler *is* a sissy sitting over an internal combustion engine, the heroes who in his behalf comb cement to the smoothness of toothpaste under the desert sun, and build his highways through the Rockies and Sierras: they are Americans too. And this leads us into a famous cliché. I hope I can then lead us out of it. (I have nothing against clichés. Most of them are true, though you have to live through the denial of them to know it.) It is the assumption that the Americans have grown soft and unable to fend for themselves, that their enslaving gadgets, through which they flip their way so expertly, are crutches or props to living, essential to a people sinking contentedly into a decadence that out-Romans the Romans.

I'm sorry to report that the Americans' devotion to urban comfort, their ingenuity with gadgets, even their reliance on them, proves no such thing. In my own experience, the Americans who are most devoted to convertible automobiles and glass-enclosed showers made no complaint on this score when they ripped up Japanese jungles for airfields or waded ashore at Okinawa. The women I know who can whip up a delicious meal in ten minutes with the skilled aid of pressure cookers, bean slicers, electric beaters and deep-frozen vegetables are also the ones who can make the best meal the slow way with none of these things. And the most skillful fisherman I know is a man who can charm a trout with his fingernail, but prefers to have a compact tackle-box along, which contains exquisite scales the size of your thumb and a leader cutter which / is a little circle of 40 plastic molds that exudes fine wire and cuts it in one motion.

Most Americans, even rich ones, were brought up in a culture that never expected somebody else to do the rough work. Most boys in college who can afford good cars can also take them apart and put them together again. This may all be changing. Still, I doubt that a devotion to gadgets is a reflection in the American character of a terrified dependence on them. They are loved for themselves, for the humorous felicity with which they dispose of elementary labor. A Texan I know, whom I would never like to meet in anger whether the choice of weapons was a jet-propelled torpedo or the back of the raw hand, put it neatly once when he said to me, "I'll ride fifty miles on a horse for the fun of it, but out of necessity I drive." One of the irritating troubles about Americans, in violation of the best advice of the best English divines, is that they just don't believe that whatever is uncomfortable is good for the character.

WHAT'S THE MATTER WITH AMERICA?

"The natives of England," wrote an Ital- 41 ian ambassador to London about four and a half centuries ago, "whenever they see a handsome foreigner, they say that he looks like an Englishman, and that it is a great pity he should not be an Englishman." In England this remark has been quoted to prove the lamentable decline of Roman susceptibilities, since a thousand years earlier the observant Gregory the Great, looking for the first time on a shipment of Britons, had made the shrewder remark: "Not

Angles but angels." This old reassurance drifted into my mind the other night when I heard over the radio an American senator, speaking from those cavernous lungs which the Almighty reserved for American senators, trumpet: "I am an American — who is there in the whole wide world that does not envy the name?" Being in a defensive mood, I was reminded in turn of a Chinese general I met here in an army camp during the war. He had just been given a heartwarming account of the economic potential 42 of China. He / made a grateful little bow, and as the American general's arm went around his shoulder he remarked: "Automobiles and cola drinks very good for Americans. But please, we should like remain Chinese."

We were going into all this the other evening, a small group of about forty Americans who meet once a week to straighten the world out before the world goes to pot. The introductory speakers were two foreign newspapermen, a Hungarian and myself. We had been extended an endearing American invitation to come and say what was an American and, if we liked, to say what was wrong with America. It had been about fifteen years since I'd played this game and I fumbled the better-known gambits. But the Hungarian had been here less than a year and was as impatient as a school chess champion.

He was a smooth, trenchant man in his early forties. In that room, where the amiable American bodies loped and leaned on chairs and tables, he was a very European figure. The creases of his double-breasted coat were horizonal, tugging at the unyielding buttons. He never unbuttoned that coat, as he faced an audience which, on a very hot night, was coatless. He had spent a lot of private time, he said, trying to find the word to define the dominant American character trait. He soon made it clear he had been pondering on a high ethical level, for he told us he wanted to find an equivalent for the three words which the Spanish philosopher Salvador de Madariaga had chosen to signify the domi-

nant characteristic of the French, the Spanish, and the Engilsh. These were: for the French — "*droit*," which it appears is an untranslatable but enviable combination of justice, right, order, and / clarity. For the 43 Spanish — "honor," which we were given to understand was familiar enough but a passion with the Spanish people. For the English, need I say, "fair play." What, then, was the word for the Americans?

Everybody was deadly still. There was an audible purr from one end of the room, from two or three of the younger men who evidently join "groups" in the expectation of hearing invited guests say the right things. I noticed a florid man near me, however, who flicked the ash off his cigar and gave me an ominous, ironical look that seemed to say, "Well, boys, you asked him here."

It will not surprise you, perhaps, to hear that the Hungarian had found the word. Somebody hinted later that he had known it before he ever took the boat across the Atlantic. The word was "salesmanship." His theory was that industrial genius is nothing in itself. Nor, it seemed, was there anything peculiarly American about a vast population of eager though slightly skeptical customers. It is the lifeline between them that counts. And that is the salesman. The product must connect with the buyer.

Elementary, maybe. But notice the snide American element in this familiar process. Where, he asked (and it must have been a rhetorical question, because he knew the answer all right), is the weakest link in the chain of supply and demand? Everybody waited politely and then let out an exploding gasp when he pronounced the word: "the idiot." The what? we hissed and muttered. "The idiot," he said sternly. "The intelligent man," he explained, "knows things the idiot does not know. But the idiot does know some things the intelligent man does not know. Therefore the idiot is the one who must be won over. At / this 44 point, the American system has to call on a body of shock troops who represent to American civilization what the Jesuits are to the Roman Catholic Church and the S.S. men were to the Nazis: the advertising men."

There was a lovely bray of laughter, which horrified the Hungarian. "You should not laugh at this," he scolded. "If you cried, that would be good." Somebody motioned to show they were laughing with him, that he had a shrewd point, that no offense was meant, go ahead. But it did no good. The Hungarian had a theory, neat and sharp as a knife. And one could only wonder what, in his chagrin, he expected his audience to do about it. Most of us who get angry at another country do so in the absurd hope that the natives will squirm and hang their heads, confess and promise to reform. It is a childish mechanism, and the foreigner is always disappointed. An American doctor said to me afterwards that expatriates in any country always have to keep up a pet peeve against the system they find themselves in, to justify their inability or unwillingness to compete in that system. It is just possible that this was the wisest sentence of the evening, though it was spoken long after the meeting had broken up.

The Hungarian's main point was conceded in theory, and in courtesy. It was then demolished. An art director with an advertising company said sure, his aim was to sell his product, or his employer's product, but his layouts and designs were not aimed at the idiot. The daily zest of his work, he said, looking steadily at the table, was to paint striking and charming designs which would set up an unconscious prefer- 45 ence for his product in just such wary / and civilized people as the Hungarian. The man next to him said all business was a form of public relations and he thought it was a waste of character and talent if you didn't try to humanize it in every way possible. Another said he didn't get the implication that there was something shameful about selling things and that the Hungarian was gravely mistaken if he thought Americans were solemnly obsessed by it. "I'd say," this man concluded, "it was more of

a game and a matching of wits." One melancholy man, whose leisure tastes ran to modern music and ballet, remarked: "All the best cracks I ever heard about advertising were made by advertising men. But it doesn't make them throw up their jobs."

All this was engrossing and good-tempered. But the meeting almost broke up in insurrection when I was called on to think aloud about the comparative significance of cricket and baseball. That afternoon I had been watching a baseball game between the New York Yankees and the Cleveland Indians. Early in the third inning a Yankee batter sent a high fly-ball soaring off, as we hoped, beyond the long white pole that marks the area between a foul and a home run. The umpire at first base whizzed around and craned his neck. The ball fell somewhere, and the spectators, being on the Yankees' home ground, roared their acceptance of the fact, which nobody had certified, that it was a homer. Then the umpire pointed this side of the pole and called a foul. He was right enough, but the crowd bellowed in pain and rage. So did the Yankee standing at first base. So did the batter. They both strode over to the umpire and spat out torrents of abuse. He / cringed for a split second. Then his 46 neck stiffened and he roared back at them. They squared their elbows back to demonstrate a merely technical respect for his person, but all the while they were shoving him along with their chests and he stumbled back under the rain of insult and calumny. The crowd loved this and egged on the three of them. When it was seen that the umpire and the players had taken over the crowd's indignation, the crisis dribbled away into waves of boos, laughter, and rippling chuckles. It was a foul.

I mentioned this to our sweating group and wondered, possibly with too much coyness, why in a cricket game the first such word out of a batsman would have caused his captain to send him off the field. Somebody remembered that a marine in the southwest Pacific, very likely prompted by a newspaperman, had said that one reason

the Americans were fighting the war was for the right to bawl out the umpire. This was too much for another Englishman present, who said that if an English marine could have been got to express himself in a printable form about the common cause he "might have said" he was fighting to have the rules respected. It was a glum moment. It appeared we had profoundly different ideas about elementary behavior. What I was really trying to suggest, from the hideous bottom of my resentment at this baseball uproar, was that Americans were not very ethical about games. The other Englishman sensed the spot I was in and came in smartly to assure the company that cricket was a rather special case. The rules of soccer, now, are set up to be obeyed, but English soccer-players often express themselves, as he put it, "very violently indeed."
47 (You / mean, threw in the Hungarian, they go "Hmmm!"?) At this point, we were in an untenable position. We were trying to prove the unprovable, namely that the British are very ethical but very virile at the same time. Our Hungarian magnanimously came to the rescue by harping again on his own more flexible theme. The Yankees, he thought, were simply using high-pressure salesmanship on the umpire. "Salesmanship," he snapped, "leading to homicide."

The evening ended triumphantly when a big swarthy man with large eyes and the bluest chin I have ever seen said in a tired way, "Speaking as a Russian Jew, my good American blood boils."

We all laughed with great relief and then, in the most patient and friendly way, he made several points that were received with general grunts of approval. He lit up just the difference, in a national attitude towards a game, that a proud Englishman might never understand and yet spend his life deploring. Every baseball player, he said, knows the umpire's word is law. But he's going to make the most of disputing it first. And the crowd expects a frequent show of indignation. Everybody knows it won't change the result. But it's a good show while it lasts and is included in the

price of admission. One of the minor therapies of baseball, it seems, is to provide for the letting off of instinctive steam — or the national yen for anarchy. It has, he pronounced, very little to do with ethics.

There was one man present who was utterly and genuinely baffled by the news of an Englishman's strict fidelity to the umpire's little finger. The idea of a captain's ordering a player from the field because he had blasted the / umpire to king- 48 dom come struck him as extraordinarily prim and solemn.

"You mean," he turned to me, "they just wouldn't do it?"

"They just wouldn't do it," I assured him down my nose.

"Tell me," he asked, brightening, and the wrinkles vanished from his forehead, "cricketers must be full of neuroses, right?"

It was getting very late.

"Right," I said. . . .

NEW YORK, NEW YORK

An English novelist came through New 101 York a little time ago and, as all travelers must, brooded awhile about our ways. When he got home he did a radio talk about it. Nothing more would have been heard about it if the script of this talk had not been reprinted in the *New York Times*. It was no sooner out than the ambulances were summoned to handle a rush of high-bloodpressure cases, and the mail-trucks dumped bags of protests on the *New York Times*. From these outcries you would never have guessed that Mr. Priestley had just been a delegate to the United Nations Educational, Scientific and Cultural Organization, and that he was a man chosen to spread light and understanding among us.

Too bad, said Mr. Priestley, that New York's skyscrapers are not dedicated "to God or to some noble aspect of communal life" but only to "buying and selling dividends." "Is that so?" asked one correspondent. "Then let me tell him that the American Bible Society, the American Association of Social Workers, the American Cancer Society, the Medical Society of

102 New York and the British / Information Services, to name only a few, don't buy and sell dividends. Mr. Rockefeller of course might plead guilty, but his conviction would carry the reminder that his skill in these things helped to cure a lot of dysentery and scurvy in tropical places and helped a lot of Englishmen to come to the United States and have the leisure, after their work with microscopes, to share some of Mr. Priestley's feelings about New York." Mr. Priestley conceded that this was "just a passing thought."

"It seems hardly worth while holding on to," snapped this New Yorker.

As for the dismal state of the drama in these parts, our man referred Mr. Priestley to the theater pages of the newspapers, "where he will note many plays he may later see in London."

New York is overcrowded, complained Mr. Priestley. Granted, said the New Yorker, but New York takes to people and likes to crowd them in.

I creep into the argument at this point only because I possess a rather dog-eared but still unexpired credential. It is that I have lived in New York steadily — continuously, anyway — for nearly fifteen years; that I came here first as a transatlantic visitor, on money dished out from one of Mr. Harkness's skyscrapers; and that in those days I saw New York much as Mr. Priestley sees it now. I think we were both wrong. And I hope it will throw light on more places than New York if I try to say why.

Neither a native nor a traveler can ever be objective about any place on the map. And all we can sensibly discuss is how true for each of them are their feelings about the place. There is a special flow of moods 103 in a traveler. / And I think Mr. Priestley now, and I nineteen years ago, were talking more about ourselves than about New York. Because travelers are never the same at home and abroad. They always think they are, but the people you travel among notice pretty soon that you have thrown off your responsibilities to your own country and don't have to take on any of theirs. This is the state of natural anarchy and for some grown-ups is the only time they know again the huge relief of kids when school's out. Travelers, however, once they are no longer young and scampy, feel embarrassed, not to say guilty, about their freedom. They can express it in one of two ways. They can be secretly frightened by the alien life around them and retreat more tenaciously than ever into habits that belong to their country and nowhere else. Hence the cricket clubs in Brazil and Hollywood, which, I have noticed, manage to recruit some Britons who would not be playing cricket at home. I have known Englishmen who in England can take their tea or leave it but who get to insist on it in the United States, precisely because afternoon tea is not a custom of the country.

The other reflex looks like the opposite, but deep in the springs of our childish fear it may be only another reaction to the same threat. It is to go out and do with much bravery all the things you do not do at home. Thus the Englishman who becomes a baseball fan or learns to shudder at Brussels sprouts. This is a plucky show that he is no longer bound by nostalgia or habit to the old life he left behind him.

I believe there is a peculiar mythical appeal to Englishman in the distant prospect of America. It may go as far / back as the 104 Elizabethans, the travelers' tales of fat turkeys, gigantic oysters, and succulent fruits, the news of an Eldorado begging for settlement. "Oh My America, my new founde land!" cried Donne, though at that particular moment he wasn't thinking of leaving home. This myth has been modified down the years, until there are at least two or three generations of Britons conditioned by a whole childhood literature about the West, and now by the glittering stereotypes of the movies, and more regrettably by the solid tradition of reporting back to England only what is corrupt or eccentric or scandalous. From this there emerges a modern myth about America, some of which is poetic and true, some of which is a punching-bag for stay-at-homes. The city of New York has come to crystallize the nightmare aspect of this dream country. It becomes a hard and hideous place, with frightening canyons of skyscrapers. Its life is, in Mr. Priestley's words, "restless . . . in its nightly pursuit of diminishing pleasures. Not a flower," he moans, "can blossom on these concrete cliffs." Well, I am told that in the granite veins of this city, on Manhattan alone, they have found a hundred and seventy varieties of semi-precious stones. Slit into this gray hunk of rock we inhabit there are garnets and amethysts and opals and beryls and tourmalines, and other jewels even less pronounceable. There are still about half as many trees as human beings. And the commonest backyard tree is the ailanthus, which — I hate to tell Mr. Priestley — the Chinese call the tree of heaven.

But this doesn't fit in with anything Europeans have been told, and the heck with it. To more Europeans than would admit it, there is always at the back of the 105 mind this / neon-lit image of New York as Babylon, where innocence is banished, where anything goes, where everything has its price, where — in the vivacious version current among my schoolmates in England — you rode a perpetual shoot-the-chutes and bounded the waves of pleasure to the music of Duke Ellington, while at your side snuggled a beautiful girl, beautiful and up to no good.

If you think I am romancing about this, let me remind you that the symbol of an island of pleasure, presided over by a beckoning female, is almost a constant of the human imagination. It was Circe in Greece, Izanami in Japan, Semiramis who built Babylon. These, you may say, are only legends. But what is more real and indispensable than the ideas that burst into life from men's imaginations precisely because they do not exist? They express the permanent dissatisfactions of man with his lot, and this particular one relieves the secret fear that, like Marley's ghost, we may be wasting our days on earth weaving chains

of bankbooks, files, ledgers, insurance policies.

When Mr. Priestley calls New York "Babylon piled on Imperial Rome," I think he is the victim of this myth. Once you stay and live in this city, you have to admit that it is nothing of the sort. The intelligentsia will claim that New York tries to be the city they would like to despise. But the intelligentsia is the same everywhere and is a poor guide to the real life of cities. And to the people who live this life, the overpowering number of middle-class New Yorkers, who have as much town pride as Leeds or Manchester, there was one sentence of old Jeremiah Priestley's that really hurt: "The lonely heart of man cannot come home here."

No? On Manhattan Island alone (and 106 Mr. Priestley was talking about only one of the five boroughs) there are two million people who won't live anywhere else and wouldn't want to, even after three drinks. New York is their home town. It is not Babylon. It is the place where we rise in the mornings to the clicking of the radiator or the bawling of the downstairs brat. We take in the milk. We descend on the schools with a rush of kisses and a greeting of neighbors. We head for the subway. We hear a great bass reverberate over the island. It is not, as Mr. Priestley might suspect, the trump of doom. It is only the *basso profondo* of the *Queen Elizabeth* going downriver. We spend the day at work, restlessly perhaps to the extent of leaving home for a distant workshop and then at the end of the day reversing the process and leaving the workshop to get home again. Maybe, if it is not slushy or damp, we decide to walk home and watch a copper sun sinking into an El Greco sky over against the Jersey shore. If the skies of New York often lift us, miserable ants that we are, into delusions of grandeur, we will often spot on the corner, as we turn to go in our building, something casual or scurrilous that restores us to the affectionate human scale. On the wall of a bricked-up lot a tiny New Yorker scribbled a typical sentence. "Nuts," it said. "Nuts to all the boys on Second Avenue" — a long straggling pause, then the concession, "except between 68th and 69th Streets."

We come in and we play with the children or bawl them out. We enjoy, if we have any sense, the variety of the people of our town, and there is often some crazy thing to tell. I have daily dealings with a score of Americans whom I shall only iden-107 tify here as an Italian shoeshine / man, a garrulous German elevator man, a warm, wisecracking Jewish newsagent, and a range of shopkeepers who span the gamut of New York names from Mr. O'Byrne De Witt to Circumstance H. Smith, a Negro with fine manners.

The thermometer dips overnight and we look forward to tomorrow, when the red ball goes up over Central Park — no signal for revolution this, Mr. Priestley, or even retribution, but the City's cue to tell us there's going to be skating. Whenever we go to the Park and find, say, there's not enough sand in the sand box the children play in, we telephone the office of Mr. Moses, the Park Commissioner. Next morning two attendants come along with replenishing boxes of sand. The city works pretty hard on the organizing of the citizen's play, and in summer there are handball courts to be repaired, there are city band concerts, city outdoor opera, city fish to be fed into the surrounding streams, and swimming for thousands who leap the trains for the vast city-sponsored lay-out of Jones Beach.

In the evening, what do we do? Well, I see from a city survey that only one in fifteen of us has ever been in a night-club. We sit and read, or have friends in, listen to the radio or look at television or go to lectures, or a movie, play pinochle or check-ers or poker, putter with this and that. And ninety-two in a hundred of us begin to go to bed around ten-thirty.

Our days and months are bound by work, and fun, and quarrels, and taxes, and movies and savings, and children and death and friendship. When we are far from home we think of New York, and it is not of Circe with a henna rinse bawling into a night-club microphone. We see in / imagination the white steam hissing 108 through the pavements. We smell the fishy smell of the Fulton Market, or the whiff of chicory over Foley Square, or the malty brew that hangs around the East Nineties. We recall the Bronx Zoo, and Mercury standing on his muscular thighs over the traffic lights on Fifth Avenue. We see in the mind's eye the magic dioramas of Africa and Hawaii in the Museum of Natural History, or the pink front page of the morning tabloids. We hear of a girl who was loaded with furs and automobiles by a sharpie using absconded funds. Over the transatlantic wires they flash her confession: "I never knew he was in an illegal business. He told me he was a gambler." Glory be! We know her for our own. . . .

Restless we *are,* and very small, threading through our canyons. But are we, as Mr. Priestley assures us we are, "full of unease, disquiet, bewilderment"? Last Summer Dr. Gallup found that over ninety per cent of us thought we were happy. Suppose we allow ten per cent for pride or bravado and another ten per cent for Mr. Priestley's trans-/atlantic insight. That still 109 leaves seventy per cent who believe, maybe wrongly, that they are happy. Better let 'em wallow in their ignorance, Mr. Priestley, these placid dopes who don't even know when they're "deeply bewildered and frustrated." . . .

Le Corbusier

Le Corbusier is the pseudonym of Charles-Edouard Jeanneret, world-famous Swiss architect and city planner, who was born in 1887. Noted for the vigor of his ideas, Le Corbusier has continually centered his interest upon the unity of the growth of cities and the development of architecture. His most famous single structure is the Pavillon de l'Esprit Nouveau in Paris; he also won first prize with his design for the Palace of Nations at Geneva, which was never erected. He planned a model community in Marseilles, and he was a member of the commission that designed the United Nations building in New York. *When the Cathedrals Were White* first appeared in French in 1937.

[NEW YORK]

39 "Like us, like Americans, my friend. You can like them, they deserve to be liked. This is a country in which there is a great deal of confusion, a great deal of activity, a great deal going on, a country in which everything is open and everything is possible. Look at New York raised up around us, carrying up to hitherto inaccessible heights a vertical city. It is natural that your spirit should often protest. Well and good! But with your heart you can understand us; with your heart you can feel that we are young, a little mad, or rather children, and that we love work and great things; and that we know nothing of discouragements. We possess a great country which has made us great; at least it has made our undertakings great. We are strong. We are driving ahead; everything is changing here; events take place in days; with you it is in centuries! Everything is changing, everything is being transformed; 40 tomorrow will be different. We have / a prodigious potential. When we shall have found our way, we shall do things that will please you.

"Come back to America, my friend, America is a great country."

A woman spoke to me thus, on my last evening in New York. My heart was a little torn by the imminent departure, a heart which had been torn every day for two months by hate and love of this new world which must be seen to be really known as it is. Hate or love: nothing more, nothing less. Daily debate. Better, debate through every minute in the midst of the stupefying city. Hours of despair in the violence of the city (New York or Chicago); hours of enthusiasm, confidence, optimism, in the fairy splendor of the city.

I am not able to bear the thought of millions of people undergoing the diminution of life imposed by devouring distances, the subways filled with uproar, the wastelands on the edges of the city, in the blackened brick streets, hard, implacably soulless streets — tenement streets, streets of hovels that make up the cities of the century of money — the slums of New York or Chicago.

I am offended by this blow at legitimate human hopes. Nevertheless, if I am observant, I discover that my despair is not always shared by the victims themselves. In New York, the people who have come in order to "make money" shake off black thoughts and, looking at the sparkle of the great avenues, the entrances of apartment houses and fine homes, think: "O.K., it will be my turn tomorrow!"

Seven million people are bound in the chains of New York, and that turn will never come unless they learn to adopt drastic measures.

Knowing quite well that that turn cannot come quickly enough for seven million beings, there are moments when I hate the city of today; clearly and coolly I know that a proper plan can make New York the city 41 par excellence of modern times, / can actively spread daily happiness for these oppressed families — children, women, men stupefied by work, stunned by the noise of the rails of the subways or elevateds — who sink down each evening, at the end of their appointed tasks, in the impasse of an inhuman hovel.

In sober offices, on the fifty-sixth floor of the newest skyscraper, men carry on business. Big business probably. I do not have a sense of figures and I know from experience that it is often more difficult to make small matters come out right than big ones. In the domain of money, the law is like that of the swing at the fair: at the beginning the effort is normal; everyone can take off and make a start. But at a certain point in the swing, when the acrobat is on the horizontal, it becomes precarious; he is too far away from the gravitational norm, and gravity acts on him. Then it takes an effort of a very particular kind to achieve a vertical position, with head down, and having passed the "meridian" of the swing, to come on around effortlessly from that point. Brute strength is not enough. The repeated attempts require a regular and harmonious progression. Harmonious, that's the word. Harmony is the cause of the success. The most difficult thing — the real difficulty — comes when you are a hair's-breadth from success: at the moment of swinging over. If you manage it, you are thenceforth launched! Many will not succeed in managing it. Those who have passed over this financial hazard owe it to their merits just as they owe it to the combination of circumstances: the things necessary to make the effort profitable, to stimulate it, to support it, were present. It was a happy conjuncture. And now the financial swing moves easily, with no further effort required except a scrupulous supervision.

That is why the skyscrapers were not constructed with a wise and serious inten-tion. They were applauded acrobatic feats. The *skyscraper as proclamation* won. Here the skyscraper is not an element in city planning, but a banner in the sky, a fireworks / rocket, an aigrette in the coiffure 42 of a name henceforth listed in the financial Almanach de Gotha.

Beneath the immaculate office on the fifty-sixth floor the vast nocturnal festival of New York spreads out. No one can imagine it who has not seen it. It is a titanic mineral display, a prismatic stratification shot through with an infinite number of lights, from top to bottom, in depth, in a violent silhouette like a fever chart beside a sick bed. A diamond, incalculable diamonds.

The great masters of economic destiny are up there, like eagles, in the silence of their eminences. Seated in their chairs, framed by two plate glass windows which fuse their rooms with the surrounding space, they appear to us made out of the substance of this event which is as strong and violent as a cosmic mutation: New York standing up above Manhattan is like a rose-colored stone in the blue of a maritime sky; New York at night is like a limitless cluster of jewels. America is not small potatoes! In the last twenty years, facing the old continent, it has set up the Jacob's ladder of the new times. It is a blow in the stomach that strikes you like a hurricane.

"I am an American."

It was not they who said it. I thought it for them.

How dare you curse New York? "Fairy catastrophe" (I shall return to that theme), unified splendor, scintillation, promise, proof, act of faith (what faith?), etc.

It is the first time that men have projected all their strength and labor into the sky — a whole city in the free air of the sky. Good God, what disorder, what impetuosity! What perfection already, what promises! What unity in a molecular state, gridiron street plan, office on top of office, clear crystallization. It is sublime and atrocious, and nothing succeeds any longer. There is nothing to do except to see clearly, think, conceive, begin over again. Of course New York is ready to begin over again. Those people have courage! . . .

83   New York is an event of worldwide importance. I have called it the first place in the world on the scale of the new times, the work yard of our era. Twenty years ago New York was still only a strange, faraway city; we had a somewhat harsh opinion of the people and their city; we said: "America, 'way off there." And we remained quiet in our acts and thoughts, bound to the old scale. But the world broke out here and there; it was swollen with sap and swollen with pus; the eruption floods the world with pus and sap. New York, strong, proud of itself, in prosperity or in depression, is like an open hand above our heads. An open hand which tries to knead the substance of today. New York has a style, has style, is mature enough to have acquired style. There are not just ragged things there; there is quality. A spirit is asserting itself; it shows itself in a section of Fifth Avenue, beside Central Park, or along Park Avenue; the people, the shops, the products, the architecture, have achieved a character which is grand, intense, and healthy. It is full of life; they are places of robust life. The Place de l'Opéra in Paris is no longer anything but a relic.

Americans tell you: "New York is not America." They are very conscious of it, they recognize themselves more readily in New England, in Boston, city of thought

84 and meditation; in / Chicago, rival of New York; in the innumerable "American" cities (ah! yes, what a unitary character in the gridiron plans, the extraordinary vigor, the activity); and then there is the diversity of this immense territory in which France, in its surface area, would be no more than a pocket handkerchief: the North with its snow, bordering on Canada; the South with constant heat in Florida — at Miami — palm trees and resort cities and water sports; New Orleans with its Negroes and the busy shipping of the Mississippi. Then the expanses of grain extending as far as the eye can see to the foot of the Rocky Mountains. The

canyons. Finally, at the very end, their paradise: California and the access to the Pacific, the islands, Tahiti, and new amusements. China faces them. Americans are thoroughly comfortable in their colonial style cottages — an architecture of high quality which expresses a healthy spirit, an ample and reasonable life.

New York, they feel, is a little bit diabolical. New York is not American. It is a world capital and has no frontier. I myself have the right to become a *New Yorker,* if I am strong enough to cut a furrow in New York. I should not thereby become an American!

For a traveler, New York is the great event of the journey. To penetrate American life — the real life — would require years — a genuine exploration. I am going to surprise you: Americans do not know America, the country is too large; they have neither the occasion nor the time, nor the means, nor any real reason to travel in their country. No more do the New Yorkers know New York. New York is too large and the day has only twenty-four hours. Travelers have a point of view about the city: we have come to see, to study, to understand, to judge. The average, ordinary life does not take up our attention. If the opportunity presented itself we could understand and enjoy the life of the cowboy on his ranch. We should find there a natural *man,* and that is the bottom of the question. In the innumerable cities of the USA we divine average societies in the process of development, on the long road of quality; the average, average situations / seem to us mediocre and they cannot hold 85 our interest. What we require is the potential which belongs to the *great cities.* Drama, intensity, violence even, human substance — the human quality which is unbridled here and which elsewhere, in the average cities, covers itself with shame. New York is a world capital and has no shame. It is raw.

Whether it is in Chicago or in New York, you will be shown only the handsome quarters; you will never be entertained ex-

cept by hosts in comfortable circumstances; very comfortable, terribly comfortable in the midst of pathetic masses. The slums of Chicago are terrible. The slums are the tragic zones where there are only hovels, lives crushed by the horror of the physical setting, lodgings which are not just burrows but instruments of torture. The slums are not simply physically ugly. Chicago, for instance, offers a striking spectacle in Drexel Avenue which is composed of private houses in the form of German Renaissance castles; some years ago it was the center of high life. One day, as a result of one of the violent shifts which are part of the destiny of cities (Paris: Place des Vosges emptied to fill up the Faubourg Saint-Germain; the boulevard of Saint Martin abandoned for the Madeleine Boulevard; then, today, a great movement toward the Champs Élysées and the creation of an important new center in the west at the expense of the boulevards which have enjoyed a hundred glorious years, etc. . . .), Chicago was cut in two: the east-west axis of the city (like the Avenida de Mayo in Buenos Aires) determined the destiny of two sections of the city. The fashionable quarter was in the south; suddenly it changed to the north. The southern part was abandoned. Who will live in these princely (and dubious) residences on Drexel Avenue? No one. Nevertheless, after a certain amount of time, the Negroes take it over. They settle down behind broken windows covered over by boards; a villa becomes a village; there are weeds in the rubbish-filled gardens, behind rusting iron fences. There is misery there. For whoever says *Negro* in the USA says pariah. This slum, then, is sinister not be-
86 cause of the place itself / but because of the kind of spirit which has sown death in this former "paradise." But there are slums in all the horror of the word: shanties of wood and blackened brick which show a neglect, a disintegration, a complete decay of that sign of vitality: maintenance. They wring your heart. They are new slums. They are from twenty to fifty years old.

The tuberculous blocks in Paris, the Barrio Chino in Barcelona (a center of prostitution), are an admission that misery is the normal lot of the cadavers of cities, of the putrefying sections of the city. It is a tragic sign of decadence: it means that something has gone wrong with the social machine, it is an accusing witness of the times which have allowed some members of society to rot for the sake of loading other, privileged persons with jewels, rings, rivers of pearls and diamonds.

I scarcely more than glimpsed the slums of New York and I believe that New Yorkers never see them in their daily rounds; they are unaware of them. If they knew the slums, it would make them sick at heart and they would make new city plans. For the world needs city planning in order to conquer human misery.

For instance, in the "moral" slums of Chicago I noticed this: laboring men and office workers are obliged to travel more than fifty miles a day in streetcars and buses in order to earn their living!

From a plane you can grasp more clearly the wretchedness of urban agglomerations and particularly the calamity in the lives of millions of Americans who are thrust into the purgatory of the transportation system. You get the idea of catastrophe, urban catastrophe — the harassed life of men, women, and children; the sections in which human wastes stagnate — the poor devils so battered by their situation that they do not have the mind, the strength, the power, or the means to get together and cry halt. The national leaders and the city fathers are unconscious of *the reality of their misery*. After a stimulating cocktail they pass through the golden portals of Grand Central Terminal into a Pullman which takes them to their car; after a ride along charm-/ing country roads they enter 87 the quiet and delightful living rooms of their colonial style houses.

Americans are eminently democratic — except about Negroes and that is a very grave question which cannot be resolved in a superficial way — they are good-natured, cordial, and companionable. The misery of our times comes from the fact that those who rule are those who have succeeded and who, consequently and quite naturally, live in conditions of material well-being. Inevitably, in spite of themselves and despite an evident good will, they are ignorant of the great charnel house of human misery. The day is only twenty-four hours long and each morning one must take up again the task left behind the evening before; it is a tiring job; thus the circuit closes, tightly, automatically. One cannot bring accusations against those who have succeeded for surrounding themselves with gracious things and thus losing sight of the urban catastrophe.

Moreover, New York is fascinating because of the other catastrophe, the fairy catastrophe: Manhattan, a city of skyscrapers, a vertical city.

The island is spread out like a sole in the water of the Hudson and East rivers. The fins along the two flanks represent the most perfect disposition of forms for a mercantile port. When you see it from a plane you think: Manhattan is a type-area for a modern city; the range of banks sheltered from the sea has the purity of a theorem. But now look at it on foot, along the avenue which skirts the river; the docks and ships form the teeth of a comb as far as you can see. The arrangement is clear, logical, perfect; nevertheless, it is hideous, badly done, and incongruous; the eye and the spirit are saddened. What could have been a communal enterprise, ordered in a serene and monumental unity, what could have been an endless jewel case for those marvels: liners or freighters — everything lacks order, everything has been badly constructed in the worst parts and even in the best ones. It was done by rapacious money-grubbers. This fringe along the water, around the whole periphery of Manhattan, is nothing 88 but dirty / scum. Nevertheless, necessity has already forced a fresh start. Since nothing had been conceived systematically, it had not been possible to look ahead. Along this too narrow waterfront avenue — which

is supposed to serve two opposed purposes: as an artery for easy circulation, and as the location of quiet basins for loading and unloading — there exists the most complete confusion. You should watch a liner unload or take on passengers with their trunks. It is an edifying sight! What a wretched business! You get by of course! Will contemporary society then go on forever in the chaos of an everlasting getting by? Will getting by be our only discipline? What a failure and what a shameful opportunity is afforded those who are unscrupulous or overcunning! Since the avenue on the river was bottled up and unusable, it was decided to construct the saving instrument of all modern city planning: the highway on piles, in the air, free, connected with the ground by ramps at appropriate intervals — the highway on which cars can travel at full speed. Above the hell of traffic, you leap forward, you escape into a real joyousness by means of the elevated highway: you see the ships, the water, the skyscrapers, the sky; you are free!

Ah! if the docks could be done over again, reconstructed in a unified way! Docks are hangars; there is no mystery about that, nor any secret of construction. Encircling all of Manhattan, more than twenty miles, pure and splendid docks would form a necklace of useful architecture around the city. It would be both efficient and profitable. My hand trembles, I am tempted to pick up a pencil. It would be so easy to do it well. That single project would illustrate the benefits of communal enterprise. Blind and self-seeking men have spoiled everything!

Within the ring of its docks Manhattan thrusts itself up into the sky. A great many skyscrapers fill the space, shut off the horizon. I did not imagine that there were so many of them; I imagined a few examples of boldness and vanity. But the whole city is vertical — or at least it seems to be, for a limited number of verticals succeed in taking up the blue of the sky.

It must be said that here the skyscrapers 89 are an architectural accident. Imagine a man undergoing a mysterious disturbance of his organic life: the torso remains normal, but his legs become ten or twenty times too long. Thus the torso of normal houses set in normal plots of ground has suddenly been raised up on an unexpected support. They have become lost in an abstract tangle of calculations. As a result of paper calculations and new methods of construction, stimulated by somewhat unreasonable considerations, they have ignored the contingencies and plunged themselves into the unknown: three hundred feet, six hundred feet, a thousand feet. . . .

The former contingencies remain and the result has been catastrophe.

The torsos of buildings were pierced with windows; the disproportionately large supports also. I have already mentioned the cottage or private-house windows, the traditional windows which belong to the period of heavy walls of brick or stone. Anachronistic windows which nevertheless have one virtue — they express the presence of a normal man, a man behind an old-fashioned window. Thus punctuating the blue sky in a very simple, regular, and automatic way — yes, a fatal and indisputable way — there are now in the sky hundreds of thousands of windows, perhaps millions. It is very moving. Mediocre and retrograde poets who write about sunsets falling on old stones, you deny that man — good-natured man, with two feet, a head, and a heart — is an ant or a bee subject to the necessity of living in a box, a case, behind a window; you ask for a complete freedom, a complete fantasy, in accordance with which everyone would act in his own fashion, carried along by a creative lyricism in ever-new paths, never beaten paths, but individual ones, various, unexpected, extemporized, endlessly fanciful. Well, here is the proof that a man holds fast to the box which is his room; and a window opens on the outside world. It is a law of human biology; the square case, the *room* is a useful creation, proper to human beings. The window behind which a man stands is a poem of intimacy,
90 of the / free consideration of things. A

million windows in the blue sky. The fairy-like atmosphere begins with them.

A hundred times I have thought: New York is a catastrophe, and fifty times: it is a beautiful catastrophe.

One evening about six o'clock I had cocktails with James Johnson Sweeney — a friend who lives in an apartment house east of Central Park, over toward the East River; he is on the top floor, one hundred and sixty feet above the street; after having looked out the windows, we went outside on the balcony, and finally we climbed up on the roof.

The night was dark, the air dry and cold. The whole city was lighted up. If you have not seen it, you cannot know or imagine what it is like. You must have had it sweep over you. Then you begin to understand why Americans have become proud of themselves in the last twenty years and why they raise their voices in the world and why they are impatient when they come to our country. The sky is decked out. It is a Milky Way come down to earth; you are in it. Each window, each person, is a light in the sky. At the same time a perspective is established by the arrangement of the thousand lights of each skyscraper; it forms itself more in your mind than in the darkness perforated by illimitable fires. The stars are part of it also — the real stars — but sparkling quietly in the distance. Splendor, scintillation, promise, proof, act of faith, etc. Feeling comes into play; the action of the heart is released; crescendo, allegro, fortissimo. We are charged with feeling, we are intoxicated; legs strengthened, chest expanded, eager for action, we are filled with a great confidence.

That is the Manhattan of vehement silhouettes. Those are the verities of technique, which is the springboard of lyricism. The fields of water, the railroads, the planes, the stars, and the vertical city with its unimaginable diamonds. Everything is there, and it is real.

The nineteenth century covered the earth with ugly and soulless works. Bestiality of money. The twentieth century

91 as-/pires to grace, suppleness. The catastrophe is before us in the darkness, a spectacle young and new. The night effaces a thousand objects of debate and mental reservation. What is here then is true! Then everything is possible. Let the human be written into this by conscious intention, let joy be brought into the city by means of wisely conceived urban machinery and by generous thinking, aware of human misery. Let order reign.

In the store windows I saw an album published for the Christmas season by Scribner's: *The Magical City.* I reflect and argue with myself. I change it to: *The Fairy Catastrophe.* That is the phrase that expresses my emotion and rings within me in the stormy debate which has not stopped tormenting me for fifty days: hate and love.

For me the fairy catastrophe is the lever of hope. . . .

EVERYONE AN ATHLETE

134   The country is covered with universities and colleges for men and colleges for women. Education is a great concern among Americans. One of the directors of Princeton University says: "We make athletes of our young men, including the puny ones."

Everyone an athlete!

The big games in America take place on Saturday afternoon and bring together in stadiums scattered all over the country crowds of sixty thousand spectators to watch the two teams. The big games are played between universities: Yale vs. Princeton, Columbia vs. Harvard, etc. . . . The study of science and arts and letters is not compromised. The day has twenty-four hours, hasn't it — time enough to furnish the spirit and develop the body?

College? Americans constantly say: "At college . . ." It reflects the presence in their hearts of a great and fine period — the fine period in their lives. Luxurious fraternities at the universities throughout the country continue to bring together serious businessmen, and prolong through life the radiance of the years of youth.

Colleges and universities, then, have a very particular char-/acter. Everything in the interest of comfort, everything for the sake of calm and serenity, everything to make solid bodies. Each college or university is an urban unit in itself, a small or large city. But a *green city.* Lawns, parks, stadiums, cloisters, dining halls, a whole complex of comfortable quarters. Often the style is Gothic — that's the way it is! — rich, luxurious, well made. There is an abundance of money. A millionaire or the widow of a millionaire gladly wills a fortune to the men's or women's college where they were so happy at twenty.

That's fine, I think. Nevertheless, during these splendid visits I think of the life of students in Paris — that of most of them: seventh floor, attic, faucet on the stair landing, Venetian heat in the summer, Siberia in the winter. Dread of solitude in the very center of the immense city. I went through it myself. Is that hard school of life a fruitful education or a public danger? The students of Paris, in poor shape physically, ill fed, living in the promiscuity of alleys and dark stairways, austerely mix the knowledge of the sciences with that of life. It is not in conformity with Taylorism and time for everything. Remaining uncertain, I refrain from passing judgment. In the copious abundance of American colleges bathed in verdure, the poor are fully welcome: there is a perhaps touching method which enables them to enjoy the benefits of college and to achieve their purpose: study, learning. They pay in kind; part of their time is spent in service, in waiting on tables in the dining hall and making up rooms. Americans are eminently democratic; no servitude is involved: I pay my way, hence I am free. Thus, equivalent rights and complete fellowship. Sectarian spirits will declare that the class struggle is involved. Objectively, in the real conditions of the USA, this seemed to me an intelligent and generous solution.

The American university is a world in itself, a temporary paradise, a gracious stage of life. . . .

I make a trip to Vassar, a college for girls

from well-to-do families. . . .

136   The buildings are scattered over lawns in a splendid park. Before my speech, I go to see the theater where I am to talk. A dozen girls are taking down the sets of a play put on the evening before. They designed and executed the sets themselves: framework, plywood panels, saws, nails, hammers, and pliers, jars of color and brushes. They are in overalls or in bathing suits. I enjoy looking at these beautiful bodies, made healthy and trim by physical training.

137   The buildings have the atmosphere of luxurious clubs. The girls are in a convent for four years. A joyous convent.

Two hours later the theater is invaded by six hundred of them. "Good heavens," I say to myself, fortified by previous experiences at American universities, "how am I going to hold the attention of those twelve hundred laughing eyes?" I talked in French throughout my tour. Make a sounding, try a facetious remark. It works! They got it, everyone understood! I never had a more responsive audience during my trip. It is a pleasure and I amuse myself by developing the bold theses for which these women will be the best propagandists. After the lecture there is a mob scene: they rush onto the platform and seize five or six large drawings I have just done. To put on walls of the dining room or study? Not at all! They rip them apart, tear them up, cut them into small pieces. A piece for each Amazon. Pens in hand, they cry: "Sign, sign!". . .

At the buffet they did almost as much for me. Some asked my companion whether I preferred blondes or brunettes, others nearly annihilated me with the weight of their questions. I am dumfounded by the nature of the questions: sociology, economics, psychology. They are well informed 138 about the serious / problems of our days. They speak impeccable French. During their college course they may spend a year in France. I have never felt so stupid: "But I am ignorant of the problems which concern you; I am only a city planner and an architect and perhaps an artist. You

overwhelm me, you are too serious, I must be excused, I am going to join the people who are eating cookies!"

There are twelve hundred girls at Vassar.

Curfew is sounded. Some of us meet for a glass of whiskey at the home of a woman who teaches art history. She says that the Ecole des Beaux-Arts in Paris has caused much trouble. A brilliant student who is present is devoting herself to a study of Caravaggio. "You women are also interested in Caravaggio? Why Caravaggio? Because of the psychological turmoil in that equivocal personality. Do you also feel a kind of frustration?" One of the men who teaches the history of art is likewise a student of Caravaggio! Caravaggio, rising from the past, nourishes a part of the American spirit; further, contemporary surrealism has won over the USA, the USA of the hesitant and the troubled.

At Vassar College you discover the hard problems of the American economy, and the uncertainty in the spirit of the American élite. These twelve hundred girls, constantly renewed, are preparing themselves for a great task. In the society of the USA women play a part through their intellectual efforts. . . .

Princeton University, a men's college, is 139 located symmetrically south of New York. An immense institution, a university city composed of parks as far as you can see. At the moment, Princeton is leading the American soccer league. That is not an insignificant fact! Holding the cup or fighting to win it is an intense springboard of solidarity and enthusiasm.

I am faced with the same question: is it a good thing for students to pass four years of happiness in a paradise; or is it better in their student days that they know the whole face of life, with its flaws, its misery, its anguish, its greatness?

These solid boys — all of them athletic — this material security, this simple joy in fellowship, this effortless existence of the young members of the tribe sheltered from contrary winds, this all-pervasive cleanliness, this exceptional domestic comfort, such are the opportunities on the credit side of the American ledger. With us the balance-sheet column is empty. On both sides, I grant that the opportunities for learning, and the manner, are in balance and they are one of the magnificent conquests of civilization.

With us there is no chance of being athletes at the end of our studies!

Throughout the USA the tribes of students camp in luxury. They have their own regulations, their own independent administration, they have the right to initiate programs, they have duties associated with sport. Someone has written that American students have good, frank heads and the eyes of calves. American students live in flocks in rich pastures; French students seem to live individually or in those small groups that form friendships; there are no rich pastures here, but only the atmosphere of lecture rooms in the midst of the arid city. I keep turning the question over, the problem I turn around. I am attracted by the pathos of life and danger; much less by the assurance of spoiled papa's boys, well fed, well washed, well buttoned up. I say 140 to / myself: they are deprived of a powerful food: difficulty. If I add up the operations involved and line them up one after another, I see quite plainly that studying is studying (nose in the books, serene mind, well-furnished stomach, warm room). And that, perhaps, there is a time for everything. When you plant beans it is not customary to put paving stones over them to keep them from growing straight.

American universities are large, rich tribes encamped in the midst of greenery, with the detachment from events which the widespread Gothic style brings. It expresses rather well a type of ideal life, Elysian, theoretical, Paradise to begin life, Hell afterward; a provisional Garden of Eden in which there would be happiness if the boys and girls did not have their own

spiritual uncertainties, like everyone else. Nothing more is needed to restore man to his torment and anxiety. . . .

In the instruction at American universi- 142 ties I think I observe a sort of fear of seeing the doors open on the unknown of tomorrow. The students are serious, balanced, calm; they acquire grades and general coverage insurance. In the halls of M.I.T. I saw huge machines hung on the walls, wash drawings, representing palaces or mausoleums. Boring, shameful. Surrounded by students and some of their teachers, I said: "How is it that you have not done away with these horrors?"

When I speak in the architectural lecture rooms of universities in the USA, I have the feeling that I am presenting dangerously disturbing ideas. They listen to me in a silence that makes me feel that I am not being understood. I throw myself into my large drawings; I put in red, blue, green, black; I write comments, figures. I conclude in a still petrified atmosphere. A student from Columbia came to my hotel to talk to me: "Your one-hour lecture was worth as much to us as three years of our regular course." — "Really?" — "Yes, and we are unanimous about it." How locked up these young people are!

In my seminar at Princeton I am discussing the plans for a villa. In them there are many charming spots designed as successive delights. I say: "It is necessary to choose and limit, to condense: of these scattered good designs, you must make *the* good design, the true one, the right one!" Expressing myself (modestly!) in the manner of Montaigne, I conclude: "Gentlemen, you never have more than one bottom to sit down on!" The teacher and the chairman of the department are present. Silence and embarrassment. — "Will you translate that, please?" — No, you will not translate such a remark in the beautiful, green, Gothic town of Princeton. . . .

Don Iddon

From "American Athletes Are Sissies" in *Coronet,* 31 (February 1952), 34–37. Reprinted from *Coronet,* February 1952 © 1952 by Esquire, Inc.

Mr. Iddon, British journalist, began working as an American correspondent for different British newspapers in 1937. Though he has been termed by some a sensationalist, his column, "Don Iddon's Diary" in the London *Daily Mail* and several other English newspapers, has been the favorite reporting from Manhattan for many British. His book *Don Iddon's America* appeared in 1951.

[THE PAMPERED ATHLETE]

34 THERE is nothing wrong with American sport that a little corporal punishment won't cure. But the chastisement should take place not behind the woodshed but in full view of the public in some stadium, preferably the one at Wembley in London.

As a British correspondent in the U.S., I have watched pampering and effeminacy creep into your ball parks and football grounds. The colossal cult of the American "Mom" and her mawkish devotion to her "boys" are sapping the fiber of the American athlete.

Almost everyone is saying that there is something rotten in American sport when basketball college players are found guilty of accepting bribes wholesale, and football-playing cadets at exalted West Point admit cheating at examinations. The British point of view is merely that your sports have gone soft.

The American athlete has become the spoiled brat of the New World, cuddled and coddled, pampered and petted. Too much money, either in salary or expenses, or both, and too much adulation are lavished on him. He has become a prince of privilege in the thriving Republic.

By contrast, in Britain the athlete remains a working bloke like the rest of the British. He receives no great sums of money for playing, no special perquisites, no fancy fees for radio and television appearances. He is not allowed to accept gifts. And he has never been known to accept a bribe.

British sports are tough, British sportsmen are tougher — probably because British sport is more adult. It is my belief that almost every major American sport derives from English children's games.

In England we call baseball "rounders" and it is played only by toddlers and young girls. Basketball is "net ball" in our language, and strictly for girls and infants. Bowling is "skittles," a juvenile or senile diversion in our islands. And / as for ice 35 hockey, allegedly the toughest of sports, this was adapted from English field hockey, the national sport of British schoolgirls.

At the risk of offending, I have to tell you that whenever an American newsreel showing American football players in their outlandish padded costumes and helmets appears on an English screen, the audience hoots with laughter. Why the armor plate? The crash helmet? The shoulder and knee pads?

We play a type of football similar to yours. In Britain it is called Rugby and it is a rugged game. No one ever wears any padding or a helmet, and it is even considered affected to put on a pair of shin guards or ear protectors. The current crop of Rugby players troop on the field and stay there (there are no substitutes), wearing a pair of studded shoes, stockings, pants, and a jersey. And that is all.

The American practice of substitutions — the incredible platoon system in football is the worst example — has little relation to sport. To replace a man because he is playing badly, or even when he is injured, would be unthinkable in Britain. The basic appeal in sport should be the sense of contest and of hazard. A team fighting with its back to the wall, perhaps short two men and with another injured, is a gallant and inspiring spectacle.

Such spectacles are common on the Rugby and soccer grounds of Britain. For a coach or manager to be able to remove a man at whim is a practice from which the British would recoil. The only time a football player, or a cricket player for that matter, is ever ordered from the field, is when he is offensive to the referee or umpire. Sometimes, of course, a player is compelled to leave the playing field because of an injury, but then he is carried out on a stretcher.

British football players have been known to carry on in many games with broken collar bones, sprained ankles, and torn cartilages. What we do is put the injured player "on the wing," where he is least likely to sustain further injury.

In recent years the British athlete has been on an austerity diet like the rest of his countrymen. While your players have been fed meat, cream, and butter, ours have nibbled at synthetic sausage, bits of vegetables, indigestible pigeon, rabbit, and a monotonous diet of fish. Fair food shares for all? Not in international sport.

Many times your athletes, particularly your golfers, have gone over to England and Scotland laden with steaks and food parcels. They have eaten the best while our men have fed on food which the average American dog might spurn. Perhaps we should not complain. This enforced Spartan diet may be one of the reasons why British athletes are tougher than American.

It seems to me that the strangest phenomenon in American sports is the coach. Apparently he is regarded as a combination of elder statesman, father confessor, and mother superior. From what I hear and see, he is also the mastermind, a repository of all the talents. I have seen him as the inspired orator, haranguing the cowed team in the dressing room, admonishing, gesticulating, sweeping from stanza to stanza until 36 the eloquent climax / with finger pointed to the field, the "go in to win for dear old ——."

We have, of course, coaches in British sports, but the man's position is not one of great power. The key man is the captain of the team, who takes the field himself. Once on the field the team is on its own. There are no orders shouted from the touch line or bench. The captain is in charge and what he says goes. And if he has a bad day and his direction is incompetent, then it is just too bad for himself and for the team.

Managers of teams give guidance and help during the days before the match, but their role is mainly administrative. The great emphasis in all British sports is on team spirit. There is an old British bromide — "the game's the thing" — and it is considered more important to play a good and fair game than to win it.

We do not pamper our players. The stars of a football team or cricket team, if they are professionals, receive no more money than a mediocre member of the team. Before the war a player in a first-division team received eight guineas a week (at that time around $33) and a bonus of one guinea for a tie and two for a win. Today, the basic salary is 15 pounds (around $42).

Even Alex James, the wonder player, whose appearance in a game added 15,000 to the gate, was paid the same salary as any raw newcomer. James earned a little on the side, writing newspaper articles and endorsing advertised products, but he never received fabulous sums on the Babe Ruth or DiMaggio scale.

Temperament and temper are not tolerated in British sports. A couple of years ago, a major-league soccer team paid a fabulous sum for an international player. Soon afterwards, the man had an argument with the referee and was ordered off the field, and his team played the rest of the game one man short.

The international player never played on that British team again. He was traded to a minor team for almost nothing, and although his genius as a soccer player was recognized everywhere, no major club has ever tried to buy him. If you don't have the guts to play according to the rules, you have no place in English sport.

James Morris

Mr. Morris, born in 1926, is on the editorial staff of the London *Times*. He has been sent over the years as a special correspondent to Egypt, Scandinavia, the Netherlands, India, and North America. Perhaps his most interesting assignment was the one which sent him with the British Mt. Everest Expedition in 1953. During 1953–1954, as a Commonwealth Fund Fellow in the United States, he gathered material for *As I Saw the U.S.A.* He was appointed Middle East correspondent for the *Times* in 1955.

[VIOLENCE]

32 . . . in America, and not least in the East, you are never far from brutality; it is part of the stimulation of the country that the old arguments of force are still, so often, tacitly valid. It is not only that crimes of violence are still so common, that feuds and acts of cruel revenge are recorded in the papers almost every day; the whole national conception of self-advancement and perpetual competition presupposes an attitude of no-holds-barred. Most Americans are accustomed to violence. Elderly ladies will drive their cars undaunted through the ghastly shoving turmoil of city traffic, readier to push than be pushed; on the frantic highways leading into the great metropolises they demand no courtesies if they stall or take the wrong turning, but simply barge back into the race again, brazenly. Indeed, Americans enjoy violence more than most people. I remember a moment in a big stockyard when, pressed to inspect the slaughtering process, I had turned away sickened at the sight; only to see a pretty young mother in a white hat holding up her child for a better view. Extortion and corruption is a commonplace (at least by hearsay) to most Americans. Mild shopkeepers in the industrial cities of the East will admit without excitement that they pay protection money to gangsters or crooked policemen. In New York recently it was announced that no less than one quarter of the city's mobile police force had been involved in a system of organized bribery. You can sense this underlying savagery, restrained, of course, but present, at many gatherings of respectable business people; among the Elks or the Kiwanians; at the dinner tables of the ambitious; anywhere in America where you feel the slogan of philosophy to be: "If you don't want to get on, move over, bud, and make way for a guy who does!". . .

[THE SOUTH]

You may well hate the South, but you 49 can never accuse it of dull uniformity, for it is a pungent entity of its own. It is not simply a region; it is an amalgam of sensations, memories, prejudices and emotions; a place of symbols, where excesses of nostalgia can be prompted by the cadence of a voice or a glimpse of a crumbling mansion. . . .

The nature of the country itself contrib- 51 utes to the oppressive quality of the South. It is, generally speaking, a wide, dry, dusty, spiritless country; sometimes hauntingly beautiful, but usually melancholy; lacking robustness, good cheer, freshness, animation; a singularly un-Dickensian country. As you drive through South Carolina (for example) on a summer day the endless cotton fields engulf you. Here and there are shabby villages, dusty and derelict, with patched wooden buildings and rusting advertisements, and with a few dispirited people, white and black, gathered outside the stores. Outside the unpainted houses of the poor whites there are often decrepit cars, and washing machines stand white among the cluttered objects on the verandas. Sometimes there is a little white church with a crooked steeple. There are frequent swamps, dark and mildewy, with gloomy trees standing in the water. The plantation mansions are sometimes magnificent, but often in depressingly bad repair.

I called at one such house for a talk with its owner and found it no more than a sad echo of a munificent past. Three generations ago the Parker plantation included some 10,000 acres, and was one of the great estates of the region. Now it is whittled down to about 150 acres, of cotton, tobacco, sweet potatoes and corn. The drive up to the house is a narrow one between pine trees, unpaved; a cloud of dust rose up behind us as we drove along it. Near the road there were a couple of small wooden shacks, one of them inhabited, for there was 52 a string of washing outside it, / the other filled to the eaves with straw; and far at the end of the drive stood the big house, crumbling, classical, reminding me of Pharaoh's Palace at Petra, seen through the crevice of the *sik*. It had a wide and splendid porch, with four pillars. Mrs. Parker thought that only Washington or Thomas Jefferson could really do justice to it, but I felt myself better qualified to sit there when I noticed that its broad steps were rickety, that the frame of its front door was sagging, and that high in its roof there was a dormant wasp nest. Inside the house was agreeably untidy; in the hall, which ran clean through the building front to back, there was an elderly harmonium, with a large hymn book propped on its music stand.

The planter, fresh from a tussle with his tractor, had greasy hands and wore a topee and an open-necked shirt. But like most southern gentlemen he had a talent for hospitality, and soon we were sitting on the balustrade of the porch, sipping long cool drinks and looking out through the pines. He told me that he ran the plantation almost single-handed, with only one full-time employee (paid two and a half dollars a day, plus a free house). His children go to the local public school and his wife does the housework. The five cabins on the estate are let to Negro families whose men work elsewhere, sometimes giving part-time help on the plantation; and "The Street," the double row of uniform cottages where the slaves used to live, is empty and tumbledown.

While we were talking on the porch a great cloud of dust approached us from the drive, and there emerged in stately motion two large mules. They were pulling a kind of sledge, a cross between a bobsleigh and Cleopatra's barge, and sitting on it, very old and wrinkled, very dignified, was a Negro in a straw hat. Round the corner he came in imperial state, the mules panting, the sledge creaking, the dust billowing all round us; and as he passed the porch he raised his hat by its crown and called: "G'd evening, boss, sir; g'd evening, Missus Parker." "Good evening, Uncle Henry," they replied.

Uncle Henry well illustrates the sad contradictions of the southern mind. He is an old retainer of the Parkers who lives almost entirely upon their kindness. He is given a house and a few acres, firewood and storage space, and a loan when he needs one. The planter would not see him in distress for the world. / He humors the old man's 53 whims, never complaining at waste nor demanding recompense; enjoying watching Uncle Henry sail by on his sledge, kicking up the dust all over the porch. He likes exchanging greetings and accepting respect. He is sincere and generous in his charity. But to suggest that Mr. Parker might invite Uncle Henry into the house, or even shake hands with him, would be more than an impertinence; it might, such is the sudden intensity of passion in the warm South, be construed as a deliberate insult. Uncle Henry will always have a home; but, after all, the race must be preserved.

So there is a tinge of cruelty even to southern kindliness; but the legend of crinolines, sweet accents and scented summer evenings is not altogether a myth. I found myself wallowing, no less, in the fabled charm of the South during a hot summer stay at Oxford, Mississippi. This is a market

MORRIS   *As I Saw the U. S. A.*   99

and university town made famous by William Faulkner, who is a native of the place; and it is bursting with the combination of sordidness and heavy beauty that is the fascination of the South. The town is built around a central square and in the middle of it all is the courthouse, center of justice and administration, solid and ornate, a-flutter with notice boards. Under the shade of the trees that surround this building the people of Oxford laze the hours away. There are innumerable old men whose chins are prickly with white stubble, wearing wide hats, chewing tobacco, spitting, and determinedly lounging. Little knots of Negroes gather separately, like boys from another form, who are not privileged to undo the second button of their jacket, or walk on the grass in Great Quad. Farmers, negligently sitting on parapets and leaning against walls, offer vegetables and fruits for sale. Little boys run up and down the steps, and through the courthouse, from one brown swing door to the other. Outside the hotel a few idle guests are reclining in chairs, smoking; a gaggle of plump women is doing its shopping in the square. On the first floor verandas of the buildings (their style reminiscent sometimes of the Wild West, sometimes of New Orleans, sometimes of the shuttered balconies of Bagdad) lawyers and realtors, in shirtsleeves, are exchanging business advice. The streets are dirty and dusty, and there is a tobacco-stained, beer-ringed ashtray atmosphere to the scene.

All around the square, though, are streets
54 of lovely old houses; / white and creeper-clad, with graceful porches and refreshing gardens; shaded by old trees in secluded corners, with tactful Negroes working in the gardens, and fountains watering the lawns. At dusk in summer these streets are suffused with an aromatic charm. The air is heavy and warm, and laden with the scent of roses and honeysuckle. Children scamper among the gardens, in and out of narrow lanes. Sometimes there is the sound of laughter from inside a house, or the raised voice of a scolding Negro mammy.

A languid content lies thickly over the town, and down in the square the old men loll silently. I can smell Oxford, Mississippi, now, 4,000 miles away — a smell compact of flowers and dust and old buildings — and still feel the lazy seduction of its manner.

Indeed, the South is full of pleasant encounters. The poor white, a shambling, ill-jointed, colorless, ungainly figure of a man, gives the region an air of ignorant meanness; but even he has his agreeable side, and when the mountaineers go square dancing they make a gay company. I remember an evening of square dancing in the streets of Chattanooga, Tennessee, in the Middle South. The roads were closed to traffic, and a hillbilly band played from the back of a truck. In the dim lights of the street lamps the dancers looked like sinewy leprechauns in check shirts and flounced skirts, prancing with an infectious abandon. They danced till late at night, and then piled into their disjointed trucks to drive back to shambling villages and isolated poor broken farmhouses, with mules and water wells, or to dirty wooden cabins hidden away in the hills.

In another kind, I recall with affection the crusty bachelor who lives alone at the mansion of Longwood, outside Natchez, Mississippi. Natchez, once a lawless river port, famous for thieves and gamblers and horsetraders, has acquired an excessive southern fragility because of its many well-preserved old houses (old, that is, by the standards of the inland South; they are mostly early nineteenth century, and, despite the hushed pride of the local ladies, are furnished much as our grandmothers' houses were furnished in England). The regional myth is thus powerful here. Racial animosities are especially bitter, and many people (seeing themselves, perhaps, as present-day O'Haras) proclaim a pride in poverty. Longwood is the oddest of the mansions of / Natchez. It was begun 55 shortly before the Civil War, a wild architectural extravaganza, octagonal, topped with a dome, surrounded by balconies.

Northern workmen were brought in to work on it, but soon after the war began they were withdrawn; they dropped their tools and left, leaving the house unfinished; and unfinished it remains, with their hammers and wheelbarrows and paint pots still lying about, with ladders propped against walls, and scaffolding still in place, exactly as they left it. It stands in a wooded garden, a grotesque monument of "steamboat Gothic," its glassless windows gaping, on its porch a dusty and disintegrating barouche. . . .

As for the country Negroes, they seem identical still with those pictured in old prints of the slave-owning times; still toiling half naked in the fields, still addicted 56 to color and gaudy / ornaments, still full of song, still ignorant and unorganized; a people of bondage, infinitely pitiful. They look like well-trained domestic animals as they board the buses, confined to the back seats, sitting blankly by the windows with their parcels on their laps; and often, when the drink is in them, they develop an animal ferocity. Few of them appear to think deeply about their social status, but they reflect it often enough in a sad apathy. I talked once with a Negro farmer in Alabama, and asked him if things were getting any better for the colored people. "Things ain't gettin' no better, suh," he said, "and things ain't gettin' no worse. They jess stay the same. Things can't ever get no better for the colored people, not so long as we stay down here." He was not so badly off, though. He owned his few acres of land, and lived in his own house. He had two mules. But he seemed incapable of ambition or aspiration, and his two sons had left him, and gone off to Chicago in an old car, to work out their salvation among its slums and rubbish. Another farmer I met seemed to think I was representing some political group, perhaps the Communist party, which has been active in the South. "We can't change things down here by ourselves," he said, and added with an unpleasantly suggestive leer: "Not by ourselves, that is, not without people to

help us." He was surrounded by a swarm of children as he spoke; poor little creatures, they were very scabrous pickaninnies, and badly needed some soap behind the ears.

The southern Negro still retains his traditional gaiety, all the same, whether expressed in riotous jazz in a New Orleans bar, or in the flashing smile of a train conductor. My wife and I once took a middle-aged Negro woman to the zoo at Jackson, Mississippi; she viewed every animal with hand-clapping delight, as pleased with the elephant as she was with the alligator, eating a messy ice cream as she wandered, in a blue floral dress and a hat with a feather in it. Another old Negro woman, encountered on the edge of a swamp in Louisiana, was fishing in the oozy water with a long home-cut rod. She had already caught a few fish, and they were floundering in the shallows tied up in a net. She told me she had been dropped there that morning from the train, which passed near by; her husband worked on the railroads, and in the evening, when the train came back / again, it would slow down past the 57 swamp and allow her to scramble aboard a freight car with her rod and her net of fish, clutching her enormous floppy straw hat. She asked me to drive a little way down the road and fetch some Coca-Cola. I bought her four bottles, and she seemed well satisfied; the last I saw of her, she was standing on the boggy bank with the rod in one hand and a bottle raised to her lips with the other; a portly, statuesque figure against a gloomy background of cypress trees.

For me, the temper of the deep South is best exemplified by the city of Memphis, on the Mississippi River. It is a sprawling place with a business district of assertive skyscrapers and a fine promenade along the river; and it is alive with the familiar associations of the South. Here W. C. Handy wrote the Memphis Blues. He is honored by a shabby little park in the Negro district. All around it the black people move with loose-limbed grace, through dirty streets full of pawnbrokers and rooming houses and cheap clothing stores, with pictures of

Negro actresses in their windows. Cotton, the master crop of the old South, rules Memphis still. Here are the offices of the great cotton brokers, and you can see bales of the stuff lying outside their doors. One of the big hotels is called the King Cotton. There is violent racial feeling in Memphis, and much political chicanery; when I was there E. H. Crump, most famous of the "bosses," was still in power, a funny old man with a wizened face and a wide-brimmed hat, who liked going to football matches; at election time one was offered a list of candidates "approved by Mr. Crump."

There was a battle of Memphis in the Civil War, and a naval engagement on the river, watched by huge crowds lining the banks. You can hardly escape the river there, for it bounds the business section, and there are always towboats passing by and hooters sounding; "river rats," shanty-men and the like live along its banks (until recently there was one slovenly shack dweller who had an Oxford degree and talked, in his cloaca, in an impeccable English accent). Memphis has its share of southern high spirits, too; the Cotton Carnival, held annually in May, is the least inhibited of American festivals. In the lobby of one of the hotels five ducks live comfortably in an ornamental fountain; each evening they waddle in file into a passenger lift and are taken up to the roof for the night.

58 Memphis is heavy with prejudice and poverty, but buoyant with a primitive gusto. For many people in several states it represents the lights and the music, excitement, opportunity, grace, culture, fun; they marvel at its flashing signs, its cool riverside parks, its hint of elegance and friendly charm; and indeed, seen at night across the dismal dust of the cotton fields, or from the steps of some miserable one-roomed hovel, it seems the very embodiment of the fabled southern flavor. . . .

[RELIGION IN THE SOUTH]

64 The most primitive white people in all America, infinitely nearer the trees than any rural ancient in England, are the mountaineers of Kentucky and Tennessee, a peasantry of the hills which has never totally accepted authority, and which manages to remain a shuttered society tucked away in remote country corners. These folk still consider taxation a wicked alien imposition, distill their own moonshine whisky in defiance of local prohibition laws, and sometimes speak an archaic Scots-Elizabethan dialect; their raggedy children run barefoot about their cabins on the hillsides, and often and again there comes news that one horny mountaineer has disintegrated another with a blast from his shotgun. When I was staying in Lookout Mountain, on the border between Georgia and Tennessee, I saw a good deal of these people, for many of them live quite close to the luxurious suburb that has been built on top of the mountain; and you could scarcely escape experiencing, in one way or another, the extraordinarily earthy force of their religion, a force that pervades the whole of the South, but is to be found in its most curious forms among these simple and conservative countrymen.

One evening my wife and I were driving down a road on the outskirts of Chattanooga when we saw, pitched beside the pavement, a dirty marquee; from it there came strains of music, played on a tinny piano and a guitar, with accompanying desultory snatches of women's voices. We stopped at once and went inside. At the end of the tent, on stage, so to speak, a very fat woman was lying on the ground quivering and shaking, sometimes tremulously, like a jelly, sometimes with sharp stabs of impulsive movement. Her dress was pulled up above her fleshy knees, sweat was on her forehead, a black hat was lying crumpled beside her, and she was breathing noisily. Two other women, wearing expressions of fanatical intensity, were supporting her head, and standing above them, waving his arms like a Paganini, prancing here and there crazily, now and then pushing back his / streaming hair with dirty-nailed fin- 65 gers, was a young man holding a guitar.

In the background a little black girl, aged about ten, was banging a hymn tune on an upright piano, and a small group of Negro women, respectably dressed, looking a trifle bored, and sometimes pausing to exchange gossip or look out of the tent flap, was half-heartedly singing some unlikely words.

The Lord is my brethren, my brethren is he;
Alone in the storm or the rage of the sea
I'll never go hungry or know poverty
So long as the good Lord is marching with
me.
Marching with me! Marching with thee!
So long as the good Lord is marching with
me!

Occasionally the young man would strum a few chords on his guitar and join in, his voice rasping and penetrative, and soon the prostrate woman, with heavings and convulsions and agonized writhing, tried to gasp a few words herself, rather as the dying man at the end of one of Poe's more terrifying stories wheezed a last phrase before dissolving into pulp. The two attendant women were galvanized. Seizing the patient (if that is the right word) by the front of her dress, they yanked her into a sitting position, and hissed urgent instructions into her ear. She was still jerking incessantly, sometimes falling sideways, to be pushed upright again, sometimes caught in mid-air as she fell backwards. "Take Him in!" said the attendants. "Take in the Lord Jesus! Roll it! Roll Him in! Take Him in! Oh Jesus! The glory of it! Rolling, rolling, rolling! Glory, glory, glory! Jesus, Jesus! Take Him in, oh! glory Jesus! Rolling, rolling, rolling!" Round and round danced the demoniac guitarist. On and on went the hymn, balefully; clang, clang sounded the old piano. The woman on the floor threw her body, as if in some hellish trance, into even more violent convulsions. "Take Him in! oh, rolling, rolling, rolling! Glory!"

There were rows of chairs in the body of the tent, and a few people were sitting in them silently, not together, but dotted about in the shadows. In front of me a middle-aged man was supporting a woman who was still jerking spasmodically from some earlier experience. A mother, gazing blankly and open-/mouthed at the specta- 66 cle, had with her two children, a small girl who sat on her chair sucking her thumb, and a boy who had reached that stage of squirming sordidness peculiar to children nearing exhaustion. A stout, sensible-looking man near the entrance to the tent told me that we were witnessing a session of Holy Rollers, a sect (he thought, he was not sure) affiliated to the Church of God. This strange church is indigenous to the South. It began as a group of fundamentalists who broke away from the existing non-conformist churches because they were losing the uninhibited emotionalism of the frontier times, and becoming more formal in their modes of worship. In Tennessee there are innumerable such dissident sects, calling themselves Pentecostal Churches, or Holiness Chapels, or a host of other grandiose titles; but the chief ones banded together to become the Church of God. It flourished, and achieved (relatively speaking) some intellectual maturity, founding a theological college at Cleveland, Tennessee. Though it had no ordained clergy, and believed in some odd manifestations of the Divine purpose, it acquired a status of local dignity. But alas! there were differences within the hierarchy, and before long there was a sprout of little, disagreeing Churches of God: the Church of God (Tomlinson); the (original) Church of God, and the Church of God With Signs Following After.

The one whose ceremonies we were watching expounded the sacred significance of the "jerks" — the convulsions, voluntary and induced, which racked the woman on the floor. She evidently suffered from some disease, and believed that if the spirit entered into her (manifesting itself in jumps, jerks, falling, rolling, the wringing of hands and gibberish) it would be cured. "And they were all filled with the Holy Ghost," says the Acts of the Apostles of the day of

Pentecost, "and began to speak with other tongues, as the Spirit gave them utterance." The followers of "the old religion," as these strange cults are familiarly called, believe that some of their number have acquired the understanding of unknown languages; and sure enough, as the hours passed, there crept into the insistent cries of the attendant women some words without meaning. Soon it was pouring out in floods from their mouths, a wild flow of words, like Romany or Lear; and occasionally even the patient herself, jerking and jumping, man-/aged to croak from her constricted throat a few totally unintelligible syllables. ("These men are full of new wine," said the mocking doubters of Jerusalem.) When we left the marquee she was still unhealed. The guitarist still whirled about her; the piano still tinnily clanged; the choristers, their great brown and white eyes rolling around the tent, still whined their listless hymn; the little boy still crawled slimily over the chairs, on and off his mother's lap; and the poor convulsed patient, all her draperies loose by now, was still urged to "let Him in, sister! Glory, glory, roll it, roll it!" by the demon women at her side.

Some of the mountain religions are even more strikingly close to the grass roots of Christianity. I remember standing in the garden of a gentle Southerner who has built his house on the sheer side of Lookout Mountain, where it runs away down to Georgia and Alabama. We were waiting for the sun to set, for he has a theory that if you look at Jupiter backwards, through a mirror, you can see her moons with the naked eye. The view was splendid. Below us, in the valley, the high road ran southwards to Atlanta; beyond it rose another range of hills, and another, wooded and kindly, with a little clearing here and there and a white farmhouse, or a cabin with its smallholding; and to our left the great rib of Lookout Mountain stretched into the distance. We stood on the precipitous edge of the garden, hoping to see a fox or a badger in the woods below, and my host said: "Ah

have lived in this region all mah life, but ah can never accustom myself to the idea that some of mah neighbors are snake-worshippers."

He was exaggerating a little, I learned on pressing inquiries (a gift for stretching the facts being one of the more endearing southern failings), but not too much. Not very far away, at the hamlet of Grasshopper, Tennessee, there had originated a sect which based its beliefs upon the last verses of the Gospel according to Saint Mark: "And these signs shall follow them that believe: In my name shall they cast out devils; they shall speak with new tongues; they shall take up serpents; and if they drink any deadly thing, it shall not hurt them; they shall lay hands on the sick, and they shall recover." Believing these words to be an injunction as well as a prophecy, members of the Church of God With Signs Following After make a practice of handling rattle-/snakes during their services. Often they are bitten, sometimes fatally, but though the custom is now illegal in Tennessee it persists widely and more or less openly. Now and again there is a news item about a particularly severe case of biting; occasionally some faded holy man appears in court; but in general it is tacitly accepted as "something that happens on the mountain." I was directed to a church, secluded among the woods, where I was told I could see this thing (the element of the circus about it, I must admit, drawing me more magnetically than any theological implications); but the place was deserted when I reached it, and a farmer sitting on the porch of a near-by shack only murmured incoherently when I asked him for advice. Such esoteric rites, though, were never far away from life on Lookout Mountain; I remember one elderly carpenter, himself an elder or preacher, prophet or evangelist, I forget which, remarking to me quite casually as he did some sandpapering: "I was brought up with the jerks, and the talking with tongues, but I don't hold with the serpents."

Even the more orthodox worshippers of the Bible belt sometimes express their devotion strangely. I spent an Easter Day in the region of Chattanooga, and wandered about during its sunny morning observing the celebrations. For many weeks people had been preparing for Easter in one way or another. The garages were full of cars being washed (for it is a matter of social prestige to drive a shining car to Easter Communion). The shops were full of excited women; the telephones were always engaged, it being a season of invitations; from every store window there glared the stony glass eyes of the Easter Bunny, the American secular symbol of the festival.

Noisy evangelism dominated the radio programs, but there was still time for a few such songs as "I was riding to Chapel on Easter Morning . . . when I saw the cutest Easter parade." When I visited the cable office to send a telegram, I was nicely asked if I would care to send an Easter Bunny-gram instead; several suitable messages were suggested, a typical one being: "The Easter Bunny is on his way — So be a good little boy (girl) every day." The city of Chattanooga was alive with activity from earliest morning. At sunrise there was a mass evangelical meeting, attended by a brigade of clerics, the Governor of Tennes-/ 69 see, and trumpeteers who greeted the sunrise with a fanfare. By mid-morning the streets were thronged with churchgoers of many denominations. Bright convertibles hurried through the sunshine, father driving in a gray suit with a carnation buttonhole, mother clutching her picture hat, Sis in a very flouncy party dress, Junior being scolded for leaning out of the car. Negro families were as bright as peacocks in smiles and fripperies, and innumerable small boys of some unidentified youth group marched about the place in white ducks and blue tunics. Sitting in a car outside the courthouse I saw a young Negro, looking extremely worried, listening to a threatening sermon (all hell-fire and penitence) on the radio. Almost everybody seemed to be going to church; leaving only a few faithless, in

grubby shirts or flowered housecoats, reading the Sunday papers on the porches of their homes.

I drove out of the town toward the Georgia border, and before long stopped at a small white wooden Baptist church on a ridge. It was a sunny day, and the door of the church was open. Outside a few boys were playing about in the dust with sticks; through the door I glimpsed a pastiche of open-necked shirts and head scarves, baggy trousers and garish cotton frocks from country stores. A very slow and tuneless hymn was being sung. A few members of the congregation stirred as I put my head diffidently around the doorpost; I caught the eye of a red-haired girl of a sluggish aspect, still mouthing the words of the hymn as she stared, but so unaccountably enthralled by my arrival that the voice faded from her throat. She nudged her husband, who whispered to an old man holding a large hymn book to the level of his eyes, who turned around with a great clattering of feet and wheezing; and presently a space was cleared for me on a bench near the back of the church. The congregation was constantly in motion. There were many young mothers with children, and whenever a baby began to cry it was carried out of the church; so that before long, out in the sunny road, there were numbers of women strolling up and down, dressed in their fineries, crooning to their babies. Now and again a couple of men went out for a breath of fresh air, or some latecomer pushed his way in with heavily whispered greetings and some muted badinage. The church was hot and airless.

The order of service was complicated. A 70 number of elderly men with grave faces took it in turn to read lessons or deliver impassioned impromptu sermons. They were called to these duties by a man who was evidently the pastor; he was fat and perspiring, dressed in a gray double-breasted suit with a garish tie, and holding perpetually under his arm a book which, by its binding and deportment, could only be of utter sanctity. He stood expansively in the middle of a raised platform at the end of the church, ushering elder after elder to the rostrum with reverent gestures. Sometimes he made an appeal for some worthy cause ("Can you sit and see, brethern and sisters, sit and see these little ones suffer? Think again, my friends, think again, dear brethern, and deliver unto us some trifle, some poor offering, some widow's mite for the Society for the Protection of Orphans of the Storm.") Sometimes he threatened those who did not regularly attend church, and on these occasions I sometimes thought the dread fire of his eye landed directly on me. "There may be some among you, my friends, I make no accusations, I say unto no one 'Thou art fit for hell-fire,' but I say again, brethern, there may be among you, here among us today, here in this sacred edifice, among these hearts lifted unto the Lord, some sinner, some poor wicked sinner, who does not come each Sabbath Day unto this edifice to offer praise and thanksgiving with us. If there be such, my friends, I say unto him, 'Brother, the sun doth not shine so hotly — nor the winds blow so cruelly — nor the ice freeze so cold — as the everlasting torments which thou art storing up for thyself in the everlasting awful halls of perpetual damnation!'"

Hymn followed hymn, and gradually I sensed among the worshippers a growing intensity of devotion. An old bespectacled farmer stood alone at the rostrum to sing an unaccompanied hymn, and during the performance some of the massed elders began to interrupt him with mournful shouts of "Amen, amen! Glory be! Amen!" These interpolations grew more frequent during the succeeding hymns, and soon the whole congregation (barring a few totally insensible yokels) seemed gripped by some undefined passion, and stood singing the hymns with a strange tenseness. Four young men with a banjo sang a long Easter hymn, *molto adagio,* and during this the elders fostered in / themselves a regular frenzy of devotion. From all corners of the room there now came deep-throated "Amens!" with supplications, ejaculations, cries of

joy and despair and awful imprecations. "Oh yes, Lord! That's right, Lord! Jesus, Jesus! Ah glory be to the Lord! Yes! Oh, oh, save us, glory be! O Lord save us miserable sinners! Oh, the hell-fire! Must we be condemned, Lord? Oh, no, glory be! The hell-fire! Glory be! Save us, save us! They shall be cast into the darkness of the pit! Hallelujah! Hallelujah, hallelujah, hallelujah, glory, glory, glory, glory be!!! Amen! Yes, Lord, glory be, amen, miserable sinners!"

By now the scene was one of general confusion. Everywhere men were raising their arms to the heavens, or clutching at their hair with both hands. Around me people were swaying from side to side, muttering snatches of prayer, or suddenly bursting into ear-splitting yells of "Glory!! Glory be!!!" The pastor strode between the ranks of his flock, the book still under his arm, alternately denouncing and beseeching its members. "Oh, you poor miserable brethern, poor suffering sheep, repent, repent! My friends, come with me and repent! Come to the altar! The fires of everlasting perpetual hell will be upon you for ever and ever! The flames of the inferno will lick you, my brethern! Oh, you sinners, you wicked children of sin, it is not too late. No! Come to the altar! Will you come, my friends? Will you come? Ah, salvation! Come, my friends, miserable sinners!" At the end of the church the quartet was now singing a syncopated hymn, to the strumming accompaniment of the banjo. Now and then, through the babel, I could hear some of its words:

> I'd rather be a beggar and live
> In a shack beside the road
> Than lay up treasure without
> Arranging for a future abode.

The minister shouted harder and more furiously, and eventually one or two elderly men, shaking with emotion, staggered out of their benches and threw themselves on the floor. Others followed, and soon from all parts of the church groups of quivering worshippers were moving toward the front,

71

72 to hurl / themselves out of my sight beyond the benches. The pastor swirled around them, shrieking commands and entreaties; the tears were streaming down his cheeks. A number of women were sobbing helplessly, and large numbers of children were screaming, and the strident cries of the elders filled the church.

At once deafened and bewitched, I left the building in a kind of blasted trance, and stood for a moment on the steps. A small boy who had been kicking stones about the road approached me with the information that, according to his mother, the pastor was a genuine saint; that he lived in the mountains and drove twenty miles to the church every Sunday; and that his grandfather was a full-blooded Cherokee Indian. I thanked him, and drove away down the country road, pursued by the raucous cacophony from the church; the faint earnest voices of the singers, the thump-thump of the tireless piano, and an occasional penetrating "Hallelujah, Lord! Glory, glory be!!"

In every hamlet and prosperous suburb, as I travelled back to Chattanooga through the sunshine, the churchgoers were on the move again, home to a handsome lunch. Whether they had echoed the cool formality of an English cathedral, or had screamed their declamations to the Almighty, they went home contented, each in his way. And perhaps nearest to the soul of the South were those determined *yogis,* hidden away in mountain cabins, who had spent their Easter morning among the serpents. . . .

HOLLYWOOD

157   Long after the Industrial Revolution in England the Pacific coast of the United States remained unspoiled and idyllic, all the way from the forests of Washington state to the Spanish shore of southern California. Times have abruptly changed, for at its most delectable point, where the mountains come down to the sea, the Americans have built Los Angeles, and for most people that hectic complexity has become representative of the region. I have never experienced a less pleasing contrast than the one which overwhelms the traveller, in his innocence, as he journeys out of Nevada across California and into the frenetic bustle of Los Angeles.

The city sprawls from the sea for many miles inland, an enormous mess of related townships, criss-crossed by big busy roads, blotched by dingy quarters of poor whites and Mexicans, given its reputation of fabulous peculiarity by the mansions of the film magnates and the glamorous streets of shops and hotels that surround the studios of Hollywood. The business area of Los Angeles is drab and ugly; the long line of the beaches has been spoiled by relentless exploitation, so that the beautiful semitropical coast, so warm and inviting, is alive with a riotous mass of feverish architecture, tarnished and corrupted by the touch of a jazzy civilization.

The pressure of life in this place is wearying, and many of its people are therefore touchy and unfriendly, not even bothering (as often as not) to summon that veneer of standard charm dictated by the American theorists of success. Irritable faces are everywhere, and hurried, waspish movements. Only the police force, one of the best in America, manages to maintain the easy courtesy one would expect of a people so happily placed geographically, and with so gracious a historical background.

Nevertheless, there is a fascination about Los Angeles, emanating chiefly from the film studios, that is not easily escaped. It / arises partly, of course, because of the extreme notability of its inhabitants. . . . 158

The stars, poor things, can scarcely resist 159 the temptations of global celebrity. Beverly Hills, the district they have built for themselves on the hillside, stretching away out of the perpetual mists of Los Angeles into the heavenly sunshine above, is a caricature of a stockbrokers' suburb, enlivened by illusions of greater grandeur. The streets are neat and symmetrical, lined with handsome trees. The garden gates are dainty, often suggestive of gnomes and thatched summerhouses. The houses are rarely blatant, but generally decorous, and usually of Olde Worlde inclinations. On the higher reaches of the hill, where the flowers are more brilliant and the air more stimulating, the houses lose some of their restraint, but most of Beverly Hills is eminently genteel, in appearance anyway. The bigger and more established the star, the more he tends to see himself as a magnate rather than an artist, and the more hierarchical his household becomes, and the more dignified and manorial his residence. How unbecoming they must think it, these constitutional monarchs of Hollywood, when the tourist guides set up their stands on the pavements, and tote their brazen signs: "See where the Stars Live: Maps and Guide Books 50 cents! Every Star's Home Marked!" . . .

160   However, I confess that despite the presence of such unattractive phenomena, I enjoyed my glimpse of Hollywood and its people. . . .

On the technical side of film production, in particular, there are many bright, able and accommodating people. You may meet them anywhere as you stroll about the studios, the English artist working for Disney, with his north-country bounce, his cheerful cockiness and his excellent tweeds; the young cameraman from Brazil, with a roving eye and a wittily disjointed style of conversation; the writer from Yale, not too cynical about his professional tasks, but deeply engaged nevertheless, in the corner of the studio, with the manuscript of a book on the Metaphysicals. I shall never forget
161 the grave pleasure with which one / of the greatest art directors accepted his winnings at a game of bingo in a club at Santa Monica, on the sea; the prize was one dollar, and he wondered anxiously (whispering about it to his wife and to me) whether he ought to go and collect it, or whether it would be presumptuous to expect the master of ceremonies to bring it to him; and he sat there indecisively until it was brought to him at last, a silver dollar at the bottom of a goldfish bowl, and he picked it out seriously and slipped it into his pocket, very pleased indeed.

The wealth of Los Angeles, and especially Beverly Hills, is incalculable. It was brought sharply home to me by the manager of an actor who suffered from recurrent illness, and was thereby handicapped in the making of films and the accretion of money. "Poor fellow," this man said, "he's going through a bad time. I don't mean he's starving, or anything like that, you know. He can manage. He gets by. He can make — poor chap, it's hard to watch — he can make one film in the year — $90,000 or so — he *manages* — but it's a bad time for him, a very bad time." This was an actor never particularly well known, a familiar face without a name; and his situation emphasized the simply fabulous resources of the top stars — wealth beyond the imagination of the old gold prospectors, and by no means to be sniffed at by many a small and moth-eaten Republic. The streets of Beverly Hills are among the most glittering in America; the shops packed with delectable items, the hotels piled deep with carpets, the boulevards wide and embellished with fine palms. Around the fringes of Los Angeles there is much dinginess, and some of the streets that link the business section with the sea are paragons of drab monotony; but Beverly Hills oozes opulence, well-being and good preservation.

Not all this money comes from films. The high company and glamour of Hollywood has lured many rich men to its precincts who have nothing to do with the cinema; and Los Angeles itself, in area the largest city on earth, is booming with industry. Several of the American oil millionaires live in Beverly Hills, as much courted by the film community as the stars are pestered by their fans. I went to a cocktail party at the house of one of these tycoons. His was a mansion built in the Spanish style, with shutters and porches and creepers, and large slim dogs standing / lan- 162 guidly near the door. In the hall, I remember, there was a large book-rest, like a lectern without its eagle, and on it, opened at the letter O, thus making a fairly symmetrical ornament, was a gigantic leather-bound copy of Webster's Dictionary. The room in which the party was already noisily proceeding was crammed with the heads of wild animals — not just the odd elk's head, or a few scattered antelope, but close, serried ranks of larger and more ferocious creatures — lions and rhinoceros and hippopotami — pushed in together, jowl to jowl, tusk to tusk, so that one beady eye seemed to run into the next, and shaggy matted ears were all but entangled with neighboring horns. Our host, a genial and robust person, was standing at the bar, built of dark oak in one corner of the room, telling a funny story to the barman. "Hi, there! Come on in!" said he, pushing me a potent Martini, "you know the General, don't you?" — and still with one arm on the bar he waved cheerfully in the direction of an elderly man whose very word (only a few years before) had been enough to summon an army or launch a campaign. So the evening began, and I found myself wandering a trifle dazed among the animals and the celebrities; the film stars, bronzed or beautiful; the captains of industry, in dark double-breasted suits, wonderfully suggestive of stocks and oil wells and astronomical incomes; the leopards; the public figures from a few years back, whose faces once looked at us from the cover of *Time* magazine, who have written their memoirs and ground their axes, and who have now withdrawn to California, with their plump wives in pale-blue cocktail dresses, and their sons on leave from Fort Knox, to mingle eminently with the party crowds, and express their ponderous opinions on the strategic value of the Pescadores.

"And where are you off to next?" asked a benign plutocrat, wearing shoes of crocodile skin.

"Seattle," I replied, "for a couple of days. I'm taking the train there tomorrow."

"Ha!" said he, "don't take the train, I'm going there tomorrow myself, on my way to visit my oil wells in Alaska, and I'm taking my private plane. Why don't you come along? It's very comfortable — it's a DC-3, boosted up, of course. I've put my own /

engines in, we should make it in three 163 hours. Okay? See you at the airport."

And so saying he wandered off, to flirt heavily with a near-by actress, and dig a friendly admiral wickedly in the ribs.

So I did, and left Los Angeles suitably. We arrived at the airport in three different cars — the millionaire, his private secretary, and I — each with our uniformed chauffeur. There stood the airplane, gleaming in a peculiar combination of colors. It was decorated with the flags of every territory it had crossed, and with the names of the various seas, and the millionaire's monogram was prominently displayed on its nose. There stood the pilot, and the co-pilot, and the steward, and the crates of good food, and the bottles and the siphons, and the napkins decorated with the millionaire's initials. There waited the various secretaries, and managers, and couriers, with last-minute advice about the state of stocks, and a few whispered queries, and a brief case full of papers.

We climbed aboard, and were soon roaring across the airfield. I noticed on the tarmac a powerful fighter aircraft of lethal aspect, clearly capable of great speeds and formidable impact. "That belongs to Jimmy Stewart," said my millionaire, leaning across my seat and offering me a cigar from a silver box. "Remember him in *Rear Window*? He's *very* fond of aviation."

MOTOR LIVING

If it is this kind of thing that gives Los Angeles its aura of affluent individualism, its air of frenzy stems directly from its position as undisputed capital of the world of the automobile. They make the cars in Detroit; but they use them, more than anywhere else on earth, in southern California, where almost everyone has a car, where the undergraduate expects one as his due, and the high school boy's popularity may depend upon the color of his convertible. The American civilization is inextricably enmeshed with the internal combustion engine. ("Now / we're in the upper-middle 164 class district," said my guide as he took me round the suburbs of Portland, Oregon, "moving up out of the Oldsmobiles into the Buicks" — and sure enough, Buicks there were, by every curb, with only an occasional Oldsmobile standing sheepishly in a garage.) To observe this phenomenon at its most advanced, you must go to southern California.

It is an old joke that the Americans are soon going to lose the use of their legs, and eventually have them reduced to vestigial remnants, like the feet of whales; but it is true that few Americans will walk anywhere if they can help it, either for practical purpose or for pleasure. You can do your banking from your car, without leaving the driving seat, by choosing a bank with a "curbside teller." You can post your letters in postboxes that protrude to the level of your car window. You can watch a film from your car in a "drive-in" cinema. At many stores you can be served in your car. At innumerable restaurants waitresses will hitch trays to the car door, so that you can eat without moving. In Florida there is even a "drive-in" church, where two or three may gather together sitting in their Chevrolets. There is no more characteristic gesture of American life than the casual rolling-down of a car window and the emergence of a hand, to grasp a hot dog or a theater ticket, a pound of apples or an evening paper, a check book or a bottle of cider from a roadside stall.

Imagine yourself, for a moment, as a travelling motorist in America. Setting off in the morning (let us say) you pull in to a petrol station for a tank of petrol. "Regular?" says the attendant, meaning the cheaper kind; and the answer he gets depends upon the locality. In New Jersey, where so much oil is refined, petrol is likely to be cheap. In Colorado, on the other hand, it can be nearly twice as expensive. If you are lucky, you may pass through a region which is enjoying a price war, and find yourself faced with a succession of scrawled blackboards, each offering petrol at more ludicrously inadequate rates, until (if you have patience) you may fill your

tank practically for nothing. "Okay," says the attendant, wiping his hands to receive the money; but in the meantime he has not only delivered the petrol; he has checked the oil and the tires, cleaned the windscreen, filled the radiator, inspected the batteries. If it is desert country, / he has topped up the water-bag you carry slung over your front bumper. If you needed maps, he has produced them free from the office. He may have given your small son a lollipop from the stock he carries in his pocket. He has certainly asked you where you are from, and has told you about how he was stationed outside Norwich with the Air Force, and how he liked the pubs, but he wouldn't go back for anything all the same, and he hopes the food situation is better now. He expects no tip, but smiles the standard American smile (so universally pleasant as to be enigmatic), and waves to the children through the back window as you drive away.

So you are off. The road is likely to be smooth and wide, and you are tempted to speed, not least because almost everyone else on the road is speeding already. The limit varies, according to the state you are in. Nevada, as we have seen, has none except in cities. In some other places you are theoretically limited to fifty miles an hour. If you go too fast, you may be stopped by the traditional "speed cop," with his howling sirens and trenchant manner, and given a little yellow ticket. It is more likely nowadays that you will be intercepted by radar. Notices will warn you beforehand — "Watch your Speed! Checked by radar!" — and your progress will be picked up by instruments mounted beside the road or in other cars, infallibly recording your speed and probably photographing your number plate.

Take no risks on the roads, especially in southern California. The American is a dashing driver, and often a reckless one; and statistics have shown that it is thirty-two times safer to fly in an American aircraft than it is to drive on an American road. Whatever you do, avoid the low-priced car driven by the single young man; he is probably a salesman, oppressed by the prosaic nature of his calling, and he likes to devise unutterable dangers on the road, as a relief to the monotony. If you see a woman driving, with small children in the back of the car, keep with her: she is probably just as skillful as the men, and, with all her responsibilities concentrated on four wheels, she is prudent too.

Do not be ensnared by the numbers and plates on other cars, which are a constant distraction. Every state has different number plates, often prettily colored, and with fancy slogans like "Minnesota: Land of 10,000 Lakes"; "Illinois: Land o'Lincoln"; / 166 "New Mexico: Land of Enchantment"; "New York: The Empire State." If it is near the turn of the years these slogans are even more diverting, for they are often changed, and it is amusing to see what horror Arkansas, for example, has perpetrated *this* time. There are many other odd things to see on the passing cars. Some people invent slogans of their own. "Official Car," says a pompous plate, aping the senatorial manner, and adds in smaller print: "Tax payer." Another popular one, during my stay in America, was: "Don't Blame Me! I voted Democratic!" Often motorists buy stickers to record the states and "scenic wonders" they have visited, and their rear windows are a gaudy mess of colored posters, with reproductions of decorative hanging bridges, Puritans, geysers, bears, country houses, the Capitol, Indians, caves and rhymes like:

There's always a welcome, early or late,
From old Minnesota, the North Star State.
In the land of the lake and the tall fir tree
Joy is awaiting both you and me.

The whole makes a pattern of souvenirs that is not only dangerous, in that it blocks the view through the car windows, but is often aesthetically indigestible.

In any small town en route you may buy an excellent cup of coffee; but be careful how you park the car. It is generally illegal to cross the road and park the car on the other side in the direction you are travelling. It is usually unpopular, in places where cars are parked at right angles to the curb, to swing around and cross to the opposite side of the road. Once you have found a place you must have a nickel or a dime for the parking meter; put the coin in the slot, and the machine records how long you have been standing there. If you overstay the limit a red flag will show, and the chances are that a slowly wandering policeman will happen by, and pause to examine the evidence, and then, laboriously extracting a notebook from his recesses, will take the number of your car in triplicate, and affix a notice to your windscreen instructing you to pay a small fine by such-and-such a time. It is a painless process, for you need not appear in court; indeed in some places you can pay the fine there and then, by wrapping your dollar in your police ticket, and deposit-/ing it in a box conveniently 167 affixed to a neighboring lamppost. In a small town in Kansas my ticket, apologizing profusely for the trouble I was being caused, instructed me to place the fine on a tray; and there I found change, in case I had only a five-dollar bill. It is an admirable device, the parking meter, relieving policemen of unnecessary duties, involving the minimum of paper work and administration, and making it easy for the motorist to comply with the law and have his coffee too.

Most of the big American roads are most skillfully signed. Large notices suggest the safe speeds for corners, and if you test them you will find that they are exactly right for the average American car, so powerful on the straight, so lumpish on the corners; go slower than they suggest, and you will be wasting time, go faster and you will feel the car heel over, and hear the tires scream disconcertingly. (They scream more easily than European tires, anyway, thus giving the impression, when some gentle old lady drives cautiously around a bend, that she is making for the Presbyterian church with an uncharacteristic abandon.) If there is a dangerous curve, or an obstacle, huge boards scream at you with bright colors or checkered patterns, not singly or in pairs, but in long rows, for several hundred yards, so that you can hardly escape their impact.

If you are color-blind, you may have difficulty with the traffic lights, for you cannot rely on the relative positions of the colors. In England I know that when the light is shining in the top hole, I must stop; and that when it shines in the bottom hole, I may go. In America there are no such certainties. Sometimes the red light is at the top, sometimes at the bottom; sometimes it is not red at all; sometimes there is no amber light. Whatever the system, there will soon be a riotous hooting of horns behind if you fail to move when you may, for the American driver has none of the fatalistic patience of the British. In San Antonio, Texas, I once found myself (in common with everyone else) faced with peculiar traffic light problems; for the whole system had gone wrong, and the lights were flashing and winking crazily, shining in the wrong order, staying for interminable minutes at red before changing momentarily to green, sometimes coming on all at once, sometimes going out all at once, till the whole city was dizzy, and portly businessmen were lying 168 back in their / driving seats in heavy hilarity. "That's Texas for you," my companion remarked, "they always overdo a good joke."

Presently it is time for lunch, and you may care to try a drive-in restaurant. Steering warily into a kind of covered stall, you blow your horn (trying not to make it sound peremptory), and soon there emerges from the central building a waitress. She is likely to be plain, but heavily prepared. Her heels are high, her skirts a little short, her nylons excellent, her manner experienced. She takes your order, and soon reappears with the food, on a metal tray which fits neatly on the door. Milk in a carton (let us say); ham and eggs on a horrid disposable plate, which makes the ham taste insidiously of cardboard; bread automatically sliced; coffee in a cardboard cup; lump sugar wrapped in hygienic paper. If you want a dessert, there are many ice creams on the menu, and always several varieties of pie; the fruit pie is a national dish — cf. the menu of the *Monarch* — and pie *à la mode* (meaning pie with ice cream) is a universal favorite. When you want to pay the bill, blow your horn again, and soon the waitress will be with you once more, smiling prettily, and examining the tip without much bashfulness as she takes the tray back to the kitchen.

When the dusk comes down, and you begin to feel the fatigue of travel, you may like to relax for an hour or two at a drive-in cinema. If you are near a town in southern California you are sure to come across one — a big stadium with a high wall, overshadowed by the screen, with the gigantic silent figures of the actors easily visible from the road. You buy your ticket without leaving the car, and maneuver your way into a convenient position. On posts dotted around the arena are loudspeakers attached to wires; reach out of the window for one of these, place it on the seat beside you, and there you are. At first it may seem a little queer having the voice beside you and the figure far away on the screen; but you will soon get used to it, mentally arranging (according to your temperament) either that Miss Monroe is really in the car with you, or that Mr. Frankie Laine's voice is up there with his larynx. It is a wonderful way to see a film, for if you are really bored you can go to sleep in the back seat, leaving your wife to endure its banalities; and from time to time, in the best drive-ins, somebody comes round with a tray of re-/freshments, 169 and knocks politely on your window. You can take your dinner with you, if you like, and eat sausages while the cowboy gets his man. Moreover, you can talk when you please, and put your feet up, and wear the most wildly extravagant of hats without being hissed at from the row behind. Only one thing can be said against the drive-in cinema; on a dark, lonely evening, in the flat and open countryside that surrounds so many American towns, there is something creepy about the sight of those silent figures on the screen, singing their silent songs, whispering their silent intimacies, hurling their soundless imprecations, as the motorist drives by outside.

Finally, at the end of your day, you decide to put up for the night. Just beyond the drive-in cinema, toward the center of the town, you will find the motels. There are rows of them, each with its neon sign, its oddities of architecture or decoration, its illuminated notice announcing a vacancy. Some are long terraces; some are a series of huts, like bathing cabins. Some, veering toward the pretentious, and going in for swimming pools and television, are liable to be expensive; others, patently frequented by cockroaches and secret lovers, are certain to be cheap. You take your choice, register at a little office, and drive to your own front door. There is no service (and no tipping), and you may have to walk down the road for a meal. But your room is probably clean and comfortable, if not luxurious, and your car is parked freely and conveniently directly outside your window.

There will certainly be a shower, and very possibly a bath. If it is a good motel, all kinds of small attentions will be paid you. The evening newspaper will be provided, and a small library will be placed beside your bed. There will be a new pair of bedroom slippers, made of a thick paper-like substance, and an unused fabric device for cleaning your shoes. Coat hangers without number hang in the wardrobe. There is a radio, and perhaps a television set. Nests of plastic cups are in the bathroom, and cakes of soap in healthful packaging. The tumblers may be enshrouded in cellophane, and the lavatory seat (as likely as not) will have a paper wrapping across it to testify to its cleanliness. Some motels, with a thought to the early traveller, provide coffee for the morning. It comes in powder form in a little cardboard cup, together with milk powder, sugar, and a cardboard 170 spoon; / and in the morning, in the cruel dawn, you have only to add hot water to this mixture (from the tap) to have a peculiarly repulsive and effective beverage.

So you sink into your soft, squashy bed, while the night traffic roars by; and in the morning, so gentle is the civilization of the automobile, you need only walk a pace or two across the carpeted floor before you can sink refreshed into the welcoming driving seat. But this manner of life, so highly refined by the southern Californians, is only a beginning. One city is installing conveyor belts to carry pedestrians along its shopping streets; they will step from their cars first onto a slow-moving belt, then onto a faster one, and so proceed in elegant ease along the boulevards. Already the Californians need rarely walk; soon, if this is any kind of portent, they will have no opportunity. . . .

CHICAGO

So we stood with this queer landlocked 207 sea behind us, and looked at the city lights. The lake front is the best façade in America; more regular and uniform than New York's, so that it presents a less jumbled and tangled mass of structures; bigger and grander than Miami's, which shines with a beckoning gaiety across the water of Biscayne Bay; less brassy and frontierlike than the waterside aspect of Seattle. Its glittering row of big buildings extends for miles along the lake, brilliantly lit; some of its skyscrapers are clean and clear-cut, some are surmounted by innumerable pinnacles, turrets and spires, so that the generally functional effect is tempered by a few touches of the educational. Beside this magnificent row there sweeps a great highway, following the line of the lake, and along it scurries a constant swift stream of lights, with scarcely a pause and scarcely a hesitation, except when some poor unacclimatized woman stalls her engine or loses her way, and is deafened by a blast of protest from behind; then the line of lights wavers for a brief moment, until with a roar of engines and a spinning of wheels the traffic diverts itself and races away, leaving the poor lost soul behind, biting her lower lip, and having a terrible time with the gears.

For Chicago is still a heartless town, in many ways. The incompetent will meet few

courtesies in its streets; the flustered will be offered no cooling counsel; it is neces-
208 sary in life to get places, / and to get there fast. Between the buildings that stand like rows of hefty sentinels above the lake, you may see numbers of narrow canyons leading covertly into shadier places behind. The façade of Chicago is supported by no depth of splendor; hidden by its two or three streets of dazzle is a jungle of slums and drab suburbs, a dirty hodge-podge of races and morals.

In the daylight, indeed, the bright glamour even of the business district is not quite so irresistible, if only because of the din and the congestion. This must surely be the noisiest place on earth. The cars roar; the elevated railway rumbles; the policemen blow their strange two-toned whistles, like sea birds lost in a metropolis; the hooters shriek; the horns hoot; the typists, on their way back from coffee, swap their gossip at the tops of their tinny voices. Across the crowded intersections scurry the flocks of shoppers, like showers of sheep, while the policemen wave them irritably on and the cars wait to be unleashed. The tempo of Chicago is terrible, and the overcrowding desperate. Just as each new plan to improve the life of the Egyptian peasant is overtaken and swamped by the inexorable march of the birthrate, so in Chicago every new parking place is obliterated, every new freeway blackened, by the constantly growing flood of motorcars. Each morning the highways into the city are thick with unwearying cars, pounding along head to tail, pouring in by every channel, racing and blaring and roaring their way along, until you think it will be impossible to cram one more car in, so bulging and swelling is the place, so thickly cluttered its streets, so strangled the movement of its traffic. It is good business in Chicago to knock down offices and turn them into parking lots. And it is decidedly unwise for the nervous or overconsiderate driver to venture into the turmoil of its streets, for in this respect, as in others, Chicago still ain't no sissy town.

Crime and corruption are still powerful influences here, and the best-laid plans of honest men to clean up the city and rid it of its crooked parasites nearly always seem to go a-gley. I talked to a number of young politicians who had such an ambition, some of them bravely outspoken in their comments on the Syndicate, the shadowy and nebulous body of corruption that still controls so much of Chicago's life. "You may say the old gags about gunmen in Chicago are exaggerated," said Alderman / Robert 209 Merriam in one public speech, "but there have been 700 unsolved murders *since* the days of prohibition and Al Capone. Perhaps the crimes of violence have diminished . . . but they have diminished only because the Syndicate has murdered its way to monopoly. Here in Chicago . . . segments of both political parties are in cahoots with this monopoly of murder." When I was in Chicago nearly everyone admitted the truth of all this, but few were ready to fight the situation; and when Merriam later stood for Mayor, he was, to nobody's surprise, defeated. People have too much to lose to meddle with such perilous matters. The big men may lose contracts, the little man the dubious co-operation of his local policemen or petty boss. Extortion, on many levels, is still a commonplace in Chicago. A policeman wrote to the *Chicago Tribune* not long ago complaining about the word "cop," which he said was derogatory. The letter brought a blistering and revealing reply from a Chicago citizen. "How do you address a you-know-what," he asked in a series of such rhetorical demands, "when he stops you without cause and questions you or searches you or your property? How do you address a you-know-what when you've been looking for one of them a long time and finally find one mooching free drinks in a saloon? *How do you address a you-know-what when one comes around to your place of business soliciting funds you don't dare refuse to give?*" Everyone knows that a five-dollar bill slipped to your examiner will help you along with your driving test. Everyone knows too, if only by reading his papers, that murders occur almost every day in Chicago; but when I talked to a senior Chicago police officer on the subject, he adroitly slipped away to the twin topics (for they seem to go arm in arm) of traffic congestion and prostitution.

All this sordid unhealthiness would be less intrusive if the city itself were spacious and wholesome of appearance. But despite the illusory grandeur of its lakefront, Chicago is a festering place. From the windows of the elevated railway, which clangs its elderly way through the city with rather the detached hauteur of a Bath chair, you can look down upon its disagreeable hinterland. The different sectors of slumland each have their national character — Italian, Chinese, Puerto Rican, Lithuanian — but externally they merge and mingle in a desolate ex-210 panse of / depression. Here is a brown brick building, crumbling at its corners, its windows cracked or shattered, its door crooked on its hinges, with a Negro woman in a frayed and messy blouse leaning from an upstairs window with a comb in her hand. Here an old Italian with long mustaches squats on the steps of a rickety wooden tenement, its weatherboards an off-white color, its balcony railings sagging and broken. Slums are slums anywhere in the world, and there are probably areas just as blighted in Glasgow; but here the misery of it all is given added poignancy by the circumstances of so many of its inhabitants, people of a score of races who came to America to be rich, and have stayed on to live like unpampered animals.

In such a climate of existence racial prejudices thrive, and you can often catch a faint menacing rumble of their dangers in a bus or on a street corner — a drunken Negro cursing the white people as he slumps in his seat, a white man arrogantly pushing his way through a group of Negro women. There have been some tragic race riots in Chicago, and there may well be more. During my stay there, hundreds of policemen were on duty each day at a big new housing project erected in an inflammable quarter of the city; for into one of the apartments a young Negro family had moved, and their white neighbors (of many national origins) had sworn to drive them out by force; so that sometimes in the evening, when the policemen were momentarily distracted, the Negroes in their shuttered rooms would hear the thud of a stone on their window, or the murmur of threats and imprecations from the street below.

Such standards of morality have inevitably eaten away like a corrosive at the old blithe and regardless self-confidence of Chicago. Not so long ago Chicagoans were convinced that their city would soon be the greatest and most famous on earth, outranking New York, London and Paris, the center of a new world, the boss city of the universe. During the period of its fabulous nineteenth-century growth, when millionaires seemed to be two a penny and the treasures of the continent were being summoned to Chicago, it was not unnatural for such an eager and unsophisticated community to suppose that the center of territorial gravity was fast shifting to the Middle West. In a sense, I suppose it has; the railway tracks, the sprawling stockyards, the factories of Chi-/cago and its sister cities 211 are the sinews of the United States, and so of half the world. But the blindest lover of Chicago would not claim for the place the status of a universal metropolis. So much of the old grand assertiveness has been lost. Nobody pretends that Chicago has overtaken New York; instead there is a provincial acceptance of inferiority, a resignation, coupled with a mild regret for the old days of wild boasts and ambitions. For one reason and another, the stream of events generally passes Chicago by, for the city is so isolated in the center of this enormous heartland, so very far from either Europe or Asia (though you can now fly to Paris direct from Chicago). Even the Chicago theater, once a lively institution, has fallen into dull days, and makes do with the second run of Broadway productions, and a few mildewed and monotonous burlesques. Despite the tumult and the pressure, Chicago sometimes feels like a backwater.

The impression is only partly accurate, for there are many wonderful and exciting things in Chicago. There are magnificent art galleries — one of the best modern French collections in existence — and splendid libraries. There is a plethora of universities, of varying degrees of academic distinction. The symphony orchestra is good, if hampered in the past by the determinedly fashionable character of its audience, which has apparently restricted some of its conductors (so intricate are the channels of snobbery) in their choice of programs.

Nor indeed has the old manly energy entirely evaporated; there is still much virility and enterprise in Chicago life. The city itself is physically expressive of this continued resilience. The huge marshalling yards lie lounging over the countryside, littered with trains. The bridges over the Chicago River open with a fascinating and relentless ease to let the great freighters through. The *Chicago Tribune,* which calls itself the World's Greatest Newspaper, is certainly among the sprightliest and most vigorous. There are brave schemes of expansion and improvement — plans to run a new highway bang through the heart of the place, to build a new suburb on an island in the lake, to erect a huge new office building astride the elevated railway, so that the trains will rattle through its open legs.

But such driving activity no longer represents the spiritual temper of the city. Chicagoans are still pursued by the demon of / progress and haunted by the vision of possible failure, so that the pressure of their existence is relentless; but the strain of it all, and the fundamental rottenness of the place, has blunted some of their old intensity and lavishness of purpose. They have accepted their station in life, no longer swaggering through the years with the endearing *braggadocio* of their tradition, but more resigned, more passive, even (perhaps) a little disillusioned. Chicago is certainly not a has-been; but it could be described as a might-have-been. . . .

212

SUGGESTIONS FOR LIBRARY WORK

In this volume it has been possible to include only a few of the many published foreign opinions of modern American culture. While the editors believe that the selections in *Modern America through Foreign Eyes* represent the range of foreign opinion fairly, they admit readily that there is a wealth of foreign writing about America which, because of space limitations, could not be included in the present volume. If you are interested in further exploration of the topic, you should read further in the books from which selections have been drawn for the text; then you should examine other foreign impressions of America such as Denis W. Brogan's *The American Character* (1944), Jean Cocteau's *Lettre aux Amèricains* (1949), Joseph Czapski's "Impressions," Jules Monnerot's "Misunderstandings," Guido Piovene's "Ungrateful Europe," Yury Šerech's "Top Hats and Dry Crusts" [the last four appear in *What Europe Thinks of America* (1953), edited by James Burnham], Ilya Ilf and Eugene Petrov's *Little Golden America* (1937), Yasuo Everett Muraoka's "American Goodwill Toward Japan" and Bernard Person's "A Dutchman Comes to New Amsterdam" [both in *You Americans* (1939), edited by B. P. Adams], Stefen Osusky's *The Way of the Free* (1951), and Stephen Potter's *Potter on America* (1957). These are only a starting list, one to which you can add extensively after library research. Broad investigation of this kind will yield material for longer and more detailed papers than the selected source materials text can provide. It will also permit you to write on topics not covered by the text.

You might, for instance, attempt to find answers to the following questions: What is the foreign opinion of the way Americans raise their children? What do foreign visitors think of American elementary and secondary schools? What is the foreign conception of the "average" American office worker or laborer? How do foreigners envision the American college professor? What do foreigners think of the American problem of juvenile delinquency? How do foreigners react to American speech in general and American slang in particular? What is the immigrant's initial reaction to America? Do foreigners describe American college life accurately? What seems to be the predominant foreign attitude toward American race problems? What have foreign visitors said of American capitalism? What is the foreign picture of suburban life in America? In what ways do foreign reactions to America reflect the native backgrounds of the foreigners? What paradoxes do foreign visitors find in the Southern United States? Why do many foreigners accuse Americans of making "cold carnivals" [the words are Simone de Beauvoir's] of historic places such as Williamsburg, Virginia? Are descriptions by foreigners of places you know well accurate and fair? What do foreigners think of the American businessman? What is the foreign opinion of American literature, art, or music? How do foreigners react to American football or baseball? What do foreigners think of Americans who travel abroad? How does American television affect the foreign viewer?

Still another area for investigating foreign attitude toward American culture is foreign fiction which deals with America or Americans. You could read Noel Coward's "What Mad Pursuit?" and Evelyn Waugh's *The Loved One* (1948). In these, foreign opinion can be seen working through characterization, plot, and theme.